"This book inspires a feeling of relief. It brings together the most pressing issues of our time – climate change, genocide, exclusionary nationalism and deep-rooted dehumanising racisms – in profoundly original ways that address power relations, exclusions, 'unhousedness' and (re)traumatisation. It faces the pain they engender while refusing familiar, patronising tropes of otherness. Its perceptive, and sometimes poetic, scholarship brings deep hope that other, genuinely psycho-social ways of living and relating are possible, despite disagreements and disappointments along the way."

Ann Phoenix, *Professor, Psychosocial Studies, UCL, UK*

"This is a profoundly disturbing book in the best sense. Chris Scanlon and John Adlam are known for their highly regarded psycho-social studies into the concept of the mind that is un-housed by trauma i.e. those experiences that dismember and dissociate people from communities, creating communities of the excluded. In this rich work, they revisit and reconsider their work, with a lens informed by a deepening awareness of the costs of cruelty; whether by white people to people of colour, men to women and all of us to the very earth we stand on. Scanlon and Adlam stand up for the value of disturbance and dissidence, in a world where what can be said aloud seems to be constrained and people who say the 'wrong' thing can be excluded or cancelled as if they should not exist. We can learn from getting closer to the unloved and unloveable and we must do so, if we are not to fragment our minds, our communities and the earth itself. All those who work with excluded should read this book, if only to remind themselves that they are part of the group that excluded the people they claim to want to help. It is not always comfortable to look in a mirror but I think we can all be grateful to Scanlon and Adlam for holding up this particular glass."

Dr Gwen Adshead, *Consultant Forensic Psychiatrist and Psychotherapist, Broadmoor Hospital, UK*

"Here we are given a mirror. In it we see something disturbing and yet hopeful about ourselves. We are confronted with the realization that healing occurs when we see that pain belongs to the collective rather than to the individuals who carry it on our behalf – a deeply knowledgeable, intensely wise and fiercely ethical exploration of today's predicament. Also one that points toward hope amidst the wreckage by suggesting how we might re-animate public spaces for reflection, empathy and understanding."

James Krantz, *PhD, Past President, International Society for the Psychoanalytic Study of Organizations*

"In this elegantly argued, carefully documented work, Christopher Scanlon and John Adlam offer a refreshing critical angle on some of the most pressing forms of social traumatization and exclusion. Going beyond 'dispossession', 'necropolitics' and 'states of exception' as means of characterizing the social injury wrought by inhospitable neoliberal sovereigns, they deploy a deeply critical, practice-based lens to looking at the suffering in our world produced by colonial and racist structures, mechanisms of dispossession and unhousedness, and ecocidal policies that are exacerbating a global migration crisis. The authors mitigate their disappointment at the persistence of oppression by proposing a blueprint for solidarity around anti-oppressive social action."

Michael O'Loughlin, *Adelphi University, New York, USA; Co-Editor,*
Psychoanalysis, Culture & Society

"Starting from homelessness and ending with 'race' this is a study of abjection and shame *and* of its refusal, the refusal to go quietly into the night and accept your place on society's outermost margins. Scanlon and Adlam examine the vexed relations between those who are cast out and those who, simply by occupying the position that they occupy, do the casting. This wonderfully imaginative and principled book draws upon a startling diversity of sources to explore the paradoxes and predicaments of structural violence."

Paul Hoggett, *Co-Founder, Climate Psychology Alliance*

"Psychoanalysis inaugurated the study of the unknown in human experience. Group analysis added the previously unexplored impact of the social and political context on personal life and relations. Now Scanlon and Adlam incorporate the ecological and architectural aspects of our lives, derived from power relations and inequalities in the distribution of wealth, which lead the casualties of the system to an un-housed, dis-membered, and dis-eased existence. This exceptional book is far from neutrality and a revolutionary contribution. Its reading is a must."

Juan Tubert-Oklander, *Psychoanalyst and Group Analyst,*
Marista University of Merida

Psycho-social Explorations of Trauma, Exclusion and Violence

The central theme of this book is the operation of intersecting discourses of power, privilege and positioning as they are revealed in fraught encounters between in-groups and out-groups in our deeply fractured world. The authors offer a unique perspective on inter-group dynamics and structural violence at local, societal, cultural and global levels, dissecting processes of toxic 'othering' and psycho-social (re-)traumatisation.

The book offers the Diogenes Paradigm as a unique conceptual tool with which to analyse the ways in which those of us who come to be located outside or on the margins of dominant social structures are, in one way or another, the inheritors of the legacies of centuries of oppression and exclusion. This analysis offers a distinctive psycho-social redefinition of trauma that foregrounds the relationship between the inhospitable environments we generate and the experiences of un-housedness that we thereby perpetuate.

Written in an engaging and accessible style, *Psycho-social Explorations of Trauma, Exclusion and Violence* directly addresses pressing global issues of racial trauma, human mobility and climate disaster, and offers a manifesto for the creative re-imagining of the places and spaces in which conversations about restructuring and reparation can become sustainable. This is an essential and compelling book for anyone committed to social justice, especially for all practitioners working in health, social care and community justice settings, and researchers and academics across the behavioural and social sciences.

Christopher Scanlon is a psycho-social consultant/researcher and consultant psychotherapist in forensic and adult mental health. He is a training group analyst at the Institute of Group Analysis and the Irish Group Analytic Society, and founder member of the Association for Psychosocial Studies.

John Adlam is a group psychotherapist and independent researcher, working mainly in the National Health Service, UK. He is a founder member of the Association for Psychosocial Studies and a former Vice President of the International Association for Forensic Psychotherapy.

The New International Library of Group Analysis
Series Editor: Earl Hopper

Drawing on the seminal ideas of British, European and American group analysts, psychoanalysts, social psychologists and social scientists, the books in this series focus on the study of small and large groups, organisations and other social systems, and on the study of the transpersonal and transgenerational sociality of human nature. NILGA books will be required reading for the members of professional organisations in the field of group analysis, psychoanalysis, and related social sciences. They will be indispensable for the "formation" of students of psychotherapy, whether they are mainly interested in clinical work with patients or in consultancy to teams and organisational clients within the private and public sectors.

Richard M. Billow's Selected Papers on Psychoanalysis and Group Process
Changing Our Minds
Edited by Tzachi Slonim

Addressing Challenging Moments in Psychotherapy
Clinical Wisdom for Working with Individuals, Groups and Couples
Edited by Jerome S. Gans

Psychoanalysis, Group Analysis, and Beyond
Towards a New Paradigm of the Human Being
Juan Tubert-Oklander and Reyna Hernández-Tubert

An Introduction to Psychotherapeutic Playback Theater
Hall of Mirrors on Stage
Ronen Kowalsky, Nir Raz and Shoshi Keisari with Susana Pendzik

Psycho-social Explorations of Trauma, Exclusion and Violence
Un-housed Minds and Inhospitable Environments
Christopher Scanlon and John Adlam

Psycho-social Explorations of Trauma, Exclusion and Violence

Un-housed Minds and Inhospitable Environments

Christopher Scanlon and John Adlam

LONDON AND NEW YORK

Cover image: Hulton Archive / Stringer; Getty Images

First published 2022
by Routledge
4 Park Square, Milton Park, Abingdon, Oxon OX14 4RN

and by Routledge
605 Third Avenue, New York, NY 10158

Routledge is an imprint of the Taylor & Francis Group, an informa business

© 2022 Christopher Scanlon and John Adlam

The right of Christopher Scanlon and John Adlam to be identified as authors of this work has been asserted in accordance with sections 77 and 78 of the Copyright, Designs and Patents Act 1988.

All rights reserved. No part of this book may be reprinted or reproduced or utilised in any form or by any electronic, mechanical, or other means, now known or hereafter invented, including photocopying and recording, or in any information storage or retrieval system, without permission in writing from the publishers.

Trademark notice: Product or corporate names may be trademarks or registered trademarks, and are used only for identification and explanation without intent to infringe.

British Library Cataloguing-in-Publication Data
A catalogue record for this book is available from the British Library

Library of Congress Cataloging-in-Publication Data
Names: Scanlon, Christopher, author.
Title: Psycho-social explorations of trauma, exclusion and violence: un-housed minds and inhospitable environments / Christopher Scanlon and John Adlam.
Description: Abingdon, Oxon; New York, NY: Routledge, 2022. |
Series: The new international library of group analysis | Includes bibliographical references and index. |
Identifiers: LCCN 2021040960 (print) | LCCN 2021040961 (ebook) |
ISBN 9781032121130 (hbk) | ISBN 9780367893316 (pbk) | ISBN 9781003223115 (ebk)
Subjects: LCSH: Social justice. | Restorative justice. | Group psychoanalysis.
Classification: LCC HM671 .S352 2022 (print) | LCC HM671 (ebook) |
DDC 303.3/72–dc23/eng/20211013
LC record available at https://lccn.loc.gov/2021040960
LC ebook record available at https://lccn.loc.gov/2021040961

ISBN: 978-1-032-12113-0 (hbk)
ISBN: 978-0-367-89331-6 (pbk)
ISBN: 978-1-003-22311-5 (ebk)

DOI: 10.4324/9781003223115

Typeset in Times New Roman
by Taylor & Francis Books

We dedicate this book to the memory of Edwin 'Diogenes' MacKenzie — and to vagabonds everywhere

Contents

Series foreword	xi
Prologue	xiii
Preface	xix
Acknowledgements	xxvii

PART I
Un-housed minds: The Diogenes Paradigm   1

1 Un-housed minds and psycho-social traumatisation   3

2 The Diogenes Paradigm   23

3 Citizens of the world?   39

4 Inhospitability, injury, insult and insurrection   55

5 Agoraphilia and agoraphobia: Negotiating fraught encounters in open spaces   74

PART II
Inhospitable environments: Traumatised and traumatising (dis)organisations   91

6 "Who watches the watchers"? (Dis)organised responses to psycho-social traumatisation   93

7 The inhospitable planetary environment: 'Climate migration', pandemic and biosphere destruction   111

x Contents

PART III
Reclaiming the agora: Activist research and anti-oppressive practice 133

8 Racial (re-)traumatisation and practices of equality 135

9 Practices of disappointment: Going along with stuff less and getting out more 160

Index 178

Series foreword

It is difficult to add very much to the enthusiastic endorsements of this contribution to the New International Library of Group Analysis (NILGA) from such highly regarded international colleagues, and to the Prologue by Anne Aiyegbusi, a Member of the Committee for Power, Privilege and Position (PPP) of the Institute of Group Analysis (UK). Nonetheless, I am pleased to align myself with their fundamental support of the project to which Christopher Scanlon and John Adlam have committed themselves.

Since its inception, Group Analysis has been challenged by the need not only to integrate its three pillars of psychoanalysis, sociology and group dynamics, but also to comprehend this new discipline in an authentic way. It is not so easy to understand that if the individual person and the group are two sides of the same coin, so too are psychoanalysis and sociology. Personal maturity is associated with the ability and willingness to take the role of citizen, and very often personal insight follows relational change, rather than the other way around. Deprivation is not only a matter of insatiability, and insatiability is not only a matter of the unconscious desire for the maternal cornucopia. These foundational features of group analytical psychotherapy can be traced more to the work of the romantic Marx than to that of Durkheim and Freud. Various sub-groups of our colleagues associate themselves with contemporary representatives of the perspectives by which the work of our founding fathers can be distinguished.

The co-authors of this passionately argued book have been influenced by, and have contributed to, a clinical sensibility associated with the practice of socio-therapy fostered more in the context of the Henderson Hospital than in many other settings. Stemming from their appreciation of the power of the unconscious restraints and constraints of the external world, Scanlon and Adlam suggest that Group Analysis should be aligned with the field of 'psycho-social studies', which in the last century was more commonly known as 'social psychology'. Despite this nominal reversal, psycho-social studies continue to privilege the 'social-a-priori'. To the recommendation – if not admonition – of Pope (1734) that, "... the proper study of mankind is man ...", we would hasten to emphasise the sociality of human nature, and the economic and political basis of sociality.

It follows that it is important to elevate the social sciences in our clinical thinking and training. Although it is vital not to confuse political practice with psychotherapy, it is necessary to reflect the metatheory of our discipline in our skills and training programmes. It is essential to honour the intellectual pillars on which Group Analysis rests.

Does this stray from the initial impulses and the hopeful visions of those who we regard as the founders of Group Analysis, such as S.H. Foulkes, Patrick de Maré and Wilfred Bion, as well as those who are our older siblings, both brothers and sisters? Not to my way of thinking. We have already influenced the development of a 'social psychoanalysis', and privileged the selection of heterogeneous groups in clinical work. NILGA is itself comprised of several sub-series involving the study of the foundation matrices of contextual societies and the dynamic matrices of organisations. Most of our authors are concerned with the causes and consequences of trauma in its broadest transgenerational sense.

I am grateful to Christopher and John for attempting to shift psycho-social studies from the periphery of our field to the very core of it. Their book will appeal to all students of Group Analysis, and to both clinicians and citizens of the profession. Nonetheless, this book demands a response from our more senior members, many of whom have undoubtedly become complacent about the realisation of our indigenous 'world-view'. We have been challenged either to develop the paradigm through which our clinical practice is organised or to acknowledge that we need a new paradigm. Either way, there is much work to be done!

Earl Hopper,
Series Editor

Reference

Pope, A. (1734). *Essay on Man, Epistle II*. Available at: http://www.gutenberg.org/files/ 2428/2428-h/2428-h.htm (Accessed: 2 January 2021).

Prologue

Dr Anne Aiyegbusi

I'm honoured to have been invited by Christopher Scanlon and John Adlam to write the foreword to their important new book. With one foot in an in-group and the other on the road less travelled, we and other fellow explorers have, for many years, tried to offer ways to understand deep and complex trauma. Understanding the rhythms of psycho-social trauma helps to elucidate the often desperate but alienating narratives associated with oppressed and marginalised persons. Meanwhile, exposing systemic contexts that erase parts of our *shared* humanity authenticates professional paradigms. At a time when the hegemony of many seminal psychotherapeutic texts and related concepts are being challenged from epistemological, ontological and social justice perspectives, the authors offer desperately required insights, especially for the discipline of group analysis.

With one foot in the road less travelled, I could consider my other foot to be located within several in-groups. For one, I am currently a member of the Board of Trustees at the Institute of Group Analysis (IGA). Significantly, I am the board member for anti-discrimination and intersectionality. So, this book has special resonance and is a timely addition to the group analytic literature. As a psychotherapeutic discipline that privileges the social and political context as well as the individual or personal, group analysis will nevertheless benefit from roadmaps for compassionately negotiating the manifold impacts of psycho-social traumas, especially those involving 'othering', which are inevitably complicated by interrelated processes of pain and denial.

The road less travelled, in the clinical field of forensic mental health and other areas of relational complexity, will inevitably lead to accounts of profound trauma. Sometimes apparent walls of it with pain and anaesthesia present in combinations that are particularly difficult to navigate. It leads to brutalising psycho-social environments that have scapegoated (some might say tried to hide) the people they have victimised into repetitive cycles of ever more traumatising experiences. Typically, these are framed as safe, caring, therapeutic enclaves, be it through systems of health, education, social and/or criminal justice. The dislocated individual is considered the problem. Is it any wonder 'Diogenesque' persons vote with their feet, exiting rejecting, invalidating and unforgiving in-groups to live in resistance against the grain and speaking truths to the often-deaf ears of power? For many, better this than the soul-destroying oppression of being the unwanted and beholden 'other' housed under sufferance. In a hopeful way, the focus of this book is firmly on the iatrogenic and damaging psycho-social processes within our groups and institutions. The authors unearth, unravel, de-code and lay bare for examination and understanding those convoluted, multi-faceted and multi-layered stories that have so often served to 'lock in' disenfranchised populations. As a result, the reader is supported to consider respectful, compassionate engagement with the vulnerability and dignity of out-group inhabitants. In other words, they outline alternative, humane routes to addressing cycles of trauma with people whose hurt and harm has actually resulted in alienation from required help.

The authors foreground racism in the book, and so will I. I describe a case of racialised trauma to encapsulate and emphasise the book's overall premise. The case in question involves the United States of America (USA), the socio-political culture of which bears a tremendous influence over the rest of the world and is considered both a model for democracy and the new Empire (Andrews, 2021). I suggest it also serves as a giant canvas upon which the universal battle to process racialised trauma is projected and enacted. At the time of my writing, relevant historic events at the heart of US politics were holding centre stage and feel so important I will record them here along with my reflections. Capturing the entire crisis and chaos of the psycho-socially traumatic moment would be impossible so I attempt to extract one distinct thread for examination. A clear new phase of the centuries long story of the nation's (and the world's) racialised social unconscious can be witnessed as repetitive, unprocessed psycho-social trauma propelling from one generation to the next.

I will begin with the background to this all too tragic human story. US history is of white supremacy, an invention by European (predominately British) settlers and exemplified by chattel slavery from the early part of the seventeenth century. As in other lands, it required the genocide of indigenous people followed by dehumanisation, terrorism, and the material and bodily plunder of Black people kidnapped from Africa to psycho-socially enhance the lives of European migrants. A bloody Civil War took place in the second half of the nineteenth century whereby the Confederacy (Southern states) fought for independence and the retention of slavery against the Union (Northern states), who were fighting for unification of the Nation and the abolition of slavery. The Union defeated the Confederacy and slavery was abolished under the Presidency of Abraham Lincoln. Shortly afterwards, Lincoln was assassinated by a high-profile celebrity intending to reclaim the Confederacy.

The South soon found itself in dire poverty and largely unable to function without the free labour of enslaved Africans. Thus, the terrorism and plunder of Black people in the Southern states began anew. Regressive laws were instituted, forcing African Americans into forms of de-facto slavery within white supremacist dominion. The pattern of Black gains followed by escalated white rage (Anderson, 2016) and enduring terrorism as part of a murderous backlash characterises a repetitive cycle that has been in motion since the abolition of US slavery in 1865 (Kendi, 2016). It contains within it an aspect of historical psycho-social atrocity in the form of blind hatred of Black success, which disrupts an internalised caste system existing in the depths of the social unconscious (Wilkerson, 2020).

Despair at the repeated pattern of hard-fought Black advancement followed by white supremacist rage, including violence and regressive policy, is offset by the often quoted statement by Dr Martin Luther King: "The arc of the moral universe is long, but it bends towards justice". Strong evidence of an arcing towards justice was perceived in 2008 in the personification of Democrat Barack Obama, an elegant, handsome, Ivy league educated and oratorically skilled Black man of dual white and African heritage, who was elected US President. It was as if the anti-racist components of the social unconscious had served up this 'best of men' as evidence of the fallacy of 'race'. His election was met with initial elation, celebrations and claims of 'post racial' societies (across the world, as well as the US). Actually, I happened to be attending a group relations event in New York at the time of Obama's election, where memories of rejoicing in Harlem and the phrase, '*I never thought I'd see this in my life-time*', which was repeated by emotionally overcome, older Black people, will stay with me throughout my lifetime.

True to history and the painful momentum of trauma though, internal backlash was soon evident. Hatred of Obama's Blackness and of his Black wife was witnessed in unrelenting racist abuse towards them. Mobilisation of right-wing conservative opposition, such as the launch of the Tea Party movement, aimed to disempower and undermine Obama, with much of his Presidency occurring in the face of steep opposition, especially after Republicans secured majority membership in Congress.

If the anti-racist components of the USA social unconscious produced Barrack Obama as the best of men, the determined white supremacist components served up Donald Trump as his 'deplorable' racist counterpoint. Trump, a high-profile celebrity and self-proclaimed property magnate, with a soiled public image, hounded Obama through the media with the so called 'birther' conspiracy. Trump seemed shamelessly comfortable as messenger for the lie that Obama was born in Africa, not the USA, and thereby ineligible for the office of President. This was, of course, a metaphor representing the racist position that, under USA 'caste law', a Black man can never be Premier. Accordingly, the Black man is always the subordinate 'other' and has no place in the 'White' House.

Tellingly, when Obama was humiliatingly cornered into producing and publicising the personal details of his birth certificate for the world to see, this didn't subdue the 'birther' lie. Beyond submitting him to a degrading racist process, it missed the point. As it was, Obama's 8-year tenure was also characterised by his intellectual and moral integrity, plus near flawless conduct. However, when his term in office ended in 2016, it seemed relevant to ask what, from a racial justice perspective, was gained by his presidency? Was it worth it given the severity of backlash, which with full double entendre viscerally resonated as an abhorrent assault? Especially as blame for the pendulum swinging chapter that followed was placed squarely on the shoulders of Obama, his presidency and the one occasion when he publicly, cleverly and eloquently retaliated against the 'birther' lie. As is so often the case, James Baldwin's astute observation may offer a better explanation:

> Well the black man has functioned in the white man's world as a fixed star, as an immovable pillar: and as he moves out of his place, heaven and earth are shaken to their foundations.
>
> (Baldwin, 1963, p. 17)

With no experience of political roles and amid charges of electoral interference, Donald Trump was carried into office as the next President having run on a campaign of 'dog whistle' racism, with a slogan to 'Make America Great Again' (MAGA). Within the not so inaudible pitch of the dog whistle, the slogan of MAGA promised the resumption of white supremacism and the caste system. White supremacy and far right politics in general were on the rise, supported by Trump with numerous armed, torch carrying, MAGA flag waving, neo-fascist and misogynist militia organisations emboldened by his racist rhetoric and posturing.

In contrast to Obama's exemplary conduct, Trump's presidency was characterised by erudite warnings from eminent mental health professionals about his malignant narcissism and unfitness for office (Lee, 2017). Special counsel investigation, imprisonment of his collaborators and an impeachment prevailed. In the glare of Trump's particularly provocative display of white privilege in all its vulgarity, violence and dishonesty, white supremacism gained ground around the world. However, it was in the US that backlash against it occurred. Another phase of the Nation's trans-generational battle to process the psycho-social trauma sequelae of its 'original sin' had been set in motion and reached its crescendo in May 2020 with the graphic modern-day lynching of a Black man, George Floyd. This led to an eruption of anti-racist protest across the USA, with allies the world over standing in solidarity. The unprecedented intensity of protest was striking by the way people of different heritages stood (and lay and knelt) side by side, rising together against violent racism at home and abroad. And in a latent sign of the moral universe arcing towards justice after all, a generation of young people of all 'races', who had grown up under the light of Obama's presidency, challenged and continue to challenge white supremacy in ways that would have been unthinkable in previous eras. Such is the USA with its sway over, and psycho-social mirroring of, world imperatives.

Just as the USA seemed to be on the brink of full-blown fascism, Trump failed in his effort to be re-elected in November 2020. Despite bold efforts to suppress the Black vote, the election was won by Joe Biden, a Democrat who had served as Vice President to Obama. Biden, in turn, selected Kamala Harris, the first woman and first person of Asian and Black heritage to hold the office of Vice President. Refusing to concede defeat, Trump set about further inciting his by now radicalised white supremacist followers with a baseless 'Big Lie' about election fraud by Democrats.

On 6th January 2021 re-election to two Senate seats in the Southern, former slave-owning, State of Georgia occurred. Georgia has long been recognised as a state where African American (predominately Democrat) voters were subject to tremendous voter suppression. Thanks to the extraordinary leadership and organisational skills of Black women, led by local politician and voting rights activist Stacy Abrams, Georgia had been 'flipped' by Democrats at the recent general election. Thanks again to this leadership of excellence, Democrats won the 6th January race, electing Georgia's first Black and first Jewish senators.

The outcome of the Georgia Senate election was announced as the ceremony to confirm Biden's presidency and Harris's vice presidency was taking place at the Capitol. Simultaneously and nearby, Trump held a rally for thousands of his supporters, including neo-fascist collaboratives. Trump then incited this crowd, who he had radicalised to his 'Big Lie', to storm the Capitol, 'Stop the Steal' and re-claim the People's House (i.e. the presidency for him). By now a seditious and murderous mob, thousands pushed and smashed their way into the Capitol building, hunting for politicians to lynch. Armed with weapons and 'flexicuffs', carrying Confederate, 'MAGA', and other neo-fascist flags, and having built a mock gallows, the marauders desecrated and vandalised the hallowed building. Five people died during the insurrection. More than a hundred sustained injuries, some severe and life changing. Two on-duty police officers have since committed suicide. Trump faces a second impeachment.

Had the moral universe arced too far, too fast, towards justice in the USA in 2020 and 2021? When viewed through the prism of large group psychology (Volkan, 2020) it had been rapid, and the combination of Trump's loss of the presidency after one term, the loss of a major Southern state to Democrats thanks to the leadership of Black women, and Trump's manipulation of a radicalised right-wing mob, their unprocessed and shared historic racialised trauma of Confederacy and Civil War loss became significant. The threat to white supremacy of a woman of colour advancing to the position of Vice President while Black women again outmanoeuvred a major plank of systemic racist oppression, leading to the election of Georgia's first Black and Jewish senators, may have been experienced as the final twist of the knife into white racism that day. The backlash and large group regression that followed, complete with time collapse (Volkan, 2020) in the form of an insurrection by a violent, delusional lynch mob, can be understood through this lens.

In the shadow of such major drama, it is easy to miss the fact that Kamala Harris's promotion erases Black women from the Senate. There are, at the time of writing, none. The arc of the moral universe is yet to bend towards justice for Black women, as a large group whose labour is so often taken for granted while our leadership so offends that, to return to James Baldwin's words, "heaven and earth are shaken to their foundations" (Baldwin, 1963, p. 17). Importantly, Audre Lorde (1997) reminds us that trauma was so severe we weren't intended to survive it. The story of the USA is the story of all of us, and we are permeated to the core (Foulkes, 1983) with psycho-social dynamics such as these. The trauma of racialised dramas is continuously replicated in our nations, institutions, large and small groups, and individual psyches. Therefore, it seems to me that if we profess to be committed to the discipline of group analysis, it behoves us to place one foot on that road less travelled and re-route to engage fully with the emotionality, complexity and detail of the various psycho-social traumas characterising our world. I'm pleased to say that this book will offer a clear point of navigation for such journeys.

References

Anderson, C. (2016) *White rage: The unspoken truth of our racial divide.* London: Bloomsbury.

Andrews, K. (2021) *The new age of empire: How racism and colonialism still rule the world.* London: Allen Lane.

Baldwin, J. (1963) *The fire next time.* Reprinted 1964. London: Penguin Modern Classics.

Foulkes, S.H. (1983) *Introduction to group psychotherapy.* London: Karnac.

Kendi, I.X. (2016) *Stamped from the beginning: The definitive history of racist ideas in America.* New York, NY: Nation Books.

Lee, B.X. (2017) *The dangerous case of Donald Trump.* New York, NY: Thomas Dunne Books.

Lorde, A. (1997) *The collected poems of Audre Lorde.* New York, NY: Norton and Company.

Volkan, V.D. (2020) *Large-group psychology: Racism, societal divisions, narcissistic leaders and who we are now.* Bicester: Phoenix.

Wilkerson, I. (2020) *Caste: The lies that divide us.* London: Allen Lane.

Preface

No man is an island, entire of itself; every man is a piece of the continent, a part of the main ... any man's death diminishes me, because I am involved in mankind, and therefore never send to know for whom the bell tolls; it tolls for thee.

(Donne, 1624, p. 103)

Pity is the feeling which arrests the mind in the presence of whatsoever is grave and constant in human sufferings and unites it with the human sufferer. Terror is the feeling which arrests the mind in the presence of whatsoever is grave and constant in human sufferings and unites it with the secret cause.

(Joyce, 1916, p. 221)

Sometimes it's hard to know when to start writing, and sometimes it's hard to know when to stop. "Like it or not we live in interesting times ... times of danger and uncertainty", said Robert Kennedy, way back in 1966, but we could certainly say the same in 2021. This has been a project born of pity and terror – if James Joyce's insight was right, and if we have lived up to its challenge – and it has been a book born into a pitiless and dissociated era.

As we began work on this book, wildfires were devastating eastern Australia while studies were showing that the Greenland ice cap was melting faster than at any time in the last ten thousand years, and a third of the ice fields in the Hindu Kush are doomed even if global warming stays below 2°C (which is now highly unlikely). Cholera, famine and internecine conflict were making a vast 'sacrificial zone' (Klein, 2015) out of the State of Yemen (while the Global North played at proxy wars and cut aid budgets in the name of austerity). Something of the order of 5,500 migrants drowned attempting the Mediterranean crossing between 2018 and 2020.

Border tensions on the borders of India and Pakistan threatened nuclear conflict, while in Myanmar the world watched (and turned away its gaze) in horror as, first of all, Aung San Suu Kyi defended her country's notorious military from charges of genocide arising out of the persecution and displacement of the minority ethnic Rohingya population; and then as she was

xx Preface

placed under arrest by those same generals in the *coup d'état* of February 2021. In China, persecution of the Uighur Muslim minority population of the north-western province of Xinjiang had extended to hundreds of thousands extra-judicially detained in concentration camps and (allegedly) large-scale sterilisation programmes.

After four years of daily commentary, bitter wrangling and acrimonious debate, a (dis)United Kingdom left the European Union with its tail between its legs – almost without anyone noticing – with the xenophobic disaster capitalists who led on 'Brexit' somehow continuing to imagine that theirs (ours?) was the post-Imperial British 'tail' that was wagging the rabid European 'dog'. The COVID-19 pandemic swept across the globe in the wake of the outbreak of the virus in Wuhan in December 2019: most of this book was written in London in extended and not-so-splendid isolation. The Conservative government in the UK, under Johnson, implemented a lamentably late, *laissez-faire* lockdown. Thousands of people died needlessly in consequence of this delay. Marginalised groups, particularly the elderly and people from Black and minority ethnic communities, were disproportionately exposed to high viral load and so died in disproportionately greater numbers. In Brazil, Johnson's fellow populist, President Bolsonaro, waged ecocidal and sociocidal war on two fronts, declining to do anything more than fiddle with the pandemic while the Amazon rainforest burned and indigenous populations were genocidally displaced. In the United States, 45's refusal[1] to accept the reality of the pandemic, and his subsequent suggestions to inject bleach as a remedy, caused hundreds of thousands more to die of neglect in the US. Arrogance born of exceptionalist nationalism led Narendra Modi to expose India to a horrifying second wave, which at the time of writing (May 2020) was seeing thousands of deaths and hundreds of thousands of new infections (under-)reported daily.

On May 25th 2020, George Floyd was murdered in Minneapolis, Minnesota, by a police officer, Derek Chauvin: suddenly, and not for the first or last time, different sorts of wildfires were raging across America and the world. National guardsmen and women were deployed in major American cities 'to restore law and order'. On 11th April 2021, Daunte Wright was shot dead during a traffic stop, and on March 29th, Adam Toledo, 13 years old, was also shot dead by police in what was initially described as an 'armed confrontation'; on April 15th bodycam footage emerged that showed Toledo had his hands up and no weapon was visible when the police officer, Eric Stillman, opened fire at close range.

Amidst this continuing State-sponsored slaughter of Black and Brown bodies across the Atlantic came the staggering news from the United Kingdom Government's quasi-independent Commission on Race and Ethnic Disparities (2021) – a report allegedly finalised before publication by No. 10 Downing Street over the heads of the Commissioners themselves – that not only was Fortress Britain *not* institutionally racist but rather, to the astonishment of many of us, that the UK was a beacon for race relations for the world. Thus does the post-modern 'culture war' violence of gaslighting arise, sneering and spitting, from the ashes of the fine art of irony.

****

James Joyce's character Stephen Dedalus proclaims in *Ulysses* that "[h]istory … is a nightmare from which I am trying to awake" (Joyce, 1922, p. 42). It was against this tumultuous, nightmarish historical *ground* that, after many months of inertia, we mobilised ourselves to address our individual and shared *disappointment* by bringing together and curating the ideas, threads and preoccupations of the body of work we have written together over the last two decades.

In this book we have consciously abandoned the 'clinical' high ground and gladly leave others to tussle for control of those generally inaccessible and mostly self-referential eyries. Instead, we have fashioned what we intend to offer as different conceptual maps and compasses with which to venture out into the wide-open psycho-social lowlands, where human beings long and belong, group, disband and re-group, make contact with each other and put distance between each other. In these lower-lands we privilege the characteristics and qualities of practice-based evidence, which tend to develop inductively and 'messily'; and we seek to conceptualise fields of psycho-social engagement that are often under-theorised. They therefore tend to become undervalued in comparison to those more technical-rational forms of knowledge, clustered under the umbrella of *evidence-based practice*, which rely upon quantification and measurement and which dominate the discourses of modern psychological, social, organisational and political life. With this in mind, we hope and trust that the reader might be ready-enough, willing-enough and able-enough to join us in rolling up our collective sleeves, in the sure knowledge that these conversations are going to get messy.

We initially considered a 'collected papers' format; but as we reviewed our 'back pages' (Dylan, 1964) we came to understand that we didn't agree anymore with some of the deliberations of our younger selves, and realised that we had not sufficiently liberated ourselves in certain ways from the discourses we were aspiring to critique. One of the things that we have learned painfully during combined careers of over 70 years in the field is that if we had been thoughtful enough to have started from a different place, we would have hoped not to have ended up here. But then again, nostalgia is not what it used to be – and perhaps we were older then, after all? The inescapable reality of the accumulating and compounding privileging of the white, male, middle-aged, educated bodies that we inhabit has finally, belatedly, inexorably commanded our overdue but now, perhaps, rejuvenated attention; although we are also confronted by the realisation, as Dylan (1965) also has it, that we still have a way yet to go and do not have any clear direction home.

We have tried not to dissociate from the truth of John Donne's inspirational protestation that *anyone's and everyone's* death diminishes us all. We have demanded, of ourselves and of each other, not only that our gaze is drawn to the minds and bodies of our fellow human beings, the predicaments in which they find themselves and the ground they find to stand on, but also that we examine our own active participation in the pervasive, pernicious psycho-social dynamics of exclusion and processes of (re-)traumatisation[2] – dynamics and processes which we are aware we risk replaying even as we seek to identify, explore and challenge them. We have tried to heed the warnings of those giants who have gone before us, not least among them the great Black American novelist and commentator James Baldwin, who memorably cautioned:

> These days, of course, everyone knows everything, that's why so many people, especially most white people, are so lost.
>
> (Baldwin, 1974, p. 59)

****

The central theme and field of study of this book is the operation, in our families, neighbourhoods and communities, of discourses of power, privilege and position, and of relations of domination between privileged in-groups 'in possession' and oppressed and dispossessed out-groups; and how these discourses and power relations exclude individuals and sub-groups of people from experiences of belonging and potentiality in ways that are not only (re-) traumatising for those who are excluded but also deeply damaging and endangering for us all. We invite the reader to join with us in engaging with the *always* distressing, and too often (re-)traumatising, impact of thinking about and working with human vulnerability.

We have set out our thinking in three parts. In Part I, as part of our own project to find our way home, we redefine our thinking about the nature of unhousedness and unsettledness in inhospitable environments, and our particular reconceptualisation of psycho-social trauma and of (re-)traumatisation. We offer a tool for the exploration of these psycho-social dynamics in the form of what we call the 'Diogenes Paradigm'. We offer our own re-re-telling – set out here in full and in one place for the first time – of the legend of the itinerant vagabond-philosopher, Diogenes of Sinope; of his encounters with his fellow citizens and his trenchant critical commentaries upon the State in which he lived. We offer our Diogenes Paradigm as a lens through which to explore the politics of otherness and unhousedness, of provisional inclusion and structural exclusion, and to analyse phenomena of reciprocal violence between in-groups and out-groups and the contested nature of the public/private spaces, within and outside the agora.

In Part II we use the lens of the Diogenes Paradigm to explore dimensions of hostile and inhospitable environments, and the ways in which traumatic experiences both shape and are shaped by the reciprocal violence at the heart of these processes. Our physio-bio-socio-ecological enquiry explores how such dynamics are played out both in the claustrum of custodial '(mis-)treatment' and the agora of societal provision for, and withholding from, the excluded. In the prevalent 'austere' socio-economic climate, all organisations and State systems concerned with the reception, accommodation, management, treatment, care or support of un-housed, displaced and dis-membered people are *increasingly* susceptible to traumatised, and traumatising, modes of disorganisation. We discuss fraught encounters between un-housed out-groups and inhospitable in-groups at the 'micro' level of the traumatised and traumatising system of health and social care, and at the 'macro' level of climate disaster and human mobility, and their intersections with carbon capitalism and empire. At both these levels of exploration, we interrogate the claim that there is 'no room at the Inn': that claim that is made by the welfare state in the grip of discourses of 'austerity' or by the 'Metropolitan' nation states of the Global North, as the unsettled peoples whom their projections of globalised power have displaced come knocking at the gate in search of shelter from those storms that 'we' of the Global North unleashed upon 'them'.

In Part III we take as our theme the challenge of how to reclaim the agora: how the ethics and the methodologies of activist research and anti-oppressive practice might enable us, and others, to push back into and against the wind of prevailing discourses. We ask what it would take for white people (and white men in particular) to give up our power, position and privilege, or whether only violence can dislodge us – and we explore whether there is any prospect of a peaceful way in which to dismantle the power structures that daily reproduce these relations of domination. We consider the day-to-day inhospitalities and hostilities that are played out in our neighbourhoods and communities, and we especially foreground issues of racial inequality, racialised trauma and the possibilities of anti-racist practice. We pay particular attention to states and practices of equality and to states and practices of disappointment, and we draw upon group analytic, systems psychodynamic and educational theories of practice to discuss possibilities for the opening up of community-based psycho-social conversations of different kinds.

****

A secondary focus of this book is to better understand the considerable challenges faced, by us all as citizens, but in particular by practitioners, teams and organisations who are tasked with reaching out to those deeply troubled (and troubling) members of our families, neighbourhoods and communities who struggle to be accommodated in, and by, these profoundly dysfunctional psycho-social groupings. One fundamental issue that follows from this is the question of language and terminology. For the most part we have sought to eschew the more esoteric 'insider' language of psychoanalytic and group analytic theory and have aimed to write in a more inter- or trans-professional language that might be more widely accessible.

xxiv Preface

We do not presume to claim that our writing style is easy: it is not and perhaps it cannot be, given that the psycho-social processes of (re-)traumatisation that we are looking to evoke and to communicate here are so complex and so painful. However, our aim in positioning ourselves here is to avoid, where possible, speaking only from an 'inside' where, for the most part and on many levels, we understand ourselves to dwell. A book about social inclusion and exclusion, and the reciprocal violence between in-groups and out-groups, had better not replay the same mistakes and more hostile power-plays that it critiques. We don't want to 'invite people in' to a conversation we might be spuriously tempted to claim as *ours.* We assume that you-the-reader are on equal terms with we-the-authors, and we address you as such. We are interested to join the conversations you are having and hope that you find something in here that resonates, challenges and stimulates and mobilises further conversation.

We have set out to communicate something of our own personal, philosophical and political commitment to keeping open questions about the relationships between those of us who, in our vulnerability, are imagined, or imagine ourselves, to be the victims of others' offensive and anti-social actions, and those vulnerable others who imagine ourselves, or are imagined, to be offensive and anti-social. We also take the opportunity to revise and redefine some of our former positions regarding unhousedness, psycho-social understandings of trauma, and our central themes bound up in the Diogenes Paradigm; to regret some of our previous silences and sins, or violences of omission, especially in the domains of racialised discourses of domination, human migration and climate disaster; and to rue our complicity in things we didn't understand or agree with – or in those conversations that didn't sit comfortably, ethically speaking, but which we went along with or turned a blind eye to, in the interests of a quiet life and a payslip at the end of the month.

Nietzsche warns that "when you gaze long into an abyss the abyss also gazes into you" (Nietzsche, 1886, p. 102). As we gaze into that abyss, we also feel mobilised to challenge and repudiate exclusive inter-personal and professional languages that label, diagnose or otherwise (unwisely) 'other' people though unhelpful name-calling of all kinds. One such dimension of professional name-calling that we have in the past engaged in, for which we now take the opportunity to apologise, and which we herewith publicly repudiate, is the tendency to 'diagnose' or 'formulate' people with 'personality pathologies' – as having disordered or deviant personalities – as if this was some sort of 'explanation' of their distress or characters or (most usually, and most pejoratively) their behaviours. We have concluded that such diagnostic name-calling is re-traumatising, stigmatising and othering, and that there is no justification for continuing to collude with this discourse (arising as it does out of the eighteenth-century attribution of 'moral insanity' (Jones, 2015)). We also note that the pejorative attribution of 'disorderliness' (in its various guises) is only ever applied 'downwards' in the societal hierarchy, from privileged, mainly white, people in power, to less privileged others with less power. If we must retain the idea of 'the disorderly', then let us (as we aim to do in this book) look 'up' the hierarchy to those generators of disorder who govern us and who thrive upon the disorder that they generate.

For these reasons we seek to paint our clinical and academic narratives and critiques with the broadest possible brush strokes and a consciously eclectic palette. We have both been group analysts of different kinds in UK public mental health, social care and criminal justice services – but we do not conceive of this as a 'clinical' text. Nor is it a text only about the UK, or only about the UK and the USA; although in large part, though not exclusively, this is a text about the violent state of the Global North. We neither of us sit squarely in any particular academic or professional discipline: we are not psychologists or sociologists or political scientists, historians or philosophers, but we think we have a bit of all of these things in us. Our shared passion is for inter-professional and trans-disciplinary communities of practice and learning. There's nothing more dangerous, for some of us, than having somebody know where you live. They might just knock on your door one night; and they will certainly take it amiss if you decide to 'up sticks' and move without first seeking their blessing.

We have, of late – and for the reasons which we have just stated – found some sort of shelter, if not yet an actual home, under the umbrella of the emergent field of psycho-social studies: an umbrella that we hope might be large and sturdy enough to offer some sort of shelter from the storm. Psycho-social studies, although relatively new as a distinct critical field of study, is solidly rooted in ancient philosophical traditions, and in its contemporary iterations is quintessentially an integrative project. It foregrounds subjectivity and affect and assumes the necessity for effective and meaningful collaboration in exploring the relationships between individual emotional life, family, group, community, organisational, systemic and social experience as shaping our wider personal, cultural and political identities. This psycho-social approach values and builds upon the integration of experientially embodied, psychological, social and ecological knowledge. It is a philosophical approach in the best sense of being loving of wisdom, with a concern for the spirit of humanity and a prizing of the value of curiosity.

Human beings have bodies and minds. Our embodiment, and embodiedness, defines who we are and how we are seen (or not seen), and therefore powerfully determines how we are treated or not treated (in every sense of this word) as well as where, and with whom, we are allowed, or not allowed, to live. This question of habitat and dwelling, then, also reminds us that the planet Earth, too, is a body and that it has an ecology within which all living things are interconnected and upon which all living things depend. On the continuing complexity-in-equilibrium of this Earth system depends the further question of whether, if and where our human bodies will continue to live at all.

We do not underestimate the individual courage or the collective organisation required to establish or maintain the type of conversations that we are promoting here. Nor do we believe that such a position can be easily achieved by isolated practitioners or from those within any single profession, academic discipline or citizen grouping. Our ongoing project is to join and to build communities of practice and learning with other professional, academic and survivor colleagues, and our fellow human beings and dwellers in Gaia, to establish and develop a psycho-social 'culture of enquiry' into the deeply traumatising and excluding processes that have been the focus of this book – with the ambition of searching for, and perhaps discovering (rather than recovering), better ways of living and working together in our families, social networks, neighbourhoods and communities, within the ecosystems upon which, for our very survival, we all depend.

Notes

1 Donald J. Trump was the 45th President of the United States, and in solidarity with African-American colleagues, and in support of creative conversations about his rise to power and his manner of seeking to retain power, we chose not to use his name but rather to refer to him 'simply' as 45. This move is also made in recognition of those nameless and all-too-numerous people who were reduced to numbers during the period of his administration.
2 Throughout the book we want to foreground the notion that for many of our fellow citizens the psycho-social processes of traumatisation that we highlight amount to repeated processes of *re-traumatisation*, which daily heap contemporary insult upon historical injury.

References

Baldwin, J. (1974) *If Beale Street could talk*. Reprinted 1994. London: Penguin Modern Classics.
Commission on Race and Ethnic Disparities (2021) The report of the commission on race and ethnic disparities. Available at: https://www.gov.uk/government/publications/the-report-of-the-commission-on-race-and-ethnic-disparities (Accessed: 15 April 2021).
Donne, J. (1624) *Devotions upon emergent occasions and Death's duel*. Reprinted 1999. New York: Vintage.
Dylan, B. (1964) 'My back pages', from Another side of Bob Dylan. LP. New York, NY: Columbia Records.
Dylan, B. (1965) 'Like a rolling stone', from Highway 61 revisited. LP. New York, NY: Columbia Records.
Jones, D.W. (2015) *Disordered personalities and crime: An analysis of the history of moral insanity*. London: Routledge.
Joyce, J. (1916) *A portrait of the artist as a young man*. Reprinted 2000. London: Penguin Classics.
Joyce, J. (1922) *Ulysses*. Reprinted 1992. London: Penguin Twentieth-Century Classics.
Klein, N. (2015) *This changes everything*. London: Penguin.
Nietzsche, F. (1886) *Beyond good and evil*. Translated by R.J. Hollingdale, 1990. Reprinted 2003. London: Penguin Classics.

Acknowledgements

We are most fortunate and honoured that two eminent figures across multiple fields and disciplines have contributed the Foreword and Prologue to this book: respectively, Dr Earl Hopper, who is series editor, and Dr Anne Aiyegbusi. Both, at different times and in their different ways, have been our comrades, friends and companions over at least two decades and we are grateful to them and look forward to adventures yet to come. We also want to pay our loving respects to Dr Estela Welldon, whose invitation to each of us separately, back in 2003, led to us writing a piece together for the journal *Group Analysis*, which, in publishing terms, was the beginning of our shared authorial journey that has led to the completion of this present volume.

We called upon several colleagues and comrades to act as 'critical friends' – to walk with us a while, anticipate some of the perils of the journey and encourage us to lean into the wind – as we prepared the different chapters that make up this book. Anthea Benjamin, Peter Finn, Wendy Hollway, Leila Lawton, Wayne Martin, Forbes Morlock and Kevin Vento all gave most generously as both friends and critics, and the book is immeasurably stronger for their care and attention. Those numerous weak spots and unguarded flanks that remain are on us, not them.

This book is, on one level, a re-view and a re-working of ideas and themes we have been exploring together and separately over the span of the last 20 years and, beginning in 2005, our joint and individual work on these themes has been published in many journals and books and presented at numerous conferences. Editors have encouraged us; colleagues have written with us; journals and institutions of different kinds have housed and published our ideas as they have developed over time; conference committees have offered us platforms of different kinds. There are far too many involved in this long unfolding process for us to attempt even a partial list, but we are grateful for all the opportunities we had to develop these ideas 'in public'. Of course, we are under no illusion that we have identified any last words on any of these subjects; and we look forward to future collaborations across fields and disciplines and cultures.

There are many others who have inspired us or guided us, put us up or put up with us along the way, and whose thought is now inextricably interwoven with ours. We use the device 'we-the-authors' in this book to signify 'the two of us' – but in truth, that is a much, much larger 'we'. We are sure that we will come to regret key omissions from the following list of people we would particularly like to shout out to here: Gwen Adshead, Mandy Allison, David Armstrong, Alison Beck, Sarita Bose, Gabrielle Brown, Joan Brunton, Gerry Byrne, Jo-anne Carlyle, Annette Clancy, Michelle Cornes, Richard Curen, Gerard Drennan, Annabella Dyer, Craig Fees, Markus G. Fiel, Mario Guarnieri, Anna Harvey, Helen Hewitt, Paul Hoggett, David W. Jones, Adam Jukes, Tilman Kluttig, Lynne Layton, Katherine Lazenby, Martin Lüdemann, Doneil MacLeod, Br John Mayhead, Diana Menzies, Ian Miller, Marina Mojović, Anna Motz, Alastair Murray, David Ndegwa, Michael O'Loughlin, Caroline Pelletier, Caroline Plumb, Mike Rustin, Ian Simpson, Annie Stopford, Elizabeth Stopford, Fin Swanepoel, Robyn Timoclea, Juan Tubert-Oklander, Kati Turner, Matt and Jess Turtle, Genevieve Wallace, Sue Wallace and Estela Welldon. Angela Signorastri held the fort throughout. Solidarity also to colleagues and friends at the *Asociación Civil Esperanza de la Amazonía* (Hope for the Amazon project), the Association for Psychosocial Studies, the Institute of Group Analysis, the International Association for Forensic Psychotherapy, the Irish Group Analytic Society, the Reflective Practice Research Network, Serbian Reflective Citizens, Turvey Centre for Groupwork and the Traumatised Organisations Study Group.

The poem 'Vagabonds' by Langston Hughes is reprinted, in full, at the beginning of Part I of the book, by kind permission of Serpent Press.

With thanks for and to Daniel Byrne and Nathan Adlam, and in memory of the Henderson Hospital Democratic Therapeutic Community (1947–2008), which sought to house un-housed minds and was always ahead of its time, not least in the manner of its passing.

Part I

Un-housed minds
The Diogenes Paradigm

We are the desperate
Who do not care,
The hungry
Who have nowhere
To eat,
No place to sleep,
The tearless
Who cannot
Weep

('Vagabonds' (Langston Hughes, 1959, from
Selected poems, 1999, p. 91))

The land shall not be sold for ever: for the land is mine; for ye are strangers
and sojourners with me.

(Leviticus 25:23 (King James Bible, 1611))

DOI: 10.4324/9781003223115-1

Chapter 1

Un-housed minds and psycho-social traumatisation

As safe as houses?

ROSALIND: Well, this is the Forest of Ardenne.
TOUCHSTONE: Ay, now am I in Ardenne; the more fool I. When I was at home I was in a better place; but travellers must be content.
(As You Like It: Act 2, Scene 4 (Shakespeare, 1623a, p. 714))

This book summarises, reframes and develops what, for we-the-authors, has been two decades of our working closely together on issues of homelessness and social exclusion, and the related phenomena of dangerousness and disturbance.

We locate 'the problem of homelessness' in the continuing inability of this society in which we live, and of those systems of care in which we have been working, to recognise and to integrate into its responses and interventions to this problem, both the sociological fact of dispossession or not having a 'fixed abode' and the psychological experience of feeling disrespected or of not feeling welcomed or accommodated. Our concern is therefore with what it might be like to not have a place to belong – with the experience and the phenomenology of 'vagabondage', in Hughes' usage in his poem that opens Part I of this book (Hughes, 1959, p. 91) – of what it might feel like to have nowhere to go and no one to turn to in order to feel *ordinarily* safe (or safe *enough*) or to find refuge or asylum.

One key challenge is to unpick our notions of 'safety' and 'security'. Is to be 'safe and secure' a fact or a feeling? As 'safe as houses', goes the old saying, but how does safety correlate to housing? Is safety a recognisable idea to somebody who does not feel or never has felt safe and does this change with the introduction of a house? Who gets to write the book on states of un-safety? This is the question incisively put by the protagonist of Ralph Ellison's *The Invisible Man* (1952):

> Where were the historians today? ... What did they ever think of us transitory ones? ... We who write no novels, histories or other books.
> (Ellison, 1952, p. 354)

DOI: 10.4324/9781003223115-2

4 Un-housed minds: The Diogenes Paradigm

How secure do any of ('we') the housed feel inside our alarmed houses, as 'we' build more and more perimeter fences and gated communities? When we speak of safety, of whose safety do we speak? Who gets to make a ruling or have the last word as to how 'safe' and 'secure' one could or should feel?

****

> In my Father's house are many mansions ...
>
> (John 14:2 (King James Bible, 1611))

Foster and Roberts (1998) wrote that "homelessness may be not only a physical reality but also a state of mind" (Foster and Roberts, 1998, p. 31) and their use of the term 'housed minds' (*ibid.*) was one of the hooks upon which we first hung our own long explorations into the multiple psycho-social phenomena which we are now grouping here under the head of the term 'unhousedness'.[1] We have previously noted the ready availability of 'house' and 'home' as metaphor for mind, especially for the mind that holds another mind in mind (Scanlon and Adlam, 2006; see also Campbell, 2019). Plato's theory of forms and the allegory of the cave that he offers in his *Republic* (Plato, 4th Century BCE) evoke both the early home of the human collective unconscious and the anguished imagining that we are all permanently and eternally displaced into a universe of shadows dancing against the wall. Saint Augustine, in his *Confessions*, likens memory to "a spacious palace, a storehouse for countless images of all kinds which are conveyed to it by the senses" (Saint Augustine, 397/8, Book X, p. 214).

Ever since the publication of *The Interpretation of Dreams* (Freud, 1900), the overlapping metaphors of house and home, housed and homely, have been beloved of psychoanalytically-inclined theorists in particular. Jung's self-reported dream (1963, p. 155) offers a vivid example of this symbol of the mind as a house with many rooms and storeys (and mansions?). For Winnicott (1986), home is *where we start from* – and so, we must psycho-socially presume, is homelessness. Bion (1962) offered the concept of 'maternal' containment in order to explore, in psychoanalytical terms, the projective, and introjective, processes whereby internal object relationships are *lodged* within the mind or *evicted* from it (note how we introduce two further 'housing' metaphors in representing his ideas in this way). Brown's edited collection, *Psychoanalytic Thinking on the Unhoused Mind* (Brown, 2019; to which we contributed (Scanlon and Adlam, 2019)), continues this tradition and reaches out beyond the consulting room to attend to the sociological realities of homeless populations and the political and cultural structures in which housing problems are located and played out.

Stuart Hall, theorising and testifying to the particular experience of being a colonial subject, states plainly that "the dynamics of displacement underwrite all social relations" (Hall, 2018, p. 76). Modern philosophy's explorations of anxieties about homelessness begin with Marx's argument that people are alienated from their labour – no longer remembering the needs and necessities and creativity that led them to take up their tools to begin with (Marx, 1844) – and follow on from Nietzsche's ideas on nihilism as the inevitable consequence of the realisation that "God is dead. God remains dead. And we have killed him" (Nietzsche, 1887, p. 203). Heidegger (1947) deconstructed what he regarded as the misconceived distinction between 'being' and 'at-homeness': a collective forgetting, sealed in language, which he felt the Platonic tradition had cemented. He proclaimed that "homelessness is coming to be the destiny of the world" (Heidegger, 1947, p. 243).

Maya Angelou wrote: "The ache for home lives in all of us. The safe place where we can go as we are and not be questioned" (Angelou, 1987, p. 214). The secure base concept within attachment theory is another way of arguing that, in ordinary development, there is a core experience of 'home' and of 'safety', of an experience of one's self as being securely housed in another person's mind.

Clinical theories of mentalisation and reflective functioning have built upon the synthesis of attachment theory with contemporary neuroscience (Bevington et al., 2017; Bateman and Fonagy, 2019). Body and mind in these accounts form a permanent home with a 'lived-in' feel, which can be valued and looked after. There is an echo here of James Baldwin's observation that perhaps "home is not a place but simply an irrevocable condition" (Baldwin, 1967, p. 88). In contrast to the jester Touchstone, we can, the more privileged amongst us, according to this theory, be confident explorers of the 'forests of Ardenne' of our own particular universes, for we have learned from experience that we can make our way back to safe territory if we feel under threat. Others, the less privileged amongst us, for all types of reasons that we shall go on to describe and explore, are less able to retreat to such places of safety.

Unhousedness

> *Jede dumpfe Umkehr der Welt hat solche Enterbte,*
> *Denen das Frühere nicht und noch nicht das Nächste gehört.*
> [Each vague turn of the world has such disinherited ones,
> to whom the former does not, and the next does not yet, belong].
> (Rilke, 1912–22)

These ideas we have briefly sketched on the question of safety and security, and how some of us might feel when we feel 'housed' – and the theme of the potential precariousness of this 'housedness' that runs along the edges of these theories – lead us into our wanderings in the uncanny woods of 'unhousedness': the exploration of which it is the object of this book to recapitulate and to revisit.

By 'unhousedness', then, we mean to denote *individual and group experiences of having been displaced, in ways that are fundamentally unsettling, from*

6   Un-housed minds: The Diogenes Paradigm

membership of communities, large or small, with which one either identifies or finds oneself problematically identified by others.

Here too, we make no claim to anything more than perhaps a new map for already well-charted territory. Berger, Berger, and Kellner (1974) argue for a psychologically and existentially framed idea of a 'homeless mind' dislocated in modernity. And here, too, is Cesarani (1999), whose biography of Koestler is entitled *Arthur Koestler: The Homeless Mind*:

> So Koestler condemned himself to homelessness. All that remained were the ideas he dragged around with him like Job ... Home finally was mind; home was homelessness; Koestler was the homeless mind.
>
> (Cesarani, 1999, p. 573)

Our deployment of the term 'unhousedness' here is carefully and explicitly psycho-social. Unhousedness is a concept identifying *experience* and has a phenomenology all its own. Under the head of 'experience', we include experiences of being subjected to acts or processes of being dis-respected, dis-possessed, dis-inherited,[2] dis-enfranchised, dis-appointed, dis-membered – different yet similar experiences of being 'dissed',[3] unheard, unseated and 'un-housed'.

In offering this conceptualisation, we note that one crucial difference between this and the more standard and not precisely overlapping term 'homelessness' inheres in the active verb 'to unhouse' (or unseat, or displace, etc) – which ensures that we do not forget that someone – those of us who constitute the in-group, in fact! – has *done* the unhousing to someone else.

> "Dispossession! *Dis*-possession is the word!" I went on. "They've tried to dispossess us of our manhood and our womanhood! ... they even tried to dispossess us of *our dislike of being dispossessed*! ... These are the days of dispossession, the season of homelessness, the time of evictions."
>
> (Ellison, 1952, p. 277)

We are therefore primarily concerned here with the *psycho-social* dynamics of two active gerunds, house-ing and unhouse-ing. By the term 'the un-housed', or 'those who have been un-housed', we certainly include 'the homeless', or 'those who have been made homeless'. However, the term will not be limited to that grouping, as there are many more 'dissed' persons who find themselves in a similar psycho-social predicament – who have never been near a soup run or a local council housing department, yet whose *embodied* experience of feeling un-housed is a result of feeling 'dissed' in ways that finds expression much further afield across time as well as within space and has very little to do with the doorways through which they currently enter and leave buildings:

So the days merge together more and more, each one like the other. You wake, rise, look for drink, fall asleep again, staring into darkness, seeing nothing, feeling nothing, hearing nothing. Time passes nonetheless.

(Healy, 1988, pp. 132–133)

Survivor testimony, such as this from John Healy's autobiographical *The Grass Arena*, does not enter so often into the 'public' domain. Experiences of unhousedness are too often unarticulated, un-remembered and dis-membered (although there is in fact a vast literature – 'grey', as the academy would warily categorise it; 'rainbow', as it might be more properly claimed – circulating at the peripheries of societal consciousness). It reminds us of the too-numerous ways in which so many of our fellow citizens are 'dissed' by dint of gender, race, religion, sexuality or other signifiers. It also reminds us that there remain homeless people who do dwell – or 'sleep rough' – on the streets, for whom psycho-social *unhousedness* is not only a metaphor.

Another point of reference here is the story of Stuart Shorter, put down on paper by Alexander Masters in *Stuart: A Life Backwards* (2006). So much is Stuart's story related to and caught up in experiences of 'unhousedness' that his whole narrative cannot be rendered in linear form (as is not uncommon) and Masters' first attempt at a biographical manuscript does not find favour with its subject. Stuart shakes his head and sucks his teeth at the author's attempts to construct a referenced, 'scientific' frame for the narrative; then:

"And another thing …" he says.
"Yes?" I sigh.
"Do it the other way round. Make it more like a murder mystery. What murdered the boy I was? See? Write it backwards."

(Masters, 2006, p. 6 [our italics])

And so he does, and Stuart's story becomes an account not only of what murdered the boy that he was but also of what killed the man he became; a double murder mystery, a narrative of unhousedness, including within it later lethal experiences of homelessness, imprisonment and substance misuse, but also of earlier murderous narratives of disability, bullying and childhood sexual abuse. It is also a narrative that, like its narrator, is itself unhoused-ness – or even unhouse-ableness – a story about the failure of health, social care and community justice structures that were called upon again and again to respond and to accommodate Stuart as both man and boy.

It is worth adding the broad categorisation of different states of homelessness which Masters offers, with Stuart's assistance. Mention is made of care leavers, ex-services veterans, ex-offenders, the poor and excluded, and the previously housed suddenly fallen on hard times, and then:

8 Un-housed minds: The Diogenes Paradigm

Right at the bottom of this abnormal heap are the people such as Stuart, the 'chaotic' homeless. The chaotic ('kai-yo-ic', as Stuart calls them, drawing out the syllables around his tongue like chewing gum) are beyond repair ... *What unites the chaotic is the confusion of their days. Cause and effect are not connected in the usual way.* Beyond their own governance, let alone within grasp of ours, they are constantly on the brink of raring up or breaking down.

(Masters, 2006, pp. 3–4 [our italics])

The structural violence of 'us and them'

They hang the man and flog the woman,
Who steals the goose from off the common,
Yet let the greater villain loose,
That steals the common from the goose.

(Anonymous, 17th century CE)

In this book we intend – but recognise that we will likely fail – to eschew the language of 'us and them'. Divisions, fear, suspicion and toxic projections as between 'us' and 'them' have become the norm. The homeless, the working classes, the feckless poor, the mob, the immigrant 'horde', the sexualised or racialised other: each or any of these 'they's' become *beyond the pale*[4] and therefore frightening to those of 'us' who are sitting pretty upon the proceeds of conquest, colonisation and domination, and are unwilling to relinquish our privilege and our ill-gotten gains. Viewed from this intersectional perspective, 'they' become not simply beyond the pale but more *beyond the beyond*. This phenomenon of toxic 'othering' is epitomised in *David Copperfield* (Dickens, 1849–1850):[5]

"It would be worth a journey ... to see that sort of people together ...".

"Oh, but, really? Do tell me. ... That sort of people. Are they really animals and clods, and beings of another order? I want to know so much."

"Why, there's a pretty wide separation between them and us", said Steerforth, with indifference. "They are not expected to be as sensitive as we are ...".

"Really!" said Miss Dartle ... "It's such a delight to know that, when they suffer, they don't feel! Sometimes I have been quite uneasy for that sort of people; but now I shall just dismiss the idea of them, altogether".

(Dickens, 1849–1850, p. 352)

We will certainly endeavour here to hold no one to be 'beyond the pale' or beyond repair, whilst also recognising that the frailty of the human body means that some, like Stuart, do not, and could not, live long enough to find healing and be restored, and that some historical injuries may require more than one generational lifetime to repair. The stories of Stuart Shorter and John Healy offer a glimpse of what it might be like to feel unseated from one's own sense of self – from the ordinary passage of time itself, even – by the dismemberment of having been psycho-socially un-housed.

Theory that is not cross-cultural and intersectional is no kind of theory at all. The language we use, and the thinking, cultural assumptions and ways of being that are embedded in language, was developed and codified and put into written form, for the most part, over the ten thousand years or so that humankind has been a species of *settler*. The words 'housed' and 'un-housed', 'settled' and 'unsettled', 'lodged' and 'dislodged', 'placed' and 'displaced', all have to do with deep-rooted assumptions or assertions about dwelling and abode, stability and permanence. However, many peoples and cultures have always been, and still are, migrant or nomadic or travelling peoples. Moreover, in a time of 'globalisation', pandemic and climate disaster the very idea of feeling 'securely housed' becomes an elusive one (see Chapter 7). Naomi Klein observes in this vein that "the state of longing for a radically altered homeland – a home that may not even exist any longer – is something that is being rapidly, and tragically, globalised" (Klein, 2016).

As many a housing worker in contemporary urban environments has learned from experience, for homeless people to be able to choose a home is difficult and painful, and sometimes even an impossible thing, and a home allocated, to whatever extent forcibly, is not by any means necessarily a home identified with. One person's secure housing may be another person's hostile environment. If such an offer of accommodation is not taken up, the offerer should pause to reflect upon the quality of their hospitality, however well-meaning it may have appeared on first inspection.

Patrick Declerck (2006) conducted ethnological field research in the early to mid-1980s into the world of the street homeless of Paris (*les naufragés*, the 'shipwrecked', as he earlier called them (Declerck, 2001, p. 163)). He did this by living amongst them, as did Orwell in the late 1920s with the 'tramping' community in England – although Orwell did so for a shorter period, with perhaps more of a safety net around him and with a journalistic more than an ethnological eye (Orwell, 1933). Declerck observed that the suffering of the homeless is felt to be 'necessary' – and societal provision kept in a state of structural inadequacy – because the *imagined insiders* feel hatred for their un-housed fellow citizens:

> We hate *them* because *they* refuse to work and because they seem to mock everything *we* hold dear: hope, self-betterment, personal relationships, procreation, bringing up children, and even simply getting up in the morning. *They* are dirty, smelly, incontinent, and unsociable, and as such *they* are a living insult to *our* aspirations and *our* narcissism.
>
> (Declerck, 2006, p. 163 [our italics])

Declerck provides a vivid example of this phenomenon at work in French governmental policy towards the homeless at that time. According to the Department for Social and Sanitary Affairs, the temperature at night had to reach minus two degrees centigrade while the day temperature needed to not rise above plus two degrees before the emergency shelters would be opened. Declerck describes this as a "thermal limit to the social contract" and shows how this policy reflected "an attempt to calculate what the well-dressed, well-fed, and well-rested perceive as cold weather" (Declerck, 2006, p. 168). It is only when the housed start to feel the chill, he argues, that the homeless are officially to be deemed to be sufficiently at risk of hypothermia (which may occur at temperatures up to 15 or 16 degrees centigrade) for the cold-weather shelters to be opened.

These are no mere abstractions. In 2019, the UK Government's best (under-?)estimate is that 778 homeless people died in England and Wales (Office of National Statistics, 2020). The mean age of these people when they died was 46 for men (against a national mean of 76) and 43 for women (against a national mean of 81) (*ibid.*; see also McClenaghan, 2020).

Structural violence

> ... riots do not develop out of thin air. Certain conditions continue to exist in our society which must be condemned as vigorously as we condemn riots. But in the final analysis, a riot is the language of the unheard ... *our nation's summers of riots are caused by our nation's winters of delay* ... Social justice and progress are the absolute guarantors of riot prevention.
>
> (King, 1967 [our italics])

These death rates for homeless people generally, and for street homeless people in particular, speak exactly to the *societal* violence described by Dr King Jr above. If we organised ourselves differently as a society, these deaths would not occur in such disproportion because we would have worked to minimise both causes and consequences of homelessness, recognising the moral unacceptability of doing otherwise. Carlen (1994) discusses the ways in which what she calls 'agency-maintained homelessness' operationalises this societal violence by means of the following:

> [t]he bureaucratic or professional procedures for the governance of home-lessness which *deter* people from defining themselves as homeless; *deny* that homeless claims are justifiable under the legislation or *discipline* the officially defined into rapidly withdrawing their claims to homeless status.
>
> (Carlen, 1994, p. 19 [italics in the original])

Our fellow human beings here, therefore, are dying of a manifest social injustice.

It was Johan Galtung (1969) who first built on these correlations to offer the concept of structural violence as coterminous with social injustice:

> The violence is built into the structure and shows up as unequal power and consequently as unequal life chances. Resources are unevenly distributed ... Above all the power to decide over the distribution of resources is unevenly distributed.
>
> (Galtung, 1969, p. 171)

Young, Lee and Lee (2018) concisely define structural violence in terms of "the avoidable limitations that societies place on groups of people, which prevent them from achieving the quality of life that would otherwise be possible" (Young, Lee and Lee, 2018, p. 31). Gilligan (1996) depicts the violence of these complex processes of psycho-social traumatisation as indicative of a lethal contagion within the political body. Gilligan based his analysis on his work as a psychiatrist working in Maximum Secure Prisons in the United States. He explores the place of shame and shaming in acts of violence:

> I have yet to see a serious act of violence that was not provoked by the experience of feeling shamed and humiliated, disrespected and ridiculed, and that did not represent the attempt to prevent or undo this 'loss of face' no matter how severe the punishment ....
>
> (Gilligan, 1996, p. 110)

Gilligan distinguishes between *structural* violence and *behavioural* violence by the latter term he means the harmful actions of specific individuals. He suggests that such 'behavioural' violence is best understood as an enacted symptom of the sense of violation, shame and humiliation of un-housed and dis-membered persons and out-groups, understood as 'parts' of the dis-eased social body. The treatment of these dis-membered parts in disconnected and split-off silos, as if they were not connected to this wider social body, serves only to re-traumatise[6] and to further isolate, exclude and *quarantine* the un-housed and the dispossessed. This is the case whether the 'parts' in question are dis-membered because of who *they* 'are' in their bodies, for instance in relation to gendered, sexual or racial differences, or whether it is in relation to what *they* 'do' with their bodies (and to other people's bodies).

For Žižek (2008), the 'systemic violence' at the heart of these processes provides the invisible structural background context of injustice, out of which acts of subjective/behavioural violence emerges: his point being that if we were more mindful of the systemic violence, if it were more visible, we would then perhaps be less startled when the subjective violence manifests itself – and so might be more mindful of how to prevent or treat it. Subjective, behavioural violence, like the 'riot', does not come out of 'thin air', as Dr King Jr notes above – it only appears to. However, in the absence of the social

12 Un-housed minds: The Diogenes Paradigm

justice that King also invokes, that might otherwise prevent the riotous assembly, organised violence becomes not a *behavioural violence* – or a riot – but rather is a legitimate reaction to the structural violence and injustices of the occupier/oppressor; a necessary 'surgical strike' towards the healing of the sick social body (Fanon, 1961).

Wilkinson and Pickett (2009) show that societies with more pronounced structural inequalities, and the adverse childhood experiences that accordingly proliferate (Felitti et al., 1998), are likely to have a larger burden of relative deprivation across a broad range of psycho-social indicators. They thus present the statistical evidence base for structural violence and the harm it causes, and they also point out that in such societies *everyone* is sicker than they would be if living in a society where wealth and resources were more justly distributed. This provides a robust challenge to the comforting self-interested assumption of many in the 'in-group' that in such societies it is only the poor who are sicker.

Our attention is thus drawn not simply to those individuals who find themselves un-housed, dis-ordered or otherwise 'dissed' (dis-possessed, dis-membered and dis-enfranchised) but also to the *psycho-socially* traumatising relationship between this dissed out-group and a societal in-group who consider the differentials between the rich and the poor, the housed and the un-housed, to be normative and acceptable. It is to the elaboration of what we mean by *psycho-social trauma* that we now turn.

A psycho-social understanding of trauma

> It's rainin' and it's stormin' on the sea
> It's rainin', it's stormin' on the sea
> I feel like somebody has shipwrecked poor me.
> (Smith, 1932; cited in Baldwin, 1962, p. 230)

It was Sigmund Freud who perhaps first noticed that the meaning of the word 'homely' (*heimlich*) "develops in the direction of ambivalence, until it finally collides with its opposite, *unheimlich* [unhomely, or uncanny]" (Freud, 1919, p. 226; Campbell, 2019, p. 22). This touches also upon Frosh's (2013) notion about *ghosts* and how we are all, in one way or another, haunted (and perhaps also hunted?) by the spectral *presence* of our forgotten (un-remembered) past – and also by the realisation that these fearful spectres will return – again and again in some terrifying horrific future – until they, and we, accommodate these ghosts in our minds and in so doing allow them to be laid to rest.

We therefore propose that *to be psycho-socially un-housed* is most often a consequence of traumatic experience; and that to live un-housedness is also always *re-traumatising* – a violent and violating psycho-social double-whammy of what went before colliding with *what is now*, in ways that are deeply damaging to the possibility of re-imagining what might be yet to come.

Whether we are settlers or nomads, to be un-housed and dis-membered is something that haunts us now, as it did in the past and always will do – until the end of human-time. A properly psycho-social exploration of traumatic unhousedness does not locate the unhousedness in the un-housed mind of the individual but in the transgenerational, psycho-social dynamics played out between those un-housed minds and the current and historical inhospitable environments that un-housed them and those who went before them (and, without intervention, those who are yet to come).

However, although there is a strong current move in UK mental health, social care and community justice services to move away from the dominance of bio-medical and diagnostic explanations of 'mental ill-health' and its 'expert' interventions, towards what is being styled as a more trauma-informed approach (see, e.g., Herman, 1997), we don't think that it moves far enough. Whilst (very cautiously) welcoming this 'turn to being trauma-informed', we note that it is hardly the first time it has happened and that there is something about the idea of psycho-social, trans-generational, trans-personal trauma that keeps being remembered and then forgotten again. We also remain concerned that this approach, though not 'diagnostic', remains, nonetheless, overly individualistic in its formulation. It therefore continues to locate the trauma inside the 'psychology' of individuals, even if 'adverse childhood experiences' are only to be understood as the *cause* of, rather than as markers, signifiers and consequences of, the wider psycho-social ailments that we are looking to describe. As we will further explore in Chapter 8, in relation to anti-racist practice, there can be peril in small or gradual changes in position when the socio-political *status quo* remains intact.

Our concern is that this *movement* in its ideology, practice and application has mostly to do with superficially de-politicised 'professional/scientific' rivalries about the nature of so-called 'evidence-based healthcare', and the professional re-positioning of 'psychology and psychologists' in relation to the erstwhile hegemony of 'psychiatry', than with the interests of citizen clients. Where once there was bio-medical medicine, so now there shall be 'psychology' – and meanwhile, structurally and politically, very little has changed. 'Trauma-informed care' ought to be such a given that it does not need to be named.

Some survivor groupings of different kinds have likewise welcomed the turn to trauma, albeit with a wariness in which we share. We fear that in any imaginable human future there will *always* be the (re-)traumatised casualties of what Žižek (2008, p. 1) refers to as "the smooth functioning of our economic and political systems", and so there will always be people who are psycho-socially (re-)traumatised through being displaced outwith the hospitality of psycho-socially traumatising structures and cultures. The suspicion therefore arises that the term 'trauma' is being incorporated into the mainstream in the same way as was the term 'recovery'; drained not only of its original meaning and its critical edge, but indeed drained of any meaning at all.

What then do we mean by a psycho-social understanding of trauma? In this book we will proceed on the basis that a psycho-social model of trauma foregrounds the objective violence of profoundly unseat-ing, unsettle-ing and unhouse-ing structures, processes, practices, acts or events that unhouse and that lead to an unhousedness for which psycho-socially informed interventions in pursuit of psycho-social accommodation are the remedy. In a psycho-social understanding of trauma, the phenomenology and hermeneutics of psycho-social traumatising – what are the experiences under consideration, and what meaning has been invested in them – are to be looked for in psycho-social domains. They are not to be found in constructs of individual 'pathology' or deficiency – nor in notions of *resilience*, which suggest that it is the responsibility of the afflicted individuals to *bear up* or *bear with* these disabling socio-political processes.

The nature of the various phenomena that lead to unhousedness therefore needs particularly to be evaluated in terms of their direct or indirect impact upon the ability of the individual or sub-group to take up their membership of community and societal groupings *on equal terms of their own defining*. Trauma, in psycho-social terms, *always* entails processes and experiences of dismembering, dislocating, displacing, unseating and unhousing. Its study (and remedy) therefore *always* entails reaching out and into the fields of invisibility and dispossession evoked by Ellison (1952) – as already noted previously – and of working to make visible again that which has been violently displaced into invisibility. The potentially traumatised/un-housed and/or traumatising/unhousing gaze of the researcher is central to a psycho-social understanding.

This is not a clinical theory or a model for clinical practice, and hence the remedy for unhousedness is not to be sought in the clinic or other socially constituted institutions – which can be, at best, only a small part of the appropriate societal response. However, the implementation of a psycho-social model of care for the psycho-socially traumatised would need to begin with a clear-eyed and vigilant sense of its own potential to deliver (re-)traumatising care, in the very same way that an active and effective anti-racist practice begins by taking as a given its own racism.

Our task then is to propose ways and means through which we might create containing structures in which to have the sorts of conversations, on equal terms and in communities of learning, about the psycho-social processes of (re-)traumatisation that are at the dark heart of our current states of mutual misunderstanding and cycles of violence. Both of us, in our different and overlapping professional roles, are also forensic psychotherapists and consultants, and the project we have set ourselves in writing this book is also, essentially, a forensic examination.[7]

We consider that at the heart of these psycho-social processes of traumatisation there is a profoundly troubling violence that demands to be better understood. Our gaze is drawn to the ways in which violent structural and institutionalised processes of (re-)traumatisation intersect, which give rise to various forms of vicious, self-perpetuating cycles of reciprocal violence (see Chapter 4). The psycho-social phenomenology of reciprocal violence is the field that, forensically interrogated, reveals the underlying dis-membering and un-housing patterns of psycho-social violence, which constitute the primary cause and so give rise to the so-called 'index offence'. The field of study can then be extended to the ecological in identical terms, and to the ways in which the offensive dangerousness underpinning cycles of violence and psycho-social (re-)traumatisation, as a 'joint enterprise' in which we are all implicated, ultimately threatens all human life on the planet (see Chapter 7).

The housed and the un-housed

> Kings will be tyrants from policy, when subjects are rebels from principle.
> (Burke, 1790, Para. 132)

George Steiner (1986) lists "five principal constants of conflict in the condition of man": between men and women, between age and youth, between society and the individual, between the living and the dead, and between men and gods (Steiner, 1986, p. 231). Marx and Engels (1872) argued that society "is more and more splitting up into two great hostile camps ...: Bourgeoisie and Proletariat" (Marx and Engels, 1872, p. 80). We propose a further constant battlefront and breeding ground for processes of psycho-social traumatisation: between the housed and the un-housed.

This particular 'binary structure' (Foucault, 1997, p. 51) vividly illustrates the dynamic that we have been sketching here between in-groups and out-groups. In Marx's polemic history (Marx, 1867), the break-up of the old feudal ties, and the expropriation of the land by the emergent European bourgeoisie, created a whole new phenomenon of homelessness. Marx showed how, as social structures moved away from feudalism into the early pre-industrial emergence of capitalism, the newly-created proletariat

> were turned *en masse* into beggars, robbers, vagabonds ... Hence ... throughout Western Europe a bloody legislation against vagabondage ... Legislation treated them as "voluntary" criminals, and assumed that it depended on their own good will to go on working under the old conditions that no longer existed.
> (Marx, 1867, p. 368)

The Poor Laws criminalised vagabondage and the giving and receiving of alms in cases where the beggar was deemed to be able-bodied (Marx used the example that a 'sturdy vagabond' arrested for a third time could be executed as a "hardened criminal and enemy of the common weal" (Marx, 1867, p. 368)). A further wave of expropriation and hostility towards the expropriated followed on the heels of the Agricultural and Industrial Revolutions in the form of the Enclosure Acts, part of a long sequence of what Standing has aptly named 'the plunder of the Commons' (Standing, 2019; see Chapter 5). The contemporary State, (in the particular form, in the UK, of the Department of Work and Pensions) continues in this grim tradition by deploying 'austerity'-driven policies and procedures; in particular by expanding the definition of 'able-bodied' to exclude from the reach of the welfare State large swathes of the workless and the psycho-socially disabled (to the condemnation of the United Nations Special Rapporteur (United Nations, 2017)). Despite, or perhaps because of, the unchanging passage of time, this violence continues unabated in our towns and cities to the present day, even if it is dressed up in the garb of a patronising neoliberal austerity rather than the executioner's mask.

The period from around the turn of the eighteenth century onwards – long before the neo-liberal turn of the late twentieth century – has been in Britain, in particular ways, a counter-revolutionary epoch; in which the 'commoner' (he who in dignified and self-respecting fashion relied upon and shared in the commons) has come to be denigrated as 'common'. An in-group called 'the housed' started to emerge into consciousness and mutual identification as 'the intentionally housed': they blessed and credited not so much their good fortune, the accidents of birth and so on, as their diligence, application and foresight, and their sense of (pro-)social responsibility.

'An Englishman's home is his castle', so the saying goes, and in this spirit we can imagine the emergent European middle classes peeping out from their castle walls to spy upon those they had displaced and beginning to share with their aristocratic landowning 'betters' a fearfulness lest they be dispossessed in their turn. We observe in this regard the increasing tendency of those of us with 'homes', literally and metaphorically, to lock ourselves into so-called gated communities, with ever more heavily guarded perimeters, in the ultimately futile pursuit of a much wished for peaceful unconsciousness; as we sleep safely in the alarmed houses that we 'hole up' in, on the other side of the ever-higher walls that we construct to protect 'us' from 'them'. The 'housed' thus become the 'not un-housed', and go on to mete out a symbolic and then structural violence against those feared others, the destitute out-group of the 'intentionally un-housed': Rilke's 'disinherited ones' (Rilke, 1912–22), or Ellison's 'transitory ones' (Ellison, 1952), or the 'shipwrecked' of Smith (1932) or Declerck (2001).

The 'un-housed', according to this discourse, must be 'doing it deliberately', and anti-socially, in order to unsettle the housed in their comfortable beds; or they must have recklessly squandered resources or fecklessly pursued vice and indulgence of one kind or another to have reduced themselves to so pitiable a state. Homelessness, rooflessness; worklessness, fecklessness, shiftlessness;[8] placelessness, statelessness: these states of displacement must apparently all be – to use the contemporary coinage – 'lifestyle choices', in which individuals are consistently blamed for their own predicament.

Here we see the operation of Nietzsche's dictum that the "concept of political superiority always resolves itself into the concept of psychological superiority" (Nietzsche, 1887, p. 19). To this day, our political classes, 'tyrants from policy', in Burke's fear-filled phrase,[9] address in their manifestos only the 'hard-working family' that is implicitly the opposite of the 'sturdy vagabond' or, in contemporary discourse, the archetypal 'benefits cheat'. Even now, to be declared to be intentionally homeless in the UK is to find yourself with only limited right to petition for temporary housing provision from the State (Ministry of Housing, Communities and Local Government, 2018).[10]

At a more macro-political level, the same dynamic was paralleled in the European colonial 'discovery' and conquest of Africa, Australasia and the Americas, which caused vast territories to be expropriated and entire populations of 'the uncivilised' to be rendered homeless. It is also currently being played out with asylum seekers and economic migrants across the world who face ever more complex and arduous scrutiny to determine whether or not, for whatever reasons, they have 'deliberately' rendered themselves stateless (we will explore these global psycho-social phenomena in more detail in Chapters 7 and 8). In the politics of the body, a similar scrutiny is intensifying from parts of a healthcare system that seeks to deny physical healthcare to the obese, to smokers and others who are 'unfit' because their very real illnesses are seen as resulting from a lack of will power, greed or laziness, rather than unhappiness, social exclusion, psychological dependency or some other psycho-social ailment. In contemporary Britain, this degrading attitude is also adopted towards the elderly and the infirm, whose vulnerability would also seem to render them undeserving of the quality of care and attention that they need in order to maintain some ordinary human dignity in their frailty (Dartington, 2010).

The un-housed have been 'othered' by the housed in the same way that the West 'othered' the Orient by "disregarding, essentialising, denuding the humanity of another culture, people or geographical region" (Said, 1978, p. 108). The 'housed' in-group, self-constructed as disciplined, logical, rational, measured, respectable, mature and, above all, *normal*, perpetrate a violence both symbolic (located in language and discourse) and structural (located in socio-political power and enshrined in law, particularly in property law) against those feared others, Burke's alleged 'rebels from principle': the displaced and destitute out-group of the 'intentionally un-housed'.

Notes

1 Our colleague Gabrielle Brown found an early Shakespearian use (albeit with a different connotation) of the term 'unhoused' in *Othello* ("my unhousèd free condition": Shakespeare, 1623b, p. 929; Brown, 2019, p. xxii).
2 Hall (2018) wrote that, "as a colonised subject, I was inserted into history ... by negation ... like all Caribbean peoples, *dispossessed and disinherited* from a past which was never properly ours" (p. 61 [our italics]).

3 In our use of the bracketed (dis) (hyphenated dis-) as a literary device we are also mindful of Dante Alighieri's evocation of the 'City' of Dis in *The Divine Comedy*: 'We started moving toward the city ... and saw, in all directions spreading out, a countryside of pain and ugly anguish. ... Each tomb had its lid loose ... and from within came forth such fierce laments that I was sure inside were tortured souls' (Alighieri, 1314, Canto IX, ll. 104–123, pp. 151–152).

4 It is worth noting that the phrase 'beyond the pale' derives from the Latin word *palus*, which means a 'stake' (hence also 'impaled'). Specifically, a *palus* is a stake in the ground that marks the boundaries of a territory, so to be 'beyond the pale' means to be from, or on the other side – the outside – of that territory.

5 Dickens has a well-deserved reputation as a social commentator and progressive campaigner and was revolted by what he saw of slavery in the United States. However, this should nonetheless not obscure his indifferent record in the matter of racial prejudice; as evidenced not only by hostile racist caricatures in some of his writing but also by the fact that he was active in the Eyre Defence Committee, led by Thomas Carlyle, that campaigned to justify, with pseudo-scientific racist smears, Governor Eyre's bloody repression of the Morant Bay Rebellion in Jamaica in the autumn of 1865 (Olusoga, 2016).

6 Throughout the book we hope to be able to hold in mind the relationship between psycho-social processes of traumatisation and the experience of traumatised people of being repeatedly and constantly *re*-traumatised through their day-to-day living in a prejudicial and excluding world. Psycho-social processes of traumatisation almost always become processes of *re-traumatisation* as repeated overt and covert triggering insults and aggressions are constantly heaped upon the original injuries.

7 The word 'forensic' derives from the Latin word *forum* (as the poet Paul Muldoon reminds us (Muldoon, 2011, p. 63)), and therefore pertains to that which is *published* – we might say, that *distress* which is thrust into the public domain – by means of an act of violence.

8 Du Bois (1903), analysing the plight of the 'Black Belt' of the Georgian cotton fields at the turn of the nineteenth century, wrote that to the mind of the 'car-window sociologist ... devoting the few leisure hours of a holiday trip to unravelling the snarl of centuries ... the whole trouble with the black field-hand may be summed up by Aunt Ophelia's word, "Shiftless!"' (Du Bois, 1903, p. 116; by 'Aunt Ophelia' he means the character Ophelia St Clare from *Uncle Tom's Cabin* (Stowe, 1852)). The racist trope of idleness was used first to justify the whip and then, following Abolition (1834) but before Emancipation (1863), to explain away the dwindling profitability of the Caribbean plantations in the middle of the nineteenth century (Olusoga, 2016; for a notorious example of pseudo-scientific racist theorising on this theme, see Carlyle, 1849). This trope has yet to disappear from contemporary discourse. Du Bois satirises the one-eyed violence of this ideological 'snarl of centuries' thusly: '"Why, you niggers have an easier time than I do.' said a puzzled Albany merchant to his black customer. 'Yes,' he replied, 'and so does yo' hogs'" (Du Bois, 1903, p. 118; see Chapter 8).

9 Burke's famous throwaway dismissal of the French revolutionaries brought outrage and opprobrium down upon him from popular pamphleteers across the UK (see Thompson, 1963, p. 98). In the original text, Burke argued that "When the old feudal and chivalrous spirit of *fealty*, which, by freeing kings from fear, freed both kings and subjects from the precautions of tyranny, shall be extinct in the minds of men", then "Kings will be tyrants from policy, when subjects are rebels from principle. When ancient opinions and rules of life are taken away, the loss cannot possibly be estimated" (Burke, 1790, Paras 131–132 [italics in the original]). He predicted that if the authority of the aristocracy and of the priesthood, who,

according to Burke, upheld learning down through the ages, is to be undermined, then "learning will be cast into the mire, and *trodden down under the hoofs of a swinish multitude*" (Burke, 1790, Para. 133 [our italics]). Not to place the two men alongside each other in terms of philosophical stature, but there is an echo of this 'stampede' in UK Prime Minister David Cameron's notoriously destructive comment upon a more contemporary 'multitude', when he remarked on ITV News that "you have got a *swarm* of people coming across the Mediterranean, seeking a better life" (Dearden, 2015 [our italics]; see Chapter 7).

10 The UK 1996 Housing Act provides as follows: 190(2): duty to provide accommodation to applicants who are intentionally homeless ... 15.13 On reaching a decision that an applicant has priority need and is intentionally homeless, the housing authority must secure accommodation for a period of time that will provide a reasonable opportunity for them to find their own accommodation. (Ministry of Housing, Communities and Local Government, 2018)

References

Alighieri, D. (1314) *The divine comedy – volume I: Inferno, Canto IX*. Translated by M. Musa, 1971. Reprinted 1984. London: Penguin Classics.

Angelou, M. (1987) *All God's children need traveling shoes*. Reprinted 2008. London: Virago.

Anonymous. (17th century CE) *The Goose and the Common*. Available at: http://www.wealthandwant.com/docs/Goose_commons.htm (Accessed 20 September 2021).

Baldwin, J. (1962) *Another country*. Reprinted 1990. London: Penguin Modern Classics.

Baldwin, J. (1967) *Giovanni's room*. Reprinted 2001. London: Penguin Modern Classics.

Bateman, A.W. and Fonagy, P. (eds) (2019) *Handbook of mentalizing in mental health practice*. 2nd edition. Washington, D.C.: American Psychiatric Publishing.

Berger, P., Berger, B., and Kellner, H. (1974) *The homeless mind: Modernization and consciousness*. London: Pelican.

Bevington, D., Fuggle, P., Cracknell, L., and Fonagy, P. (2017) *Adaptive mentalization-based integrative treatment: A guide for teams to develop systems of care*. Oxford: Oxford University Press.

Bion, W.R. (1962) *Learning from experience*. Reprinted 1984. London: Maresfield.

Brown, G. (ed.) (2019) *Psychoanalytic thinking on the unhoused mind*. London: Routledge.

Burke, E. (1790) Reflections on the revolution in France. Available at: https://www.bartleby.com/24/3/ (Accessed: 1 January 2021).

Campbell, J. (2019) '"There's no place like home": On dwelling and Unheimlichkeit', in Brown, G. (ed.) *Psychoanalytic thinking on the unhoused mind*. London: Routledge, pp. 19–35.

Carlen, P. (1994) 'The governance of homelessness: Legality, lore and lexicon in the agency maintenance of youth homelessness', *Critical Social Policy*, 14 (1), pp. 18–35.

Carlyle, T. (1849) Occasional discourse on the Negro question. Available at: https://en.wikisource.org/wiki/Occasional_Discourse_on_the_Negro_Question (Accessed: 10 January 2021).

Cesarani, D. (1999) *Arthur Koestler: The homeless mind*. London: Vintage.

Dartington, T. (2010) *Managing vulnerability: The underlying dynamics of systems of care*. London: Karnac.

Dearden, L. (2015) 'David Cameron says he did not dehumanise migrants with "swarms" comment', *The Independent*, 15 August. Available at: https://www.independent.co.uk/news/uk/politics/david-cameron-says-he-did-not-dehumanise-migrants-swarms-comment-10456984.html (Accessed: 1 January 2021).

Declerck, P. (2001) *Les naufragés: Avec les clochards de Paris*. Paris: Plon.

Declerck, P. (2006) 'On the necessary suffering of the homeless', in Scholar, R. (ed.) *Divided cities*. Oxford: Oxford University Press, pp. 161–176.

Dickens, C. (1849–50) *David Copperfield*. Reprinted 1985. London: Penguin Classics.

Du Bois, W.E.B. (1903) *The souls of Black folk; with 'The talented tenth' and 'The souls of white folk'*. Reprinted 2018. London: Penguin Classics.

Ellison, R. (1952) *The invisible man*. Reprinted 1965. London: Penguin Twentieth Century Classics.

Fanon, F. (1961) *The wretched of the earth*. Translated by C. Farrington, 2001. London: Penguin Modern Classics.

Felitti, V.J., Anda, R.F., Nordenberg, D., Williamson D.F., Spitz, A.M., Edwards, V., Koss, M.P., and Marks, J.S. (1998) 'Relationship of childhood abuse and household dysfunction to many of the leading causes of death in adults: The adverse childhood experiences (ACE) study', *American Journal of Preventive Medicine*, 14 (4), pp. 245–258.

Foster, A. and Roberts, V.Z. (1998) '"Not in my back yard": The psycho-social reality of community care', in Foster, A. and Roberts, V.Z. (eds) *Managing mental health in the community – chaos and containment*. London: Routledge, pp. 27–37.

Foucault, M. (1997) *Society must be defended*. Translated by D. Macey, 2004. London: Penguin Books.

Freud, S. (1900) *The interpretation of dreams*. Translated by J. Strachey, 1953. Penguin Freud Library, Volume 4, 1991. London: Penguin.

Freud (1919) 'The uncanny'. *Standard Edition*, 17, pp. 217–256.

Frosh, S. (2013) *Hauntings: Psychoanalysis and ghostly transmissions*. Basingstoke: Palgrave Macmillan.

Galtung, J. (1969) 'Violence, peace, and peace research', *Journal of Peace Research*, 6 (3), pp. 167–191.

Gilligan, J. (1996) *Violence: Reflections on our deadliest epidemic*. Reprinted 2000. London: Jessica Kingsley Publishers.

Hall, S. (2018) *Familiar stranger: A life between two islands*. London: Penguin.

Healy, J. (1988) *The grass arena*. Reprinted 2008. London: Penguin.

Heidegger, M. (1947) *Letter on humanism*. Translated by F.A. Capuzzi with J. Glenn Gray, 1993. Reprinted in Krell, F.D. (ed.) *Martin Heidegger: Basic writings*. 2nd edition. San Francisco, CA: Harper Collins, pp. 217–265.

Herman, J. (1997) *Trauma and recovery: The aftermath of violence – from domestic abuse to political terror*. New York: Basic Books.

Hughes, L. (1959) 'Vagabonds', in *Selected poems*. Reprinted 1999. London: Serpent's Tail, p. 91.

Jung, C.G. (1963) *Memories, dreams, reflections*. Translated by R. and C. Winston, 1963. London: Collins.

King James Bible (1611) *Standard Version*. Available at: https://www.kingjamesbibleonline.org/ (Accessed: 2 January 2021).

King Jr, M.L. (1967) 'The other America'. Available at: https://www.crmvet.org/docs/otheram.htm (Accessed: 1 January 2021).

Klein, N. (2016) 'Let them drown – the violence of othering in a warming world', *London Review of Books*, 38 (11). Available at: https://www.lrb.co.uk/the-paper/v38/n11/naomi-klein/let-them-drown (Accessed: 1 January 2021).

Marx, K. (1844) *Economic and philosophical manuscripts*. Translated by G. Benton. Available at: https://www.marxists.org/archive/marx/works/1844/epm/index.htm (Accessed: 1 January 2021).

Marx, K. (1867) *Capital*. Translated by S. Moore and E. Aveling. Available at: https://libcom.org/library/capital-karl-marx (Accessed: 1 January 2021).

Marx, K. and Engels, F. (1872) *The Communist manifesto*. Translated by S. Moore, 1967. London: Pelican.

Masters, A. (2006) *Stuart: A life backwards*. London: Harper.

McClenaghan, M. (2020) *No fixed abode: Life and death among the UK's forgotten homeless*. London: Picador.

Ministry of Housing, Communities and Local Government (2018) Homelessness code of guidance for local authorities. Available at: https://www.gov.uk/guidance/homelessness-code-of-guidance-for-local-authorities/chapter-15-accommodation-duties-and-powers (Accessed: 1 January 2021).

Muldoon, P. (2011) 'Humours of Hakone', in *Maggot*. London: Faber and Faber, pp. 42–50.

Nietzsche, F. (1887) *On the genealogy of morals*. Translated by M.A. Scarpitti, 2013. London: Penguin Classics.

Office of National Statistics (2020) Deaths of homeless people in England and Wales: 2019. Available at: https://www.ons.gov.uk/peoplepopulationandcommunity/birthsdeathsandmarriages/deaths/bulletins/deathsofhomelesspeopleinenglandandwales/2019registrations (Accessed: 1 January 2021).

Olusoga, D. (2016) *Black and British: A forgotten history*. London: Pan Macmillan.

Orwell, G. (1933) *Down and out in Paris and London*. Reprinted 2001. London: Penguin Modern Classics.

Plato (4th Century BCE) *The Republic*. Translated by D. Lee, 1955. London: Penguin Classics.

Rilke, R.M. (1912–22) *Duino elegies: The seventh elegy*. Translated by A.S. Kline. Available at: https://www.poetryintranslation.com/PITBR/German/Rilke.php#anchor_Toc509812221 (Accessed: 1 January 2021).

Said, E. (1978) *Orientalism*. Reprinted 2019. London: Penguin Modern Classics.

SaintAugustine (397/8) *Confessions*. Translated by R.S. Pine-Coffin, 1961. London: Penguin Classics.

Scanlon, C. and Adlam, J. (2006) 'Housing "unhoused minds" – inter-personality disorder in the organisation?', *Housing, Care and Support*, 9 (3), pp. 9–14.

Scanlon, C. and Adlam, J. (2019) 'Housing un-housed minds: Complex multiple exclusion and the cycle of rejection revisited', in Brown, G. (ed.) *Psychoanalytic thinking on the unhoused mind*. London: Routledge, pp. 1–18.

Shakespeare, W. (1623a) *As you like it*. Reprinted 1986. In Wells, S., Taylor, G., Jowett, J., and Montgomery, W. (eds) *William Shakespeare: The complete works*. Oxford: Oxford University Press, pp. 705–733.

Shakespeare, W. (1623b) *The tragedy of Othello the Moor of Venice*. Reprinted 1986. In Wells, S., Taylor, G., Jowett, J., and Montgomery, W. (eds) *William Shakespeare: The complete works*. Oxford: Oxford University Press, pp. 925–964.

Smith, B. (1932) 'Shipwreck blues'. 10-inch single (78 rpm). New York, NY: Columbia.

Standing, G. (2019) *Plunder of the commons: A manifesto for sharing public wealth*. London: Pelican.

Steiner, G. (1986) *Antigones: The Antigone myth in western literature, art, and thought*. Oxford: Clarendon.

Stowe, H.B. (1852) *Uncle Tom's cabin*. Reprinted 1995. Ware: Wordsworth Classics.

Thompson, E.P. (1963) *The making of the English working class*. Reprinted 2013. London: Penguin Classics.

United Nations (2017) Report of the Special Rapporteur on the right of everyone to the enjoyment of the highest attainable standard of physical and mental health. UN General Assembly – A/HRC/35/21. Available at: https://undocs.org/A/HRC/35/21 (Accessed: 23 January 2021).

Wilkinson, R.G. and Pickett, K.E. (2009) *The spirit level: Why more equal societies almost always do better*. London: Allen Lane.

Winnicott, D.W. (1986) *Home is where we start from: Essays by a psychoanalyst* (Edited by Winnicott, C., Shepherd, R., and Davis, M). Harmondsworth: Penguin.

Young, J., Lee, B.X., and Lee, G. (2018) 'From human violence to creativity: The structural nature of violence and the spiritual nature of its remedy', in Adlam, J., Kluttig, T., and Lee, B.X. (eds) *Violent states and creative states: From the global to the individual. Volume 1: Structural violence and creative structures*. London: Jessica Kingsley Publishers, pp. 29–44.

Žižek, S. (2008) *Violence*. London: Profile Books.

Chapter 2

The Diogenes Paradigm

In-groups and out-groups

ALEXANDER: Dost thou not know that I am able to give thee a kingdom?
DIOGENES: I know thou art able, if I had one, to take it from me; and I shall
never place any value on that which such as thou art can deprive me of.
(Fielding, 1743)

This book is about fraught encounters in liminal spaces where two or more
bodies, groups or social worlds intersect or collide – about what happens
when un-housed minds encounter inhospitable environments.

A 'fraught encounter' could involve an outreach worker kneeling down
beside the tent of a street homeless or an assessment appointment in a spe-
cialist service for people with 'complex needs'; or it could involve hired hands
of Agribusiness, or Big Oil, torching acres of Amazonian rainforest or pushing through a pipeline to the Alberta tar sands under the outraged or des-
pairing gaze of indigenous peoples whose homes, culture and languages are
being destroyed; or it could involve a barrel bomb spiralling down from the
skies to burst upon some rebel-held suburb of Aleppo.

The Italian political philosopher Giorgio Agamben observes that
"[E]very limit concept is always the limit between two concepts" (Agamben, 1995, p. 11). To delineate and mark the boundary of a concept, so as
to more effectively describe that which it includes and encloses, necessarily
also denotes and differentiates that which comes to be defined as located
on the other side, the outside, of these boundaries. This is the case whether the territory thus delineated is conceptual or geographical. Where 'I'
ends, there 'not-I' begins; and so it is also with groups, communities,
societies and countries, even if it is sometimes harder to determine exactly
where the boundary may lie.

Declerck (2006) writes that cities are "the site of a deep division between a
socialised majority and a desocialised minority", and that this division is no
accident but rather "a structural necessity … cities are the stage on which

DOI: 10.4324/9781003223115-3

society chooses to display the price paid by those who do not accept – because they cannot – the obligations of social existence" (Declerck, 2006, p. 161).

In this book we take Declerck's observation as our starting point for a wider-ranging psycho-social enquiry into the nature of fraught encounters between territorial and conceptual in-groups and the membership of out-groups who must find themselves, and each other, whilst on the outside.

The particular group that takes up the work of defining the limit concept – that work, which at the State level, pertains to what Foucault calls 'biopolitical power' and the operation of 'discourse' (Foucault, 1997) – is necessarily defining itself as the 'in-group'. The membership of the 'out-group' thereby consists of those who are not in a position to join in the work of definition: the work of identifying, describing or explaining *themselves* in their own terms.

Tom Main, who was Medical Director at the Cassel Hospital, an internationally renowned multi-disciplinary psychoanalytic inpatient treatment service, described a particular *ailment* that was characterised by processes of fragmentation and subgrouping in the treatment team (Main, 1957). Main and his colleagues observed that an in-group of medical practitioners would come together in subliminal identification and collusive self-satisfaction to pronounce on 'what was really going on'. Other members of the multi-disciplinary team (such as nurses and social workers) came together in more loosely formed out-groups elsewhere, united not only by their sense of seeing the clinical situation differently but also by their frustration that they were excluded from the places and spaces where this 'privileged knowledge' was produced. For the in-group, once it has constituted itself, the work of defining who or what lies beyond its limit – outwith the city wall – tends to assume ever-increasing importance in order to bolster and boost the spurious belief, upheld by the in-group, of the rightness of their thinking.

This is a form of violent exclusion in which the work of the in-group becomes less a question of asking 'who are we (all)?' and more a process of identifying and defining 'who is not with us and is therefore against us'. It is about an exclusivity that, at its most benign, is always infused with superiority and a patronising *noblesse oblige* and, at worst, is a clear and present manifestation of relations of domination, coercion and control of those 'without'. At the State level, Agamben (2003) identifies the 'state of exception', in which the rule of law in certain circumstances can be suspended (for example, the suspension of the rule of law at Guantanamo Bay) as *the* defining mechanism by which power is manifest in the modern nation State. In such a state, the in-group has free rein to exercise its powers as it pleases – or indeed as it dis-pleases.

These processes within the in-group, in turn, give the (by now) more scattered membership of the out-group a chance to cohere in identification, around the hypothesis that 'he who is not against me must be with me'. Fearful feelings congeal into massified, hostile ideologies; 'chosen glories' and 'chosen traumas' are distributed (Volkan, 2009); blows are substituted for (harsh) words. Before anyone quite understands how we got here, boundaries have become barriers, walls and fortifications are being built and barbed wire is being stretched across their ramparts and parapets. In Foucault's words, "a battlefront runs through the whole of society … There is no such thing as a neutral subject. We are all inevitably someone's adversary" (Foucault, 1997, p. 51). A *reciprocal violence* begins to manifest itself – we will come back to this idea in more detail in Chapter 4.

In this context we wish to re-present two questions, rehearsed earlier in Chapter 1, that we see as intrinsic to these particular kinds of fraught encounters. Firstly, how can we re-think the challenges involved in seeking to promote social inclusion without perpetuating social exclusion as we do so? And how can we re-think the challenges involved in out-reaching to the un-housed, abject, excluded and 'hard-to-reach' out-group, in circumstances where the 'terms of engagement' for 'coming in from the cold' may just be too much for the members of those out-groups to bear or to swallow?

Here we face a central dilemma: how to speak about these psycho-social dynamics and dilemmas without replaying the oppressions we are trying to challenge and overthrow. The French philosopher Jacques Rancière counsels us to avoid the perils and pitfalls of ventriloquism when 'philosophising the poor' (Rancière, 1983). In the context of the difficulties we are trying to map here, there can be no substitute for first-hand survivor testimony. The problem is that the un-housed are mostly not seen, their stories are not spoken, and so, not heard. We find ourselves ethically constrained from ventriloquising other peoples' life stories in the form of 'case histories'; and so, we turn to story-telling of a different kind.

In our work together over the last two decades, we have used stories from history, literature and legend to illustrate the psycho-social realities we are trying to explore. We have in mind here the use of the story as 'mutative metaphor' (Cox and Theilgaard, 1997), which might both depict and elaborate the fraught encounters that we have experienced and observed in our own practitioner experience of working in health, social care and community justice settings over (too?) many decades. It is impossible here to do justice to the vast literature that opens up under that head. However, one such story – one-third myth, one-third legend, one-third history – that has been (re)told many times over the last 2500 years, and continues to grow in the telling, concerns the life and times of Diogenes of Sinope. It is to this tale that we now turn.

Defacing the currency

The Diogenes Club is the queerest club in London … There are many men in London, you know, who, some from shyness, some from misanthropy, have no wish for the company of their fellows …. It is for the convenience of these that the Diogenes Club was started, and it now

26 Un-housed minds: The Diogenes Paradigm

contains the most unsociable and unclubbable men in town. No member is permitted to take the least notice of any other one.

(Conan Doyle, 1893)

The 'Diogenes Club' was favoured by Sherlock Holmes' brilliant older brother Mycroft as a form of psycho-social retreat from the social niceties and hypocrisies of the wider societal context (a main condition of admission was that no member must speak with another, on any subject, ever). In 2004, the embalmed body of a homeless man named Edwin 'Diogenes' MacKenzie (to whom this book is respectfully dedicated) was discovered among the possessions of the painter Robert Lenkiewicz, who had died two years previously. Lenkiewicz's 'Vagrancy Project' collected paintings of and testimonies from the many street homeless people who had clustered around his various studios, and he had established a series of informal housing provisions in derelict warehouses that might then have been described as 'doss-houses'. His protégé MacKenzie, who was born in 1912, was a homeless man who lived in a concrete barrel in Chelson Meadow on the estuary of the River Plym. Lenkiewicz painted his portrait many times and, for some while, MacKenzie acted as supervisor of one of Lenkiewicz's 'doss-houses'. Lenkiewicz later recalled:

> I called him Diogenes after the philosopher who lived in a barrel because I found him living in a concrete barrel, a circular container, in the crook of a tree looking down onto Chelson rubbish tip, a precipitous drop, and he had lived in there for nine years. I remember lifting up some of the coats that he slept on to find the whole thing teeming with maggots, so he was a pretty rough and ready character. He certainly looked like your archetypal medieval scholar ...

(Lenkiewicz, 1997, p. 34)

MacKenzie died in 1984 – and in accordance with his own wishes his corpse was embalmed and retained (and hoarded?), in defiance of various scandalised relevant authorities. It also happens that 'Diogenes Syndrome' is an informal term for the diagnostic term 'syllogomania', or 'pathological hoarding', a practice common to many of the un-housed who, perhaps partly in parody of the manner in which the housed accumulate possessions in capitalist societies, surround themselves with what the housed may regard as 'rubbish' but which, for the individual in question, may represent intensely felt layers of meaning.

Our story is the story of the man whose name, in these and other ways, has been handed down through the ages: Diogenes of Sinope, a wandering Cynic[1] philosopher and manic street preacher; and of his interactions with the people that he encountered and engaged with on his travels. (For sources from antiquity on the life and times of Diogenes, see Diogenes Laertius (3rd century BCE) [DL when specifically cited in what follows] (no relation, by the way!);

Dio Chrysostum, 2nd century BCE; Plutarch, 1st century CEa; 1st century CEb; Navia, 2005).

Sinope, now known as Sinop, is an ancient and strategically significant coastal town on the northernmost promontory of the northern Turkish coast, roughly due south of Sebastopol across the Black Sea. It was a prosperous port, situated along major trade routes, and famous for minting coins. In ancient times it was occupied and colonised by Greek, Macedonian, Persian and Byzantine imperial powers before becoming part of the Ottoman Empire in the twelfth century: this is important to note because the psycho-social trauma that underpins and emerges from experiences of oppression, appropriation and colonisation is a fundamental part of our story.

Diogenes was born in Sinope right at the end of the fifth century BC (Diogenes Laertius suggests 413 BC). At this time, Sinope was a democracy, established by Pericles of Athens. Diogenes and his father, Hicesias, had made themselves a tidy pile by getting themselves put in charge of minting the city's highly esteemed and much-prized currency (coins bearing Hicesias' name have been found at various sites (Navia, 2005, p. 226, n. 2)). Think of this father-son duo as perhaps the ancient world equivalent of white-collar criminals: they were caught defacing the coinage and had to disappear into exile. There are conflicting reports as to who actually did what – Diogenes Laertius cites competing authorities (DL, 6.20; Navia, 2005, p. 205). According to one account, it was Dad who brought disgrace upon his son – others maintain it was the other way around, and Diogenes Laertius suggests that Diogenes himself confessed to the offence in one of his now lost writings.

The Greek wording also leaves room for interpretation about whether the coinage was defaced, the precious metals 'skimmed off the top', or whether father and son minted counterfeit coins alongside their official output. We could even read into the story that Hicesias and Diogenes were not so much white-collar criminals as covert activists, protesting Greek domination of their city by undermining the currency of empire. Freedom fighters or dodgy dealers, all that matters, for purposes of the story we wish to tell, is that Diogenes became a displaced person. One way or the other, he had given offence and was publicly shamed and driven into exile and homelessness (and Hicesias was thrown in jail).

Shamed but not necessarily ashamed, Diogenes Laertius suggests that when later, in Athens, Diogenes was confronted with his 'shame-ing' in Sinope, he countered that "it was precisely through that ... that I became a philosopher"; rather than having been condemned to exile by his ertswhile fellow citizens, he instead "condemned them to stay in Sinope" (DL, 6.49; Navia, 2005, p. 214). Diogenes, in his attitude on this score – and on shame generally, as we shall see – was rather one who might say, 'you may decide that I have been shamed, but it's my life and I'll think my own thoughts about it, and I decline to be troubled by what you or anyone else may be thinking about it all'. *Anaideia* – shamelessness – would come to be a core value embedded in Diogenes' *praxis*, his way of being coherently in the world.

But we are jumping ahead. Here, for the moment, we find him, newly a fully-fledged member of the out-group, leaving Sinope with a criminal record, or at any rate under a storm cloud of calumny, still eight hundred or so miles from Athens as the crow might have flown, and needing direction or inspiration. When in doubts and uncertainties, in those days, the thing to do was to consult the oracle (although Diogenes would later reportedly be disparaging of this practice (Navia, 2005, pp. 30–32)). There actually was a Delian oracle in Sinope; but in the version of the story we prefer to imagine, Diogenes finds his way to Delphi. There he puts his question to the Pythia, the high priestess of the oracle.

According to Diogenes Laertius (DL, 6.21; Navia, 2005, p. 205), he specifically asked how he might win the greatest reputation (shame, in his own mind, thus already repudiated). Conceive of his surprise and mystification, then, when the response he receives is the quintessentially Delphic advice that he should 'deface the currency'! 'I've already done that – *and* I've already been *done* for that!', we might imagine him protesting. However, the Pythia will not deign to parse the message of the Gods: Diogenes must figure it out for himself.

And this is the inspiration he finds: he will set out now to deface the *political* currency of the day. He will make his way to Athens and he will hold no truck with social niceties and with the discourses of the in-group. So, they would kick him out of their way, would they, like a dog (an animal strongly associated with shame in ancient Greek culture), expect him to cower, shamed, in some corner? Well, maybe dogs know a thing or two about how to be in this world – he will model his *praxis* upon theirs. (The townspeople of Athens will later ask him what he did to deserve being called a dog, and he will retort: "I brown-nose those who give me alms, I yelp at those who refuse, and I set my teeth on those who are rascals" (DL, 6.60; Navia, 2005, p. 218).) He will stand in the marketplace and call things as he sees them – let people say what they may. He will question everything, take nothing as read. Surrounded by dogs, he will be himself *dogged* in pursuit of the truth. The Greek word *kynikos* means 'doglike'; therefore, Diogenes the Dog[2] also became known as Diogenes the Cynic (literally, 'a man from God who acted like a dog' (Navia, 2005, p. 7)). An image of a homeless man, then, and a befriender of dogs: a persistent portent and foreshadowing of relationships between gods, dogs and men that we see, or more often look away from, on the streets of our towns and cities today.

Diogenes' barrel and the hospitality of the agora

> Our city is open to the world.
> (Words attributed to Pericles by Thucydides, 5th century BCE, p. 146)

The scene now shifts to the Athenian *agora* or marketplace, which was the central public place where goods, services and ideas were exchanged (and of which we shall have much more to say in Chapter 5). For present purposes, it is enough to note that a certain ethos of hospitality was upheld, as Thucydides suggests, in the Athens of those days (allowing that this Athens was a slave State whose immense wealth was built from the fruits of war and plunder). A displaced person down on his luck, such as Diogenes, would very likely have found his way to the *agora* on arrival in the city – and would not necessarily have encountered a hostile environment or found himself processed through databases via CCTV and escorted to the gates by corporate security patrolmen of severe mien and unsettling livery, as is so often the fate of so many of his modern homeless counterparts.

Diogenes was an educated and previously prosperous man with a fair bit of intellectual and social capital at his disposal. He had very possibly been to Athens before and had connections he could have looked up if he'd been of a mind and had wanted to seek accommodation. Offers came his way and Diogenes Laertius reports that he considered a cottage at one point (DL, 6.23; Navia, 2005, p. 206). But Diogenes found he could not live under a roof of any permanent nature – it weighed in too heavily upon him, we might imagine, and loomed too oppressively between him and the open sky.

He took up his abode in a barrel, or tub, in the *agora*. Today you can still visit the site of the *agora* in the centre of modern Athens and visualise, amid the ruin of crumbled stone, the spot where roughly he thus made his camp. There are varying versions of what kind of vessel it was that he inhabited: the Greek word '*pithos*' might suggest something more like a very large ceramic jar used for storage – and thereby connects Diogenes' tub to other mythological places associated with turbulent states of mind and disturbances, such as Psyche's jar and Pandora's box.

Discarded *pithoi* in some early Mediterranean cultures were used for burial purposes (an echo here of the embalmment of Diogenes MacKenzie?) and so there is something here about the ambiguity and potential darkness or dangerousness of the term 'container' and of what it might hold. Diogenes, who had a gift for parody, which we shall explore further, may have been making play with ideas of safety as well as ideas of what a home 'should' look like when he crawled into his tub with his dogs and his rags, right in the centre of the ancient *agora*, pronouncing himself uninterested in more worldly notions of resettlement. As already suggested, the Athenians took him largely to their collective bosom and Diogenes Laertius relates how they once replaced his tub for him and punished those who had smashed up the old one (DL, 6.43; Navia, 2005, p. 212).

In his own subversive way – in the only way that was consistent with his practice; the only way, we suggest, that he felt was open to him – Diogenes proceeded to make himself at home. He lived a dog's life in full view, not so much (a)shamed or shameless as declining to attach any importance or to confer any authority upon discourses of shame. He spat, and shat, and masturbated in his barrel; and when challenged on that latter act of self-soothing,

30 Un-housed minds: The Diogenes Paradigm

Diogenes is supposed to have countered that he wished it were as easy to relieve his hunger by rubbing his stomach. When Plato is supposed to have called him a 'dog', Diogenes retorted: "Quite true, for I come back again and again to those who have sold me" (Critchley, 2009).

Diogenes Laertius coyly suggests that, rather like the dogs surrounding him, Diogenes may also have performed sexual intercourse (the "works of Aphrodite") in public (DL, 6.69; Navia, 2005, p. 221); although his tub may not have been quite large enough for this activity. At any rate, this biographical allusion earns its subject a disapproving rebuke down through the ages from no less an authority than Saint Augustine, who grumbles that Diogenes imagined his world view would gain more traction,

> if its indecency were more startlingly impressed on the memory of mankind ... the Cynics did not continue this practice, and modesty, which makes men feel shame before their fellows, prevailed over error – the mistaken idea that men should make it their ambition to resemble dogs.
> (Saint Augustine, 1467, p. 582)

Diogenes in much of his *praxis* was perhaps consciously following in the footsteps of Socrates, who famously stretched Athenian hospitality beyond its breaking point, and whom Plato portrays as saying,

> [t]o put it bluntly ... God has assigned me to this city, as if to a large thoroughbred horse which because of its great size is inclined to be lazy and needs the stimulation of some stinging fly.
> (Plato, 4th century BCE, p. 57)

Plato indeed is supposed to have described Diogenes as "a Socrates gone mad" (DL, 6.54; Navia, 2005, p. 216). Certainly, 'making himself at home' seemed, for Diogenes, to entail making as much of a nuisance or gadfly of himself as possible – 'defacing the currency' turned out to be a full-time job (O'Loughlin, 2011).

From the base camp of his barrel, Diogenes maintained a questioning and challenging stance towards the society that surrounded him. His protest took the form of a running commentary on the hypocrisies inherent in the relationships between people and how they were played out in the organisation of the social world. He would wander the streets in broad daylight carrying a lamp before him (the inspiration for Seamus Heaney's sublime poem *The Haw Lantern* (Heaney, 1987)), claiming to be in search of 'one honest man' and belabouring with his stick anyone upon whom his disapproval became focused. He would call for men to listen to him and then set upon them with his staff, saying, "I called for men, not for scoundrels" (DL, 6.32; Navia, 2005, p. 209).

He was, in short, "great at pouring contempt upon his contemporaries" (DL, 6.24; Navia, 2005, p. 206). If ever you-the-reader have found yourself accosted and harangued on the city streets by some fierce, bedraggled and unworldly stranger, on a subject matter you hadn't remembered raising in conversation (or, indeed, if you at any time have stood in that stranger's shoes yourself), then you will know something of how Diogenes busied himself in the Athens of his day at the full-time job of thinking his own thoughts and standing in his own shoes.

****

We trust by this point that the shape of our story is becoming clear. Our principal protagonist is a *dogged* and psycho-socially traumatised human who, shamed into exile and flight, becomes homeless and displaced. Stripped of citizenship, he is *homo sacer* (Agamben, 1995), which is to say, 'bare life', a Stateless subject. He quickly becomes deskilled in the practices of the in-group, as street homeless people very often do, but he finds other resources inside him and around him – he *resists*. He goes to advice agencies (the oracle!) but he's too far out in the cold to be able to come back in again in any way that feels congruent for him. He comes to the big city and sets up his camp in the marketplace amongst his pack. There, after his own fashion, he makes a life for himself; outside of the conventional world, but in caustic, ironic and parodic relationship with it.

Diogenes declines all ambiguous worldly offers; and plenty of them come his way, along the lines of, "here, kindly accept your proper portion of shame and shame-ing", or, "now, graciously receive your portion of resettlement, without quibbling as to the terms and conditions". He's having none of it, and why should he? The in-group experiences him as 'treatment-refusing', but he has his values and his ethics and he feels that the ground he stands upon is the *only* ground he can stand upon. He is neither hero nor anti-hero. The historical Diogenes by most accounts was, of his time perhaps, both toxically misogynistic as well as acidly misanthropic – and we-the-authors don't suppose, either, that we would much have relished him setting about us with his stick. The reader must form their own view. For our part, he has our empathy and our respect (which is probably what matters most), and even our admiration – but not necessarily or unequivocally our endorsement – neither, we must acknowledge, would he or should he have cared in the slightest what we thought of him.

By withholding recognition to the laws and mores of his society, Diogenes sets out to provoke reflection upon the limitations of those laws and mores. As such, Diogenes takes his place in a long and honourable tradition of wandering Cynic philosophers and street preachers, like Antisthenes and Socrates before him, and onward via 'the historical Jesus' (Crossan, 1992), through to Mahatma Ghandi or Dr Martin Luther King Jnr. A contemporary example might be found in the figure of Greta Thunberg, who set up her metaphorical barrel outside the Swedish Parliament, on Friday 20 August 2018, for a solo 'school strike' protest against indifference to and authorship of climate disaster at both a State and a global level. She handed out leaflets proclaiming that the reason for her strike was that, "you adults are shitting on my future" (Crouch, 2018). This was Cynical *praxis* at its purest. Just over a year later, on Friday 20 September 2019, millions of people across 185 countries joined her in her weekly Friday climate strike (Laville and Watts, 2019).

Diogenes and Alexander

KING LEAR: First let me talk with this philosopher.
(*The Tragedy of King Lear*: Act 3, Scene 4 (Shakespeare, 1623, p. 1084))

Now it is time to introduce into the story our other lead character. The powerful combination of social challenging and Cynical enquiry we have been describing comes into focus in Diogenes' fraught encounter with Alexander the Great, the mighty son of the mighty Philip of Macedonia. Macedonia was the great imperial power of its day and Alexander was the most powerful man in the world; perhaps the most powerful man that ever lived. His empire, when he died in 323 BCE at the age of thirty-two, covered more than two million square miles.

In the winter of 336–335 BCE, when this meeting is supposed to have taken place, leaders of the several Greek city-states had met in conference near Corinth and voted to join forces with Alexander and to propose him as commander-in-chief for the planned conquest of Persia (Plutarch, 1st century CEa, p. 266; Lane Fox, 2004, p. 71). Diogenes meanwhile was hanging around a suburb of Corinth[3] called Craneion,[4] lying in his barrel with his dogs. The power differential between the two men, on the face of it, could not have been wider. We suggest, therefore, that the story of their encounter may stand as a paradigmatic tale for all encounters between the out-reaching, colonising, inhospitable in-group and the alienated, resisting, un-housed out-group – between 'sovereign power' and 'bare life' (Agamben, 1995).

The great and the good of the military-philosophical complex came to the city of Corinth in the weeks that followed the conference at the Isthmus of Corinth in order to congratulate Alexander. Alexander had heard tell of Diogenes' exploits and track record and found himself piqued that the latter had, perhaps dangerously, declined to pay homage. He decided to go down to Craneion to do a bit of outreach. To begin with, it doesn't go very well (perhaps this is often how it goes, when, as is not infrequently the case, the would-be outreach worker is less than half the age of, and has a fraction of the lived experience of, their target won't-be client). "I am Alexander the great king", he begins. "And I am Diogenes the Dog", comes the response (DL, 6.60; Navia, 2005, p. 218). A tumbleweed moment, if ever there was one.

However, the two men recognise something in themselves and in each other, and perhaps something of themselves in each other – some kind of wary identification and commonality of outlook, even if their two positions are irreconcilable and mutually exclusive – and they end up talking at length. Alexander has himself recently been under the tutelage of the young Aristotle (Lane Fox, 2004). He is a man who claims to value friendship above all other goods, and he finds much to discuss with his resisting 'client', a man who (apocryphally) has exchanged barbed words with Plato and had been the disciple of Antisthenes, a student of Socrates (DL, 6.21–25; Navia, 2005, pp. 205–207).

Alexander finds himself impressed, not only by the abject state of Diogenes' living conditions but also by his wit, his intelligence and fearlessness – in Plutarch's words, "for the hauteur and independence of mind of a man who could look down on him with such condescension" (Plutarch, 1st century CEa, p. 266). He asks if there's anything he can do for him; perhaps he suggests, in so many words, that Diogenes deserves better, if only he would pull his finger out (and maybe ditch the hounds ...) and that he, Alexander, is just the man to fix things for him. Diogenes replies from his barrel, in terms familiar to any outreach worker who has knelt down alongside a homeless person's 'bash': "Yes, stand aside a little, for you are blocking the sun" (Lane Fox, 2004, p. 71).

The Diogenes Paradigm

> For leaning out last midnight on my sill
> I heard the sighs of men, that have no skill
> To speak of their distress, no nor the will!
> (Owen, 1918)

This encounter, then, offers us an archetypal and fundamentally psycho-social image to represent two worlds colliding. This image is both clinical and societal, personal and collective. Diogenes stands for our latter day socially excluded: the homeless, the displaced, the truant, the starved, the addicted, the anti-social, and all those others of us who in their 'un-housed' states of mind, literally and/or metaphorically, do not find themselves accommodated either in the formal structures of the social world or in the minds of that in-group's members. It stands for those more *ordinary* members whose experience is of being 'dissed' by virtue of the body they inhabit, the class into which they were born, the god to whom they pray, or who more mundanely find themselves unable or unwilling to take up the role and position allocated to them by the self-defining in-group.

Diogenes' instruction to Alexander to get out of his light constituted a profound and powerful philosophical, psycho-social challenge to worldly authority as represented by the 'greatness' of Alexander. Power and powerlessness collided – and suddenly it was not so clear which was which.

34   Un-housed minds: The Diogenes Paradigm

Diogenes, not for the first or the last time, declines to be resettled. He is experienced as (rashly) refusing a 'reasonable offer', but it's more that he simply doesn't recognise an offer that's worth his while considering.

To anticipate a just criticism here: we must distinguish 'being articulate (in the adjectival sense of being eloquent and expressive) in one's protest' from being able or willing to 'articulate a protest' (in the verbal sense of putting together and projecting). You don't have to have studied with Plato in order to fix one of our latter-day Alexanders with your beady eye, or even to tell him to sling his hook. You can doggedly glue yourself to the pavement and not say a word. You need colossal courage and a strong sense of the ground you stand upon in order to speak truth to power from the wrong end of a significant power differential (the practice of *parrhesia*) (Foucault, 1983).[5] But you don't need to be a Philosopher with a capital 'P' (nor a Poet) to do so.

Standing in relation to these latter-day socially dis-advantaged, dis-placed and dis-membered Diogenes, Alexander comes to represent both the might and the impotence of the citizenry and its systems of care. What then becomes of *us* in the in-group when our authority is disregarded and our currency defaced by *them*, the dis-membered out-group. If we stand in Alexander's shoes, do we force Diogenes to emerge from his barrel and deal with the dangerous and endangered 'real world' – and to deal with it on our terms, not his? Do we seek, as we did with other historical 'troublesome priests', to be rid of him, through metaphorical (or literal) assassination or 'social/ethnic cleansing'? Alternatively, do we, like Pontius Pilate, wash our hands of him, pass by on the other side, try to take no notice of him, beyond being mindful of our own personal safety, and leave him, as a perverse sacrifice to Mammon, to freeze to death in a doorway?

One thing seems clear: after, and in response to, such an exchange of *truth*, nothing is ever quite the same again, even if we of the in-group, in turn, decline to recognise this new worldview, turn away from it or abstain from thinking it through. The *parrhesiastic* Cynicism of the out-group comes to be experienced as perhaps as dangerously contagious as the more prosaically cynical turning away from the truth of the in-group. According to Diogenes Laertius, things were never the same for Alexander. In his profound identification with Diogenes, Alexander is reported to have remarked, "had I not been Alexander, I would have liked to have been Diogenes" (DL, 6.32; Navia, 2005, p. 209; Plutarch, 1st century CEa, p. 413). This brings to mind Bob Dylan's warning not to mock 'Napoleon in rags' (Dylan, 1965) – Alexander in rags may be just as dangerous a proposition as Alexander in armour, and he may be mocking you much more effectively.[6] Foucault (1983) describes the 'parrhesiastic contract' as one in which the figure of the sovereign, "the one who has power but lacks the truth, addresses himself to the one who has the truth but lacks power, and tells him: if you tell me the truth ... you won't be punished" (Foucault, 1983, p. 32).

The Diogenes Paradigm   35

This ethos or unwritten rule binds Alexander and Diogenes together, and it also takes confidence and moral courage for Diogenes to take up the licence to tell that truth, and for Alexander to hear and respond to it:

> [DIOGENES (to ALEXANDER)] ... if it be your pleasure, run me through with your spear; for I am the only man from whom you will get the truth, and you will learn it from no one else. For all are less honest than I and more servile.
>
> (Dio Chrysostom, 2nd century BCE, pp. 196–197)

Indeed, so powerful was their truth-ful identification with each other – at least in the minds of their chroniclers – that it was said that they died at the same time on the same day – and in circumstances of equivalent mystery. Alexander's death was shrouded in secrecy and conspiracy, such that rival accounts of the cause of death (food poisoning, alcohol poisoning or murder by poisoning) still do battle with each other (Lane Fox, 2004, pp. 461–472). Likewise, Diogenes Laertius (DL, 6.77; Navia, 2005, pp. 223–224) can't decide, from the records available to him, whether Diogenes died of food poisoning from an octopus or septicaemia from a dog's bite, or whether he suffocated himself; or whether – a pleasingly symbolic if physically implausible explanation – he brought about his own demise in a supreme act of self-control, by holding his breath.

****

Diogenes' moment of transformation, in our story, comes when he is challenged to deface the currency by the Pythia at Delphi. He seems to come then to understand that, if people were offended by him, his dogs and his barrel, this was not his problem. However, if he found himself offended by what he saw in the world around him, in the societal container, then this *was* his problem and his task was to engage confrontatively with this offensiveness – to *resist* – and to manage himself as best he could in this one-man resistance movement.

In this way Diogenes took up a threshold position in relation to the world, the only truthful position that was available to him – one that was neither in nor out. His position was necessarily anti-social, and was experienced as inherently dangerous and threatening to the *status quo* (even though the Athenians took the 'Buchwald' road and made him one of theirs),[7] so much so that eight hundred years later, Saint Augustine still reckons he'd better put Diogenes back down in his place, lest his particular brand of subversion spread.

And we think Saint Augustine was right to be vigilant, for there is perhaps an ethical stance embodied by Diogenes that retains its force down to the present day: to refuse accommodation from societal systems that we may perceive to be fundamentally untruthful and hypocritical; to speak truth to power without fear or favour; to live out the Delphic prophecy by defacing the political currency.

36 Un-housed minds: The Diogenes Paradigm

Notes

1 Diogenes abhorred all system and was therefore more a forefather of Cynicism than strictly speaking a Cynic – we shall have more to say about this in Chapter 3. In most of what follows, when we describe a practice as Cynical, we essentially intend to evoke his particular practice of creatively questioning everything and taking nothing for granted. We will try to distinguish carefully between this and cynicism with a small 'c', in which the value of everything other than self-interest is indifferently and destructively dismissed.
2 Among literary iterations of the Diogenes legend, mention should be made of Diogenes the Dog in *Dombey and Son* (Dickens, 1848). Dickens portrays him thus: 'Diogenes was as ridiculous a dog as one would meet with on a summer's day; a blundering, ill-favoured, clumsy, bullet-headed dog, continually acting on a wrong idea that there was an enemy in the neighbourhood, whom it was meritorious to bark at ... he was far from good-tempered, and certainly was not clever, and had hair all over his eyes, and a comic nose, and an inconsistent tail, and a gruff voice' (Dickens, 1848, pp. 279–280).
3 In some accounts, this fraught encounter took place in Athens, and elsewhere we have told that version of the story. Here we've decided, on balance, not to risk any quarrel with Plutarch.
4 Navia (2005, p. 229, n. 44) records that Diogenes Laertius' reference to the 'Craneum' is to a gymnasium outside the city walls of Corinth. The name means 'skull', as does the Aramaic word 'golgotha'. There is therefore a powerful echo between the place where Diogenes is supposed to have died (DL, 6.77; Navia, 2005, p. 224) and the place where the historical Jesus is supposed to have been executed.
5 Foucault describes the practice of parrhesia as one in which "the parrhesiastes is always less powerful than the one with whom he speaks" (Foucault, 1983, p. 18), and in which "the speaker uses his freedom and chooses frankness instead of persuasion, truth instead of falsehood or silence, the risk of death instead of life and security, criticism instead of flattery, and moral duty instead of self-interest and moral apathy" (Foucault, 1983, pp. 19–20). A practice and a value set that, in contemporary public life, we can't but feel has diminished, is diminishing, and ought to be increased.
6 The possible discomfort of role reversal is brought out by Rabelais' novel *Pantagruel* (1532), in which Diogenes and Alexander are glimpsed in the underworld: 'I saw Diogenes strolling about dressed magnificently in a great purple robe, holding a sceptre in his right hand, and driving Alexander the Great mad with his scoldings when Alexander hadn't repaired his trousers properly – all he got in payment was a great whacking from Diogenes' stick' (Rabelais, 1532, p. 110).
7 If this integrative or benignly incorporative strategy of accommodation be sovereign wisdom of a kind, then it may have also passed down through the centuries. Consider the Roman historian Suetonius' account of an encounter between the Emperor Vespasian and another Cynic outcast: "... when Demetrius the Cynic, who had been banished from Rome, happened to meet Vespasian's travelling party, yet made no move to rise or salute him, and barked out some rude remark or other, Vespasian merely commented: 'Good dog!'" (Suetonius, 121, p. 281).

References

Agamben, G. (1995) *Homo sacer: Sovereign power and bare life.* Translated by D. Heller-Roazen, 1998. Stanford, CA: Stanford University Press.

Agamben, G. (2003) *State of exception.* Translated by K. Attell, 2005. Chicago: University of Chicago.

Conan Doyle, A. (1893) *The adventure of the Greek interpreter*. Available at: https://en. wikisource.org/wiki/The_Memoirs_of_Sherlock_Holmes_(Gutenberg_edition)/The_Greek_Interpreter (Accessed: 1 January 2021).

Cox, M. and Theilgaard, A. (1997) *Mutative metaphors in psychotherapy: The Aeolian mode*. London: Jessica Kingsley Publishers.

Critchley, S. (2009) *The book of dead philosophers*. London: Granta.

Crossan, D.M. (1992) *The historical Jesus: The life of a Mediterranean Jewish peasant*. New York, NY: Harper Collins.

Crouch, D. (2018) 'The Swedish 15-year-old who's cutting class to fight the climate crisis', *The Guardian*, 1 September. Available at: https://www.theguardian.com/science/2018/sep/01/swedish-15-year-old-cutting-class-to-fight-the-climate-crisis (Accessed: 1 January 2021).

Declerck, P. (2006) 'On the necessary suffering of the homeless', in Scholar, R. (ed.) *Divided cities*. Oxford: Oxford University Press, pp. 161–176.

Dickens, C. (1848) *Dombey and Son*. Reprinted 2002. London: Penguin Classics.

Dio Chrysostom (2nd century BCE) *On kingship*. Translated by J.W. Cohoon. Available at: http://penelope.uchicago.edu/Thayer/E/Roman/Texts/Dio_Chrysostom/Discourses/4*.html (Accessed: 1 January 2021).

Diogenes Laertius (DL) (3rd century BCE) The Life of Diogenes of Sinope. Translated by R.D. Hicks. Reprinted in Navia, L. (2005) *Diogenes the Cynic*. New York: Humanity Books, pp. 203–235.

Dylan, B. (1965) 'Like a rolling stone', from Highway 61 revisited. LP. New York, NY: Columbia Records.

Fielding, H. (1743) 'A Dialogue between Alexander the Great, and Diogenes the Cynic'. Available at: http://en.wikisource.org/wiki/A_Dialogue_between_Alexander_the_Great,_and_Diogenes_the_Cynic (Accessed: 1 January 2021).

Foucault, M. (1983) *Fearless speech*. Reprinted 2001. Los Angeles, CA: Semiotexte.

Foucault, M. (1997) *Society must be defended*. Translated by D. Macey, 2004. London: Penguin Books.

Heaney, S. (1987) 'The haw lantern'. In Heaney, S., *The haw lantern*. London: Faber and Faber, p. 8.

Lane Fox, R. (2004) *Alexander the Great*. London: Penguin.

Laville, S. and Watts, J. (2019) 'Across the globe, millions join biggest climate protest ever', *The Guardian*, 21 September. Available at: https://www.theguardian.com/environment/2019/sep/21/across-the-globe-millions-join-biggest-climate-protest-ever (Accessed: 1 January 2021).

Lenkiewicz, R.O. (1997) *R.O. Lenkiewicz*. Plymouth: White Lane Press.

Main, T. (1957) 'The ailment', *Journal of Medical Psychology*, 30, pp. 129–145.

Navia, L. (2005) *Diogenes the Cynic*. New York: Humanity Books.

O'Loughlin, M. (2011) 'Commentary on Scanlon and Adlam: [Anti?]social critics – mangy curs or pesky gadflies', *Group Analysis*, 44 (2), pp. 149–154.

Owen, W. (1918) 'The calls', in Stallworthy, J. (ed.) (1994) *The war poems of Wilfred Owen*. London: Chatto and Windus, pp. 49–50.

Plato (4th century BCE) Apology. Translated by H. Tredennick and H. Tarrant, 2003. Reprinted in *The last days of Socrates*. London: Penguin Classics, pp. 39–70.

Plutarch (1st century CEa) Alexander. Translated by I. Scott-Kilvert, 1973. Reprinted in *The Age of Alexander*. London: Penguin Classics, pp. 252–334.

Plutarch (1st century CEb) *On the fortune or the virtue of Alexander.* Translated by B. Perrin. Available at: https://penelope.uchicago.edu/Thayer/E/Roman/Texts/Plutarch/Moralia/Fortuna_Alexandri*/1.html (Accessed: 2 January 2021).

Rabelais, F. (1532) *Pantagruel.* Translated by A. Brown, 2003. London: Hesperus.

Rancière, J. (1983) *The philosopher and his poor.* Translated by J. Drury, C. Oster, and A. Parker, 2004. Durham, NC: Duke University Press.

SaintAugustine (1467) *City of God.* Translated by H. Bettenson, 2003. London: Penguin Classics.

Shakespeare, W. (1623) *The tragedy of King Lear.* Reprinted in Wells, S., Taylor, G., Jowett, J., and Montgomery, W. (eds) (1986) *William Shakespeare: The complete works.* Oxford: Oxford University Press, pp. 1063–1098.

Suetonius (121) *The twelve Caesars.* Translated by R. Graves, 1957. London: Penguin Classics.

Thucydides (5th century BCE) *History of the Peloponnesian war.* Translated by R. Warner, 1954. Reprinted 1972. London: Penguin Classics.

Volkan, V. (2009) 'Large-group identity: "Us and them" polarizations in the international arena', *Psychoanalysis, Culture and Society*, 14 (1), pp. 4–15.

Chapter 3

Citizens of the world?[1]

A pillar in the desert

> ... thrice ten years,
> Thrice multiplied by superhuman pangs,
> In hungers and in thirsts, fevers and cold,
> In coughs, aches, stitches, ulcerous throes and cramps,
> A sign betwixt the meadow and the cloud,
> Patient on this tall pillar I have borne
> Rain, wind, frost, heat, hail, damp, and sleet, and snow ...
> (Tennyson, 1833, ll.10–16)

Thus far, we have been considering the absent or unseated or un-housed individual as a problematic or dismissed figure in the mind of the in-group and exploring how conceptualisations of this figure develop over time, and how the attitude and approach of the in-group changes accordingly. Our focus now shifts to how the excluded monadic outsider experiences the figure of the in-group and the varying extent of his identification with the scattered membership of the out-group. We are building here on the group dynamic theories of Wilfred Bion (1961), S.H. Foulkes (1948) and their followers, and their shared insight that none of us find group membership straightforward: that there are universal complexities at play in the myriad manifestations of group membership and multiple ways of managing the tension between the claim to a group identity and the assertion of individuality.

In many forms of structured group activity, there is an apparently clear idea of who is or is not a member, and this idea is itself one of the forces that structures the group activity in question. In such a group, the designated group leader, on behalf of an in-group, will leave one or more empty chairs around the table or in the circle in order to signal the absence of a particular person. The chair, in effect, comes to represent the absent member: this is to say, the group comes to feel that the *absentee* has placed the chair in order that he may be symbolically represented. Other members, when referring to the absentee, will often nod in the direction of the chair, as though somehow including him in the conversation. In this sense, the chair represents or

DOI: 10.4324/9781003223115-4

substitutes for the absentee's *presence* in the circle and can be seen as a kind of gloss upon or a dismissal of possible ways of recognising and understanding the reality of his absence.

The in-group *establishes the norm from which the group deviates* (Foulkes, 1948) through a tacit acceptance that the absent member is symbolically present in the empty chair despite his insistence on being absent. Emergent ambivalent or hostile feelings towards the person whose presence the chair has thus far represented are kept under the radar of the group and so are slower to find expression. After all, the in-group, consisting of those regularly present, *feels* that it knows where he is (as though to say 'we know where you live – we can come after you if we need to'). However, if he persists in being absent a second or a third time and his 'alibi' – his status of absenteeism and 'elsewhere-ness' – starts to feel unclear or suspect, then the idea quickly develops that he has fallen off, thrown himself off or been thrown off the edge of the world of the group. He is felt to have become 'un-housed'.

The chair, increasingly provocatively, now has come to represent his *absence* in the circle; and not only this, but also his giving of offence to the group by seeming to disdain it. Taking up this offensiveness, there follows a dismissal or denial of the possibility that he is taking up his membership by not being present and a gulf begins to open up. He is now not merely absent but has become *wilfully* absent. Although he does remain a member, at least formally speaking, it is clear that he has transgressed; even if, or especially if, the nature of the transgression is not clear. His apparent insistence, therefore, on taking up his membership of the group by declining to attend, comes in turn to be experienced as a kind of anti-social *refusal to attend*.

The group leader, as representative of the *normative* values of the group, attempts to re-engage the absentee by means of various, more or less, coercive 'outreaching' techniques: a phone call, a letter, the offer of an individual meeting, the assertion of a deadline for returning. These various kinds of intervention are generally mandated by the group. The more authoritarian interventions are mandated even in situations where we might perceive that the absentee has been covertly (unconsciously) authorised by the group to enact something on their behalf;[2] the gentler interventions may come into play even if the absentee has become the semi-consciously designated scapegoat for the group, or is experienced as a bully – or has become the (pitied) *identified patient*.

However, sometimes his absence – and the tension in the in-group in relation to his absence – is prolonged beyond the capacity of the group (or the leader) to tolerate. The group's desire to 're-member' the absentee, to bring him back in from the cold and into conformity with the group norm (in this case, the acceptable way to take up membership is to be present) is exhausted and the endeavour relinquished. Any residual sympathy has then to be disavowed, perhaps in order that the 'in-group' can overlook the possibility that his absence was, at least in some part, a very justifiable response to a pre-existing tendency to relate to him as 'not properly joining in' in the first place.

We would see this as a manifestation of a difficulty of the group and its failure to *accommodate*, rather than a difficulty in the troublesome individual. However, all too often this psycho-social problem does become located in the individual and is experienced by the established membership of the in-group as a problem of, and for, the absent individual to manage. The difficulty is (dis-)located in the individual member by imagining the refusal to take up a place to be *his* difficulty rather than a difficulty *of* the group. The absent individual's membership is then actively revoked and he is evicted, or deemed to have forfeited his place; the 'chair' is removed and the absentee is un-seated. Consigned to the out-group, he then becomes the disavowed, un-housed and dis-membered 'other'.

Whether at the family/small group or the macro socio-political level, it is the examination of these psycho-social processes of inclusion/exclusion that is at the heart and soul of this text.

****

We would like now to revisit these dynamics using a vignette from another very old (hi)story; and this story is perhaps more about a 'holy fool' than a Diogenesque 'street philosopher' (Kociejowski, 2016). The ascetic early Christian saint, Simeon the Elder, was born around the end of the fourth century CE in Sis or Sisan, now the Turkish town of Kozan in Anatolia (roughly 400 miles due south from Diogenes' hometown of Sinop). Simeon converted to Christianity in early adolescence and withdrew to a monastery aged sixteen; but his practices of extreme, almost suicidal asceticism (starvation, prolonged sleeplessness, self-mutilation, hiding in snake- or scorpion-infested hollows) disturbed his fellow monks beyond even their own considerable endurance (Kociejowski, 2016, pp. 259–278).

Simeon therefore sought a more complete retreat from the world. He found it atop a pillar of rock in Taladah, near Aleppo in the north-eastern corner of Syria. He became not a *pithos*-dweller but the founder of a long tradition of pillar-dwelling hermits known as the Stylites (derived from the Greek *stylos*, meaning pillar). The remains of Simeon Stylites' pillar still stand today, although the site was bombed in 2016 during the Syrian Civil War by Russian warplanes. Gibbon, in his *Decline and Fall of the Roman Empire* (1781), reports:

> In this last and lofty station, the Syrian Anachoret resisted the heat of thirty summers, and the cold of as many winters … He sometimes prayed in an erect attitude, with his outstretched arms in the figure of a cross, but his most familiar practice was that of bending his meagre skeleton from the forehead to the feet; and a curious spectator, after numbering twelve hundred and forty-four repetitions, at length desisted from the endless account.
>
> (Gibbon, 1781, Vol. 3, Chapter XXXVII, Part II)

Simeon Stylites, meditating upon a pillar of rock in the desert, gives every appearance of having nothing to do with any kind of group experience. He would appear to be the paradigmatic exception to the poet's rule that no man may be 'an island, entire of itself' (Donne, 1624, p. 103). Yet he seems to be defining himself as an ascetic isolate *in relation to* a societal grouping (in this case, the entire world) whose values he rejects. He ostensibly denies his membership of that in-group, but in his *praxis* of pursuing his monadic, hermit lifestyle, he cannot but express his membership of the societal group upon which his continuing corporeal existence depends. Even atop his tallest pillar – supposed to have been as much as fifty feet high – there were still ladders up which disciples might approach him, or pulleys in order that he might winch up food to sustain him; just as Diogenes in his barrel also relied on alms for his day-to-day survival. Simeon depended upon the visiting populace to provide those foodstuffs, even as he was daunted and disheartened by their intrusion upon his meditations. Simeon Stylites on his pillar, like Diogenes in his barrel, 'cannot help being a member of a group' (Bion, 1961, p. 131). Neither figure is any less a member of the societal group, any less 'a piece of the continent, a part of the main' (Donne, 1624, p. 103), than anyone else.

Simeon Stylites' pursuit of a mystical, solitary and uninterrupted relation to his God can be seen as an extended study in necessary interdependence and the limits of autonomy in a social world infused with reciprocal dynamics of repudiation and longing. His first attempt to retreat from the world fell foul of societal normativity, even in a community so small and austere as that particular monastery within whose walls and practices he sought refuge. His subsequent early attempts at living and pursuing his devotions as a hermit were beleaguered by crowds of worshippers eager to enter the presence of a reputed miracle worker. Just as Diogenes *needed* the crowds of the agora, even if only to harangue them, Simeon on his pillar needed the throngs of worshippers milling around him in the desert sands, even if only to show them the error of their ways. The religious authorities, like some ancient Care Quality Commission, sent delegations to ascertain his obedience ratings. His autonomy, in short, was compromised by his societal membership just as much as was, for example and by way of contrast, the then Eastern Roman Emperor Theodosius II (who is known to have deferred to Simeon's teachings and once sent bishops to try to talk him down from his pillar to receive medical help – Simeon of course was having none of it and stayed where he was).

Both Diogenes and Simeon position themselves in relation to a societal in-group or, in our contemporary terms, a system of care, by finding that the only place they can take their stand is at the very edge of it. Both men endured, to the last, unimaginable hardships, with immense self-discipline.[3] Both men, also, were *parrhesiastes* (Foucault, 1983), giving of their caustic wisdom indifferently to the Imperial great as to the lowly – and both men earned and built what trust came their way by virtue of their truth-telling. The in-group might move either to (re-)incorporate them or to rescind their formal membership, by excommunication, exile, execution, or some other similar technological means – but not, it would appear, on terms that the member thus coaxed, coerced or dis-membered would feel the need to recognise as valid. There is an impasse: the irresistible force has met with the immovable object. To explore the nature of this impasse more deeply, we need to go back to Diogenes, and to his famous claim to be a 'citizen of the cosmos' (Navia, 2005, p. 233, n. 97).

Metropolitan lines and Cosmopolitan circles

> To the question, "Where do you come from?" [Diogenes'] reply was "I am a citizen of the world".
> (Diogenes Laertius, 3rd century BCE 6.63; Navia, 2005, p. 219)

In these stories we are re-narrating around what we are calling the Diogenes Paradigm, we hope it is possible to discern a thematic progression. We begin with the conventional hierarchical relationship between power and powerlessness, and its correlation with the dynamics of shame, shaming and shamelessness. We note the humiliating interdependency that can obtain between the powerful and the powerless (in Hegelian terms, the master–slave dialectic (Hegel, 1807: see Chapter 4));[4] and then we explore the creativity inherent in the possible inversion and subversion of these relationships and in the flattening of the hierarchy that is at their core.

None of Diogenes' purported writings have survived, but this claim to be a 'citizen of the world', which has been attributed to him, marks him as the originator of the term 'cosmopolitan'. He makes this claim, and when he tells Alexander to kindly step out of his light, he is not 'merely' being a nuisance or offering some random provocation. He has a coherent critique of the societal world as he finds it: a critique which is condensed in some of the epigrams attributed to him, but which is most clearly expressed in his *praxis* of seeking always to speak truths equally to the dogs, to the living gods and to all who would exercise their power without noticing the extent to which they are privileged in their self- or other-appointed positioning (see also Stevenson, 2020).

Alexander stands in the centre of – and embodies and epitomises – the dominant socio-political structure of the Ancient Greek system of city-states, the *metropoles* of Athens, Sparta, Corinth, Thebes, Syracuse, Rhodes and a thousand or so others. This system is no mere historical footnote, as its direct descendant is the 'Westphalian' State, equal with all other States, irrespective of size, and exercising absolute and exclusive sovereignty over its own territory.[5] It is also the structure that scaffolds the definitory activity of the in-group: its claimed authority to confer citizenship to some whilst denying this privilege to others. To delineate this boundary of inclusion, to draw a Metropolitan line, as the city-state did – a geographical boundary, and a psycho-social boundary within it of citizenship – is also to place people outside of it; to exclude them and deny them.

44 Un-housed minds: The Diogenes Paradigm

Alexander takes up that Metropolitan authority in his offer to Diogenes to come back in. 'Alexander' – that is to say, the *figure* of Alexander in our paradigm – represents the power and the assumption of the power of inclusion of the in-group, as well as the ambiguous offer of the societal system of care to those whom it has, in one way or another, excluded. "Join me", we might imagine him saying, "leave your barrel and come in from the cold, and various provisions of housing, welfare and education that are in my gift, shall become yours by right". Beneath his apparent generosity and good intentions (tacitly but openly backed by overwhelming force), he takes as axiomatic the legitimacy of the dividing line between a citizen and a non-citizen, and his own authority to draw that line as between those allowed to contribute to affairs of State and those who are disallowed. He is *sovereign* in this matter, as in all matters.

Alexander's 'Metropolitan' vision is of a unified world pacified by his enlightened leadership and patronage, with the boundary line demarcating only unconquered territory or terrorised enclaves (Agamben's 'states of exception' (Agamben, 2003)). Indeed, such was Alexander's omnipotence that, according to Plutarch (1st century CEa), when he saw the breadth of his domain, he was said to have wept because there were no more kingdoms to conquer. Channelling Metropolitan power, the figure of Alexander does not question the structural violence he embodies or the discourses of aggression, conquest, pillage and enslavement that underpin this world view because his world view, militarily, politically and ideologically, is not merely the right one: it is the *only* one. Might is right and right is mighty.

This assumption of absolute authority is exemplified in the story of how Alexander responded to the challenge of the 'Gordian knot'. Gordium was of old the capital of Phrygia, not far from what is now the Turkish capital city of Ankara. The Gordian knot was made of cornel bark and had been used to tie a chariot to a yoke outside the palace. Rather like the Arthurian legend of Excalibur embedded in the rock, it was supposed that no man could loosen it, but that anyone who succeeded in doing so would rule all Asia. Alexander gathered a large audience to witness him making the attempt but found the knot too intricate for the puzzle to be solved, and so took his sword to it in order to avoid losing face. He thus bypassed the problem instead of solving it; but given that this was Alexander (and he was still holding his sword), all present prudently agreed that this was a satisfactory fulfilment of the prophecy (Lane Fox, 2004, pp. 149–151).[6]

In this ruthless aspect, Alexander anticipates the assumption of divinity by the Roman emperors and Western European monarchs that followed him. His campaigns of conquest are also the forerunners of the rampages of the ecocidal neoliberals of late capitalism. In late modernity, the Metropolitan wielding of the power of the boundary maker draws less distinct, more abstract lines than the rivers or mountain ranges, or city walls of ancient times, but what gets left outside and excluded are what Naomi Klein (2015) calls the 'sacrificial zones' of ecologically devastated sites and populations.

It is therefore perhaps profoundly disconcerting for Alexander to encounter Diogenes; for the figure of Diogenes in our paradigm, standing for the socially excluded and psycho-socially traumatised 'outsider', *does not recognise* Alexander's 'greatness', nor even his Sovereign authority. Diogenes is determinedly unimpressed – although he does recognise Alexander the man. In Fielding's imagined dialogue:

ALEXANDER: ... dost thou not know us?
DIOGENES: I cannot say I do: but by the number of thy attendants, by the splendour of thy habit; but, above all, by the vanity of thy appearance, and the arrogance of thy speech, I conceive thou mayst be Alexander the son of Philip.

(Fielding, 1743)

Diogenes knows only that Alexander has the power to undo that which he offers – to unhouse him once more if the whim should move him or the wind should turn. Disdainful of that power to wield force, Diogenes denies Alexander authority and, in the process, asserts what *later* takes the shape of a 'Cosmopolitan' counter-claim: he has the status of 'a citizen of the world' (*kosmopolites*: for an extended analysis of the dynamics between Cosmopolitan and Metropolitan ways of seeing the world, see Pelletier, 2011). Diogenes' proclamation is of a wider circle that entirely surrounds and contains Alexander's Metropolitan power; his own 'proper place', to borrow the Platonic notion (Plato, 4th century BCE), is as wide as the universe itself. 'Draw your line however you wish', we might imagine him countering Alexander, 'my circle surrounds it, and both you and I, your retinue and my dogs, we are all of us inside *this* circle'.

The figures of Diogenes and Simeon live in apparently 'abject' circumstances, in a state of being cast off or outcast. Nonetheless, for them, as well as for all their un-housed brothers and sisters in philosophical, artistic, poetic and political resistance down through the centuries, the question of 'citizen or non-citizen of the Metropolis' simply does not arise. They take up positions of psycho-social resistance to the hostile environment of the Metropolitan in-group and to its very assertion of the right to arbitrate or give a ruling as to who is *inside* and who is to be cast out. Alexander doesn't even get a direct response to what is, in effect, his highly conditional offer of *help*: all Diogenes has to say is 'get out of my light, I can't be doing with any such negotiation'. Foucault (1983, pp. 120–121) notes that Diogenes specifically stakes what we are calling his proto-Cosmopolitan counterclaim by asking Alexander to step out of his light because, in so doing, Diogenes claims not only that we are all equal under the sun, but also challenges Alexander's (in our reading) quintessentially Metropolitan claim to be a God-King, and so a personification of the life-giving Sun.

Diogenes' resistance is in proto-Cynical identification with the shamed and shameless dog and with the 'doggedness' of aspiring to speak truth to power without fear or favour, to stand on his own shoeless two feet. He doesn't see why he need allow limits to be placed upon his capacity to think his own thoughts; upon his freedom of expression; upon how he occupies himself or what he does with his own body. In this sense, he declines to "render therefore unto Caesar the things which are Caesar's" (Matthew 22:21: King James Bible, 1611). As far as he's concerned, he's going to be neither included nor excluded. No 'Metropolitan' or 'statist' attempt to enclose the free universe of man and animal is going to cut any ice with him, any more than it would with his hounds.

Communalism and universalism

> God loves from whole to parts: but human soul
> Must rise from individual to the whole.
> Self-love but serves the virtuous mind to wake
> As the small pebble stirs the peaceful lake;
> The centre mov'd, a circle strait succeeds,
> Another still, and still another spreads;
> Friend, parent, neighbour, first it will embrace;
> His country next; and next all human race ...
> (Pope, 1734, Epistle IV)

We have already noted the threads of identification that bind together the figures of Diogenes and Alexander. Both hold a particular kind of world view and we can make use of the clash of those views in our paradigm to shed light upon the nature of present-day systems of care, particularly in the fragile democracies of the old 'West', and upon the problems of out-reaching to the out-cast and the out-group.

These systems of care can be understood as fundamentally 'Metropolitan' in their essence and ethos; whereas critiques and movements of resistance to 'the system' tend to be more 'Cosmopolitan' (Extinction Rebellion or the Climate School Strike would be good contemporary examples of this). As Navia (2005) points out, Diogenes' challenge to the Metropolitan order of the city-state emerged at a time when the city-state system was being challenged more widely in the old Western world, both by emergent nationalism and by Alexander's attempt to colonise and dominate the entire known world.

We have been exploring the nature of the transaction and the fraught encounter between, on the one hand, 'metropolitan' systems of care, which defensively and, we argue, *offensively* define their boundaries in ways that exclude (or that set unacceptable terms of inclusion) and, on the other hand, the excluded, 'cosmopolitan' seekers (or avoiders) of different kinds of *asylum*: 'citizens of the uni-verse' who withhold their allegiance to any particular earthly power. There are, therefore, more or less Metropolitan and Cosmopolitan ways of ordering things, and yet each may consider the other to be in a more or less offensive state of dis-order.[7]

If Alexander the Great's ruthlessness was centred, as at Gordium, around the denying of complexity and therefore of any possibility that there is any sort of limit to his power and prowess, then the figure of Diogenes stands for the weary yet wary wisdom that the system of care is not there so much to help him as to limit or to hinder him, and that any real or metaphorical soup proffered should be supped with an extremely long spoon.

The Cynics and the Stoics

> ... each of us is, as it were, circumscribed by many circles ... the first, indeed, and most proximate circle is that which everyone describes about his own mind as a centre, in which circle the body, and whatever is assumed for the sake of the body, are comprehended. For this is the smallest circle, and almost touches the centre itself ... the outermost and greatest circle, and which comprehends all the other circles, is that of the whole human race ... it is the province of him who strives to conduct himself properly in each of these connections to collect, in a certain respect, the circles, as it were, to one centre, and always to endeavour earnestly to transfer himself from the comprehending circles to the several particulars which they comprehend.
>
> (Hierocles, 2nd century CE, pp. 106–109)

Diogenes may have coined the nominative term 'a cosmopolitan', in the sense of 'a citizen of the cosmos' but, as we have already noted, he was no proponent or adherent of ideological systems of any description. He is supposed to have considered that "the only true commonwealth ... is that which is as wide as the universe" (DL, 3rd century BCE 72; Navia, 2005, p. 222); but this is not quite the same as advocating its institution. It was the Stoics, in particular Zeno of Citium, who started to teach in Athens around 300 BC, who developed a coherent philosophy of Cosmopolitanism with a capital 'C'. Plutarch, writing some four centuries later, suggested that Zeno offered "a dream or, as it were, shadowy picture of a well-ordered and philosophic commonwealth" (Plutarch, 1st Century CEb, p. 398) based around a core principle:

> that all the inhabitants of this world of ours should not live differentiated by their respective rules of justice into separate cities and communities, but that we should consider all men to be of one community and one polity, and that we should have a common life and an order common to us all, even as a herd that feeds together and shares the pasturage of a common field.
>
> (Ibid.; also cited in Martin, 2015, pp. 347–348)

As Martin goes on to explain, Zeno's position is one of ethical *universalism*. It answers the question, "'To whom, exactly, do our ethical standards apply?' Here Zeno's answer seems to be: *everyone*" (Martin, 2015, p. 348). 'Metropolitan' moral systems that limit the reach of ethical commitments to a

48   Un-housed minds: The Diogenes Paradigm

designated grouping, be it family or tribe or State (or the 'employed', or the 'sane'), from which some or many are, by definition, excluded, are here subjected to a fundamental challenge.

The Stoic philosopher Hierocles (quoted earlier) who was writing probably in the first half of the second century CE, offers the image of concentric circles – the smallest being the body-mind, the psyche-soma as it were, of the individual, expanding outwards through familial and tribal and citizenship ties to the largest circle: the human race itself. Hierocles added that the dilution of blood ties might naturally correspond to a diminution in warmth of attachment:

> for something of benevolence must be taken away from those who are more distant from us by blood; though at the same time we should endeavour that an assimilation may take place between us and them.
> (Hierocles, 2nd century CE, p. 110)

However, the ethical challenge, if we accept this metaphor of concentric circles that Pope's poem offered earlier deploys, concerns whether it is possible to aspire to an unconditional (and, with due respect to Alexander and Plutarch, non-coercive) communalism within which all are equally interdependent and equally connected to any given *random* point that might be subjectively identified as the centre; rather than to define the terms of inclusion and citizenship according to the capacity to 'know one's place' within the particular circle in which one is positioned, or by measuring one's distance from this illusory centre.

Ground to stand on and shoes to stand in

> But if you believe you're a citizen of the world, you're a citizen of nowhere. You don't understand what the very word 'citizenship' means.
> (Theresa May: *The Independent*, 2016)

We have here offered three contested and contesting ways of conceptualising the psycho-social dynamics of the relationship between, on the one hand, in-groups in the form of States and systems of care (and 'would-be helpers' positioned as agents of State) and, on the other hand, out-groups in the form of populations finding themselves located at the margins of, and denied access to, these social systems – either absolutely excluded as non-citizens, vilified for being 'out-of-place', or inhabiting the more liminal neither-in-nor-out territory inhabited by Diogenes or Simeon Stylites. It is our fundamental contention that there are, essentially, no problems or challenges of health and social care, or the wider social systems within which these problems are situated, that are not bound up, like a colossal Gordian knot, in these psycho-social dynamics associated with the withholding, the offering, the receiving or the rejection of a care or concern for both our near and more distant neighbours.

In the first of these three conceptualisations – in the 'Metropolitan' corner – there's a line in the sand (or the concrete) denoting who's 'in' and who's 'out'. If you're on the wrong side of that line, you're the wrong end of a significant power differential; but unless a state of exception (Agamben, 2003) obtains, you may still 'come in from the cold' *on the condition* that you accept the terms of the invitation. Usually this involves fairly detailed and demanding small print about cleaning up, shutting up, knuckling down, learning the language, passing the 'cricket test',[8] toeing the line and *knowing one's place.*

In the second, 'Cosmopolitan' view of things, there are some nuances distinguishing different accounts and practices, but essentially there's a 'comprehending circle' involved. Either there is a 'universalist' position in which ethics apply equally to all, whatever the distance from the given individual centre (let's call this the 'Zeno' position); or there is a model of a kind of social inclusion by osmosis in which one's duty is gradually to reduce the distance between the individual and members of the outer ring of a system of concentric circles (we'll call this the 'Hierocles' position).[9]

Diogenes, in his defacing of the political currency, 'coined' the term '*a* cosmopolitan' as a rebuke and a challenge to the *Metropolis*, and at times he has been strongly associated with the 'Zeno' position (in the past we have also conceptualised his practice in this way). However, it is perhaps truer to the spirit of that ancient Dog to say that the 'Diogenes' position is a *third* position or non-position: "much more of an anti-political stance than some sort of banal internationalism" (Critchley, 2009, p. 31). Navia (2005) suggests that Diogenes' 'Cosmopolitanism' (and, we might add, that of Simeon Stylites) was essentially a refutation of membership of any particular kind of community, including the familial group. Like Groucho Marx, Diogenes wasn't interested in belonging to any kind of club that would have him as a member.

Diogenes' practice of resistance towards both 'us' and 'them' simultaneously embodies a *macro* commentary and critique of the systemic socio-political currency and a *micro* commentary and critique of the psycho-social arrangements of our personal, interpersonal, family, group and community lives. In this view, the figure of Diogenes has no part of any political or ideological system. He (or she or they) is beyond such systems or orderings of things – a monad, and a vagabond – and our Paradigm here retains some of its symmetry in that Alexander, in some ways, is a figure who also transcends his (Metropolitan) position, out of the sheer grandeur and sweep of his vision of conquest.

We contend that it is particularly crucial to hold in mind these different psycho-social framings because in late capitalism it is perhaps harder to spot the line in the sand, or to define the public/private circle in the organisation-in-the-mind (Armstrong, 2005), than it was in the times of Diogenes and Simeon. As Bauman (2000) suggests (see Chapter 5), in our times of liquid modernity the 'interested citizen' has evacuated the agora and is holed up in cyberspace, while Alexander has also taken his phalanxes and disappeared into extra-territorial space, where he can wield power covertly and much more easily (for no *parrhesiastes* can even find him, let alone confront him).

At the inter-State and trans-national level, with the possibility for instant mass communication, the globalisation of capital and the concentration of power in multi-national, offshore corporations, one could be forgiven for imagining that, at least temporarily and superficially, the Cosmopolitan project has been finally realised and we are all indeed 'citizens of the world'. This superficial perspective can of course only be achieved by turning two blind eyes to the colossal power differentials and to the cynicism of the in-group in what Latour (2017) terms 'globalisation minus'. As Edgerton (2019) concisely observes *à propos* the 'Brexit' debacle, "London is a place where world capitalism does business – no longer one where British capitalism does the world's business". The corollary at the level of the system of care in the UK is that it is now next to impossible to tell which bits of the National Health, Social Care and Community Justice Services operate as public services and which take public money to operate in the rapidly proliferating and flourishing private, for-profit sector; a *free market* that may then allow globalised health providing companies to monopolise and control who is allowed to be 'healthy' and who must perish.

****

Lastly (and 'lastly' may be the operative word) our analysis must also include the impact of trans-national, carbon-fuelled capitalism and 'extractivism' (Klein, 2015) on the climate and our ecology (see Chapter 7). We now live in the age of the Anthropocene, one in which humankind (and humankind's recklessly accelerating consumption of resources) is the principal agent of geological change – not only in the 'known world' upon which Alexander set his sights, but also Heirocles' outermost circle: the planetary system or 'Gaia' in its entirety (Lovelock, 2007).

Many Metropolitan powers are responding to this crisis by seeking to assert lines in the sand (and boundary walls) in order to stem the feared (and, in the West, *securitised*) flow of climate migrants displaced by anthropogenic climate change or by the wars fought for 'extractivist' carbon plunder. As Baldwin and Bettini (2017, p. 2) argue, "the relation between climate change and human migration must be understood foremost as a relation of power". Fröhlich and Klepp (2018) further suggest:

> [t]he territoriality which is inherent in the Westphalian state model is fundamentally questioned and challenged by large-scale migration movements ... Migrants – regardless of whether their movement is voluntary or forced – challenge national boundaries, defy legal and political categories and question dominant understandings of national belonging and citizenship. The migrant thus becomes a figure that questions a state's ability to control its borders, political institutions and citizenship regulations.
>
> (Fröhlich and Klepp, 2018, pp. 4–5)

However, even if our fellow human beings can be turned back and sent 'home' [*sic*], the Metropolitan powers that endeavour to do so can claim no authority (a point well understood by King Canute) over wind, sea levels, carbon particles, micro-plastics and other presences and forces within the Gaia system: "migrations without form or nation" (Latour, 2017, p. 10).

There are both Metropolitan and Cosmopolitan responses to global or Gaian problems, but they can be increasingly seen to be inadequate, perhaps more clearly than ever before. The COVID-19 crisis certainly points to such a conclusion. The 'Westphalian' system of separate sovereign States, each asserting their right to act alone or to deny and procrastinate, is being challenged by climate disaster (and the pandemic), which does not recognise or respect national boundaries or Sovereign States. On this view, the Metropolitan system of power that emerged towards the later stages of the Holocene is also now, in the Anthropocene, unhousing us all. We are all at risk of being contaminated by – and spreading the contamination of – these insurgent biological and psycho-social forces.

Latour (2017) argues that the very notion of 'homeland' is in flux but that the human need for ground to stand upon, the "basic right ... to feel safe and protected" (Latour, 2017, p. 11) is therefore all the more fierce and intense. Dangerous attempts to stem the relentless tide will still call for Cosmopolitan responses and our Paradigm will still hold, but as the ice melts and the waters rise, the 'securely housed' may yet have need of, and even have cause to envy, the mindset and the skill set of the displaced. Baldwin and Bettini (2017, p. 17) urge that "[l]ife adrift is thus not some fatal condition. To be adrift is to be overfull with potential and with life". The Diogenes position may beckon to us all.

Notes

1 We are very grateful to Caroline Pelletier, with whom we have worked together on these themes and whose thought is therefore interwoven with our own in much of the ground covered in this chapter in particular (see Adlam, Pelletier and Scanlon, 2010).
2 In Bion's 'basic assumption' theory (Bion, 1961), this would be a situation in which the absent member is the unconsciously appointed leader of the fight/flight group mentality that is at odds with, and resistant to, the designated task of the group. There is tacit agreement that the absent member is the only one doing the right thing ('old so-and-so had the right idea, missing this meeting') – it is as if he is taking a stand on behalf of the whole membership – but the group's support for his doctrine remains disavowed and unacknowledged. The absent leader is a leader in name only and no one will actually follow him out into the cold.
3 In Moby Dick (1851), Melville writes of Simeon that: 'in him we have a remarkable instance of a dauntless stander-of-mast-heads; who was not to be driven from his place by fogs or frosts, rain, hail, or sleet; but valiantly facing everything out to the last, literally died at his post' (Melville, 1851, p. 158).
4 Diogenes apocryphally was himself a slave for some part of his life, after he left Athens. He is supposed to have been captured by pirates and sold to a citizen of Corinth named Xeniades. Asked by the slavemaster if he had any particular skills

that could be put to use, Diogenes replied "to govern men", and when he then spotted Xeniades in the crowd, he told the auctioneer to sell him to that customer, "because he needs a master" (DL, 3rd century BCE 29; DL, 3rd century BCE 74; Navia, 2005, pp. 208, 223). Xeniades forthwith made Diogenes governor of his children. Eventually he made him a free man again, and this is how it comes to pass that we next encounter Diogenes back in his pithos in Craneion.

5 The Peace of Westphalia was concluded in 1648 and marked the end of the bloody and devastating Thirty Years' War, waged mostly across the territory of what is now Germany, between numerous European powers of that time, empires, kingdoms and principalities alike. The conceptual structure of the treaty predicated upon the principle of non-interference by other States in the domestic business of any individual State and obtained in the West largely unchallenged (at least, considered as a principle of international law) until the second half of the twentieth century.

6 There is an echo of the Gordian legend in the Star Trek mythological story of the Kobayashi Maru 'no-win' training exercise. Captain James T. Kirk (the Alexander of the Federation?) is reputed to have dealt with the challenge by reprogramming the computer scenario so that it could now be solved – which earns him a commendation for original thinking rather than dismissal for cheating. He is supposed to have claimed, Alexanderesquely, not to believe in the very existence of such a thing as a 'no win' scenario (https://en.wikipedia.org/wiki/Kobayashi_Maru).

7 At one point, Plutarch approvingly offers a very Metropolitan take on the method of social inclusion implicit in Alexander's conquests, suggesting that: '[t] hose who were vanquished by Alexander are happier than those who escaped his hand; for these had no one to put an end to the wretchedness of their existence, while the victor compelled those others to lead a happy life' (Plutarch, 1st century CEb, pp. 395–396); and that if Cosmopolitanism dreamed of a Commonwealth, 'it was Alexander who gave effect to the idea ... as he believed that he came as a heaven-sent governor to all, and as a mediator for the whole world, those whom he could not persuade to unite with him, he conquered by force of arms, and he brought together into one body all men everywhere .... He bade them all consider as their fatherland the whole inhabited earth' (Plutarch, 1st century CEb, pp. 398–399).

In this version of social inclusion, force and coercion are unproblematic means to a good end and the socially excluded are those unfortunates whom the in-group has simply not yet got around to subduing and incorporating into the mainstream.

8 In the UK in 1990, the Conservative MP Norman Tebbit claimed in a newspaper interview that many British people of Asian heritage would fail to pass the 'cricket test' because they would cheer for India or Pakistan in test matches rather than for the England team – thus suggesting that (to his mind, and in our terms) they had failed to understand the conditional nature of the Metropolitan offer of citizenship and to relinquish their 'former' identities and allegiances.

9 Evelyn Baring, Lord Cromer, gives the following illuminating distortion of the term 'Cosmopolitan' to justify Empire when discussing the subjugation of the Egyptians, a project of which he was in personal charge of on behalf of the British Empire for a quarter-century from 1882: "the real future of Egypt ... lies not in the direction of a narrow nationalism, which will only embrace native Egyptians ... but rather in that of an enlarged cosmopolitanism" (Baring (1913), quoted in Said (1978, p. 37)).

References

Adlam, J., Pelletier, C., and Scanlon, C. (2010) '"A citizen of the world": Cosmopolitan responses to metropolitan models of social inclusion', in Institute of Education/

Normal University of Beijing, *Education and Citizenship in a Globalising World.* London, November 2010. doi:10.13140/2.1.3846.9764.

Agamben, G. (2003) *State of exception.* Translated by K. Attell, 2005. Chicago: University of Chicago.

Armstrong, D. (2005) *Organization in the mind: Psychoanalysis, group relations and organizational consultancy.* London: Karnac.

Baldwin, A. and Bettini, G. (eds) (2017) *Life adrift: Climate change, migration, critique.* London: Rowman and Littlefield.

Baring, E., Lord Cromer (1913) *Political and literary essays, 1908–1913.* Reprinted 1969. Freeport, NY: Books for Libraries Press.

Bauman, Z. (2000) *Liquid modernity.* Cambridge: Polity Press.

Bion, W.R. (1961) *Experiences in groups.* London: Tavistock.

Critchley, S. (2009) *The book of dead philosophers.* London: Granta.

Diogenes Laertius (3rd century BCE) *The Life of Diogenes of Sinope.* Translated by R. D. Hicks. Reprinted in Navia, L. (2005) *Diogenes the Cynic.* New York: Humanity Books, pp. 203–235.

Donne, J. (1624) *Devotions upon emergent occasions and Death's duel.* Reprinted 1999. New York: Vintage.

Edgerton, D. (2019) 'Brexit is a necessary crisis: It reveals Britain's true place in the world', *The Guardian*, 9 October. Available at: https://www.theguardian.com/comm entisfree/2019/oct/09/brexit-crisis-global-capitalism-britain-place-world (Accessed: 2 January 2021).

Fielding, H. (1743) 'A dialogue between Alexander the Great, and Diogenes the Cynic'. Available at: http://en.wikisource.org/wiki/A_Dialogue_between_Alexander_ the_Great,_and_Diogenes_the_Cynic (Accessed: 1 January 2021).

Foucault, M. (1983) *Fearless speech.* Reprinted 2001. Los Angeles, CA: Semiotexte.

Foulkes, S.H. (1948) *Introduction to group-analytic psychotherapy: Studies in the social integration of individuals and groups.* London: Heinemann.

Fröhlich, C. and Klepp, S. (2018) 'Climate change and migration crises in Oceania'. Policy brief No. 29. Tokyo, Japan: Toda Peace Institute. Available at: www.toda.org (Accessed: 2 January 2021).

Gibbon, E. (1781) Decline and fall of the Roman empire. Available at: https://www.sa cred-texts.com/cla/gibbon/03/daf03041.htm (Accessed: 2 January 2021).

Hegel, G.W.F. (1807) *The phenomenology of spirit.* Translated by A.V. Miller, 1977. Oxford: Oxford University Press.

Hierocles (2nd century CE) 'How we ought to conduct ourselves towards our kindred'. Translated by T. Taylor, 1822. Available at: https://en.wikisource.org/wiki/Political_ fragments_of_Archytas_and_other_ancient_Pythagoreans/How_we_ought_to_con duct_ourselves_towards_our_kindred (Accessed: 2 January 2021).

King James Bible (1611) *Standard Version.* Available at: https://www.kingjamesbi bleonline.org/ (Accessed: 2 January 2021).

Klein, N. (2015) *This changes everything.* London: Penguin.

Kociejowski, M. (2016) *The street philosopher and the holy fool: A Syrian journey.* London: Eland.

Lane Fox, R. (2004) *Alexander the Great.* London: Penguin.

Latour, B. (2017) *Down to Earth – Politics in the new climatic regime.* Translated by C. Porter, 2018. Cambridge: Polity.

Lovelock, J. (2007) *The revenge of Gaia.* London: Penguin.

Martin, W. (2015) 'Stoic transcendentalism and the doctrine of Oikeiosis', in Gardner, S. and Grist, M. (eds) *The transcendental turn*. Oxford: Oxford University Press, pp. 342–368.

Melville, H. (1851) *Moby Dick*. Reprinted 1994. London: Penguin Popular Classics.

Navia, L. (2005) *Diogenes the Cynic*. New York: Humanity Books.

Pelletier, C. (2011) 'Beating the barrel of inclusion: Cosmopolitanism through Rabelais and Rancière – A response to John Adlam and Chris Scanlon', *Psychodynamic Practice*, 17 (3), pp. 255–272.

Plato (4th Century BCE) *The republic*. Translated by D. Lee, 1955. London: Penguin Classics.

Plutarch (1st century CEa) *Alexander*. Translated by I. Scott-Kilvert, 1973. Reprinted in *The age of Alexander*. London: Penguin Classics, pp. 252–334.

Plutarch (1st century CEb) *On the fortune or the virtue of Alexander*. Translated by B. Perrin. Available at: https://penelope.uchicago.edu/Thayer/E/Roman/Texts/Plutarch/Moralia/Fortuna_Alexandri*/1.html (Accessed: 2 January 2021).

Pope, A. (1734) *Essay on man*. Available at: http://www.gutenberg.org/files/2428/2428-h/2428-h.htm (Accessed: 2 January 2021).

Said, E. (1978) *Orientalism*. Reprinted 2019. London: Penguin Modern Classics.

Stevenson, S. (2020) 'Psychodynamic intersectionality and the positionality of the group analyst: The tension between analytical neutrality and inter-subjectivity', *Group Analysis*, 53 (4), pp. 498–514.

Tennyson, A. (1833) 'St Simeon Stylites'. Available at: https://en.wikisource.org/wiki/St._Simeon_Stylites (Accessed 2 January 2021).

The Independent (2016) 'Theresa May's keynote speech at Tory conference in full', 5 October. Available at: https://www.independent.co.uk/news/uk/politics/theresa-may-speech-tory-conference-2016-in-full-transcript-a7346171.html (Accessed 2 January 2021).

Chapter 4

Inhospitability, injury, insult and insurrection

Reciprocal violence

> The rich man in his castle,
> The poor man at his gate,
> God made them, high or lowly,
> And ordered their estate.
> (Alexander, 1848, p. 27)

In Chapter 1 we looked in detail at theories of structural or objective violence as different ways of conceptualising violent states and their relationship to violent actions (Young, Lee and Lee, 2018). Destructive acts of behavioural violence rarely, if ever, come 'out of the blue': they necessarily involve 'a doer' and 'done to', but they can only be *understood* as emerging within a relational, social and political context (Benjamin, 2018). The behaviourally violent act emerges from, and is an external expression of, an internal state of mind; it is, at the same time, an expression of social violence that emerges from, and occurs within, the psycho-social matrices and ecologies of the socio-political hostilities within which we are all mired.

Just as an individual can be in a violent state of mind, so too these systemic and societal structures are 'violent states' (Adlam, Kluttig and Lee, 2018). Primo Levi wrote that violence "snakes either through sporadic and private episodes, or government lawlessness" (Levi, 1986, p. 167). This analysis extends not only to politicised constructs such as that of the 'Rogue State', but also includes the *micro-aggressions* that reveal the ageism, racism, anti-Semitism, Islamophobia, misogyny, homophobia and gendered violence (re-)encountered by so many on a minute-to-minute and day-to-day basis. These same violent states also inhere in the majority-voted populist socio-political policies that justify and legitimise the types of 'hostile environment', born of greed, intolerance and denial, which lead inexorably not only towards a socio-economic 'austerity' that attacks the many whilst enriching the few, but towards a biosphere destruction that might yet destroy much or all (human) life on earth.

Against this background we might understand that those who lost their lives in the Grenfell Tower fire in London in 2017 did not die 'simply' of

DOI: 10.4324/9781003223115-5

smoke inhalation, or even of an unworkable fire safety strategy. They died of an ongoing *slow-burning* 'structural violence' built out of racism and xenophobia, and an 'exterminism' (Thompson, 1980) in which some lives are viewed as less 'deserving' of the ordinary standards of housing and protective function afforded to their 'more deserving' and 'more worthy' fellow citizens. In the same way, the victims of Hurricane Katrina in New Orleans in 2005 did not die of drowning, nor even of climate disaster (Baldwin and Bettini, 2017). They were killed by the structural violence manifest in the failure of the authorities to repair the Mississippi levees and the clustering of the Black urban poor in inadequate housing in low-lying areas of the city. What both these man-made disasters have tragically in common is the racial segregation, social ostracism and (c)overt social engineering that serves to maintain 'the bright and beautiful' power differentials that keep 'the rich man in his castle and the beggar at his gate'.

This way of understanding fraught encounters between in-groups and out-groups foregrounds the psycho-socially traumatising impact of violent processes of inclusion/exclusion and dis-memberment, and violent responses to the violence of power differentials and relations of force and domination. From this perspective it is impossible to consider the attacks on the New York World Trade Centre in September 2001 (out of that impossible clear blue morning sky) without reflecting on the context of fossil capitalism in the Middle East, the House of Saud's control of Mecca and a whole millennium of aggression, attack and counter-attack between the West and Islam going back to the First Crusade. Similarly, it is impossible to consider the waves of migration from Africa and the Middle East separately from the long history of Western imperialism and the legacy of colonialism, racism and the slave trade (see, e.g., Du Bois, 1903; Fanon, 1952, 1961; Danewid, 2017). The Metropolitan powers 'securitise' (construct as a threat) these flows of displaced peoples but not (alas!) the imperialist history that caused or contributed to the currency of their displacement:

> ... the migratory patterns that currently reflect the anxieties of globalization are fears about what might happen if 'they' come 'here'. The historical consequences for 'their' societies when, uninvited, 'we' went 'there' earlier are not to be remembered ...

(Dalby, 2017, p. 47)

It is a paradoxical quality of these fraught encounters, therefore, that the plaintive, reciprocal cry forever rises up (whether at the interpersonal or the inter-State level): "they started it"; "we were only defending/protecting ourselves". In order to distinguish between the antagonists, we must be careful to remember and attend to historical and current power differentials. Within the frame of our paradigm, we can observe, in the fraught encounter between the figures of Diogenes and Alexander, how each gave offence to the other – each experiences the other as a nuisance and a menace to the order of how things should be. Alexander finds Diogenes' abjection and homelessness offensive; Diogenes finds Alexander's shameless projection of imperial power offensive. According to legend, Alexander is piqued that Diogenes doesn't stand up to salute him and furious when Diogenes casts aspersions on Alexander's greatness and assumed divinity, but stands respectfully aside when told to step out of Diogenes' light.[1] Each at different times elects *not* to take offence and to remain interested in what the other has to say. In this 'parrhesiastic game' (Foucault, 1983) there is a shared understanding of the steps of the dance between them: a tacit licence for truth-telling because it reflects well upon the honour of both parties that the truth be allowed to be told (and that the power differentials will nonetheless remain intact).

Diogenes doesn't beat Alexander with his stick (as was sometimes his way of taking and then giving offence) and Alexander doesn't run Diogenes through with his sword (as was very often his way of winning an argument). An uncomfortable peace is maintained, even if threats and insults are central to this fraught encounter. Despite their mutual respect and identification (as we explored in Chapter 2), we can see that nonetheless a state of *reciprocal violence* obtains between them. The psycho-socio-dynamics of reciprocal violence constitute a societal ailment: a violent state indicative of a disturbance of what Bion (1961) called 'groupishness'; and what Foulkes (1948, p. 127) described as the location of this disturbance. In our paradigm, this 'groupish' disturbance is located both interpersonally and in dynamics of reciprocal violence played out across power differentials between in-groups and out-groups, and the psycho-socially traumatising processes of exclusion and dismemberment that are at its roots and in its branches. At the 'macro' level of racist imperialism, these dynamics of reciprocal violence are nowhere better encapsulated than in the writings of Fanon:

> The violence of the colonial regime and the counter-violence of the native balance each other and respond to each other in an extraordinary reciprocal homogeneity.
>
> (Fanon, 1961, p. 69)

If the ethic of reciprocity – the 'Golden Rule' of reciprocity, fraternity, neighbourliness and respect – is the model for all human relationships across almost all major religions and philosophical systems, then perhaps this is precisely because the tit-for-tat talion principle of reciprocal violence and retaliation is the universal norm.

Practising self-harming

> … as soon as Alyosha had gone, Lise unbolted the door, opened it a little, put her finger in the crack, and slamming the door, pinched her finger with all the force at her command. Ten seconds later, releasing her

finger, she went back to her chair slowly and quietly, sat up erect in it, and began examining intently her blackened finger and the blood that oozed from under the nail. Her lips quivered, and she whispered rapidly to herself: "Mean, mean, mean, mean!"

(Dostoyevsky, 1880, p. 687)

Simone Weil defines force as "that *x* that turns anybody who is subjected to it into a *thing*" (Weil, 1939, p. 3 [italics in the original]). Within the frame of our 'Diogenes Paradigm', we propose a *gestalt* configuration in which the 'figure' of the injured or injurious individual is set against the 'ground' that is the societal violence of 'force' (in Weil's particular use of the term) and the relations of domination and subjugation within which this violence is embedded. Our attention may be psychologically (or judicially) drawn to the figure of the behaviourally violent individual or act (for example, the asphyxiation of George Floyd by Derek Chauvin in Minneapolis on 25 May 2020); or socio-politically to the ground of the structurally violent system (the long history of slavery and racist violence upon which the prosperity of the British and American Empires is founded). It may even be that, at times, our attention can float between figure and ground, but this is much harder to sustain because we are all also participants in these transactions and, as such, our perception is necessarily affected.

How much offence 'we' may give or take depends on the ground upon which 'we' stand. Whether it's the proverbial mote or beam that we have in our respective eyes, none of us can see clearly. The more intense the retaliation to the perceived offence, the more likely it is (to borrow the aphorism often misattributed to Gandhi) that an eye for an eye will leave everybody blind. If the psycho-social trauma established and sustained within dynamics of reciprocal violence is the defining problem of our age (and, at the global level, the clear causal connections between imperialism and fossil capitalism on the one hand, and mass displacement and climate disaster on the other hand, support the idea that it is (Angus, 2016)), then finding a way to think about such matters without perpetuating them becomes an urgent challenge to be addressed.

Lear (2017, p. 80) observes that unjust societies (such as we hold ours to be) "tend to cloud the minds of those who live within them" and that trauma (in our sense of psycho-social trauma, although he does not use that term) "does not befall individuals alone; the conceptual life of a culture may suffer a traumatic blow" (Lear, 2017, p. 9). He goes on to wonder:

> … if we live in an unjust society, we have reason to think that our own thought-processes have been distorted …. Could it be that our concept of justice is unjust? If so, how would we be able to think this if the very concepts with which we think are distorted? We need somehow to be able to recognize the injustice *from inside* the unjust thinking – and do so in a way that at least holds out the prospect of rectifying our thought.

(Lear, 2017, pp. 9–10)

Emboldened by Lear's proposition (2017, *ibid.*) that poetry and storytelling are technologies that may usefully be deployed to try to pull off this difficult trick, we want in this chapter to use the Diogenes Paradigm to re-imagine understandings of a particular dimension of reciprocal violence – the issue of practices of 'self-harm', and hostile and inhospitable societal responses to those practices, including the pathologisation of personality, as enacted by systems of care. We will explore the reciprocally violent, isomorphic relationship between, on the one hand, the violent states of mind and violent self-harming practices of individuals in societal out-groups and, on the other hand, the societal violence of the in-group, the body-politics of the State, and the experience of those of us who, as its representatives, are engaged in relations of colonisation, domination and subjugation. With one eye still on the problem of hypocrisy and the perils identified by Lear (2017), it is important to own here that, in the kinds of fraught encounters we are trying to understand, we-the-authors have been, and continue in different ways to be, in the position of agents of the (British) State and its system of health and social care – and therefore implicated in its failures of hospitality and abuses of human rights.

Just as bodily attacks may be played out within and between members of out-groups and in-groups, we might also notice the ways in which the violent State may offensively maim, harm or injure its own political body ('herd immunity' or 'no-deal Brexit', anybody?). Criminal law in the West developed in relation to the concept that an attack upon the body of a subject of the King was a treacherous and seditious injury *and* insult to the body of the Sovereign himself (Foucault, 1975). This principle at the heart of the Law, then, constituted practices of domination by authorising formally decreed retaliatory assaults, by way of vengeance as well as deterrence, upon the body of the offender. In the same way, self-harm and suicide were, and in many cultures still are, considered to be both sinful and a crime, as not only do such practices offend the sovereign-God but also deprive the 'kingdom' of a 'worker'.

Motz (2008) argues that attacks upon one's own body and attacks upon others' bodies are likewise both experienced as forms of violent and offensive behaviour, as 'crimes against the body'. The degree of offensiveness is experienced differently by different beholders at different times; consequently, *we* (the societal 'we') authorise different parts of the system of care to take offence and to take the responsibility to deal with this offensiveness and alleged immorality on 'our' behalf. Attacks on the body of others are problematised (or legitimated) by the criminal justice system; attacks upon one's own body usually become the responsibility of systems of health and social care (albeit often working hand-in-hand with forensic systems of care).

Our focus is partly on single acts of violence towards the self, but we are mostly concerned here with multiple and recurring patterns, practices and habits of self-harm, self-injury and with differently fashioned psycho-social processes of *re-traumatisation*. If single acts of self-injury can be experienced, by both the sufferer and the observer, as emerging 'out of the blue', then repeated violence, almost by its very nature, risks ceasing to be experienced as violence at all – from either perspective. It is a normative project fraught with great difficulty, both conceptual and ethical, to pronounce on whether a given survival strategy or safety practice is 'adaptive' or 'maladaptive'. However, our proposition is that such practices, in any case, emerge from psycho-social processes of (re-)traumatisation, and while they all involve a violence of some kind, they might all be understood as survival strategies; as ways of managing within the matrices of violence described above.

We include here acts of self-neglect, which, although enormously damaging, might not reach thresholds of interest for access to the system of care (whether or not the terms of the offer would be acceptable to the individual). The self-neglectful sufferer – for example, the substance-using rough sleeper – is thus all too often neglectfully deemed to be 'making a lifestyle choice' and thereby doomed to be left to freeze or starve to death in a doorway.

Our business here is to explore the psycho-social frame and phenomenology of these practices, rather than to view them through a 'clinical' lens. Our use of the term 'practice' rather than (for example) 'behaviour' is intended to bring out this crucial distinction, as well as to make the link back to Diogenes' or Simeon Stylites' practices of resistance (and perhaps even parody). We also offer the term 'practice' in order to evoke the discipline, application and focus involved in the repetition of certain actions. Practices of self-harming, like the practices of the gymnasium, or of chess, or of playing a musical instrument, may require a highly disciplined self-denial (*askesis*, a Cynic virtue exemplified by both Diogenes and Simeon Stylites), as well as a determination to overcome, to prevail – perhaps even to triumph. In the instance of practices more troublesome for the individual and more ambivalently entered upon, the secondary problem which then arises is the force of habituated patterns of activity that become embedded in the *praxis* and which then make it difficult to vary or relinquish such practices, even if they no longer serve their purpose.

Considering such actions as a *praxis* also allows us to remember that these self-harming or self-neglectful practices can, from time to time and to varying extents, become culturally accepted modes of expression (Turp, 2002). Practices of self-decoration or body modification by piercing or tattooing, like prolonged fasting and abstinence, are then perceived to exist at an uneasy intersection between violence and play (see, e.g., Lemma, 2010). At times and in places, reciprocally injurious acts performed by 'consenting adults' are often (but not always) deemed to be 'private matters' that attract little, if any, attention, regardless of the degree of damage and self-and-other injury. The extreme asceticism of Simeon Stylites exemplifies another obvious and widespread example of the pursuit of ecstatic or devotional practices of self-harming in religious observances, from penance, fasting and self-denial to flagellation: practices that are not censured but often celebrated.

Certain acts of politically motivated protest, for which we may take the figure of Diogenes as exemplar, may also be vilified or revered according to the eye of the beholder. The death of Simone Weil offers an example of spiritually inspired practices of self-denial intersecting with a political commitment. Weil died of complications related to tuberculosis, having imposed upon herself a minimal calorific intake in solidarity with the inhabitants of occupied France in World War Two. In this, Weil can be located within a genealogy and ascetic as well as aesthetic practice going back to the (anti-) heroine of Sophocles' *Antigone* (Sophocles, 442–441; see also Steiner, 1986). We are arguing here against *any* kind of colonising 'pathologisation' of these psycho-social phenomena, which arbitrarily splits off one-or-other practice and construes some as 'symptomatic behaviour' and others as 'exotica' (or erotica). Still other practices are thus constructed as creative or sublime mystical expression on the part of, or for the entertainment of, the in-group, which arbitrates and sits in judgement upon these different, 'other' *praxes*.

Reflexive violence

> [T]he ego can kill itself only if … it can treat itself as an object – if it is able to direct against itself the hostility which relates to an object and which represents the ego's original reaction to objects in the external world.
>
> (Freud, 1917, p. 261)

Practices of self-harming (including self-neglecting), which we are here construing as a psycho-social phenomenon indicative of a group or societal ailment, are generally held to present particularly difficult challenges to systems of care and control. Like many other forms of violence, they can helpfully be understood as emerging from violated states of mind and body (see, e.g., Herman, 1997; Motz, 2008). The individual, understood in these terms, is most often in a violent state of mind in the 'here-and-now' because this state of mind has been violently pushed into them, and internalised through traumatogenic (often trans-generationally transmitted) 'there-and-then' experiences of exclusion, violation and neglect in their own familial, communal, cultural and ethnic (and racialised) biographies.

We have previously proposed the term *reflexive violence* to convey the sense of a violent and impulsive action – both the injury and the insult – unconsciously and reflexively turned back upon the embodied self (Scanlon and Adlam, 2013). Diogenes here is a paradigmatic figure, in that, in refuting the imperialist violence that would 'pathologise' the out-group, his dangerous and endangered practice is to use his own (self-neglected?) body to mimic and to parody[2] ways in which the in-group wields force. In this analysis, the practices of harmed or neglected bodies evidence and bear witness to the operation of the social forces that have objectified these bodies and so reduced the humanity of the subject. The scars and wounds are sometimes (though not always) visible; but the invisible ink of the discourse of domination always reveals itself, in a certain light, upon the tormented skin and flesh of the subjugated.

That hyphen that is hard to avoid in the terms 'self-harming' or 'self-neglecting' allows us to emphasise how reflexive violence might be understood to be directed both at the individual's own 'embodied multiple selves', and at the internalised selves of historical and contemporary others. By this we mean to suggest that Diogenes, in his abjection, is publishing an appraisal of the state to which the Metropolitan powers of his day and his yesterdays have reduced him. However, he is also making a kind of counterclaim. He is not only, or even not mainly, protesting his marginalisation – well, we'd have to ask him! But our sense is that he is also pushing back, proclaiming that these are his values, this is what he considers a virtue. He's not only 'gone to the dogs'; he is dogged, and the values of the 'natural' state are his values, and the virtues of animals are, in his view, worth upholding.

Although such practices of self-harming or neglectful-ness are often covert and hidden from view, they are 'written on the body' nonetheless (Adshead, 2010), and as such constitute a form of *publication*, even if no outside eye is able to see the invisible ink or decipher the text when it is revealed. The canine and human faeces smeared around Diogenes' barrel; the maggots writhing in Simeon's wounds when he bound rope tight into his flesh; Lise's finger smashed in the door jamb in *The Brothers Karamazov*; these are performances or instances of practices that can all then be understood as publications or texts, or as codified ciphers that need to be decoded. If these were subjected to hermeneutic analysis, they could reveal the contextual meanings of such acts, even if these meanings are not (yet) available to the apparent protagonist of the story. These three examples, from legend or literature, all in one way or another serve to bear witness to experiences of abjection (Kristeva, 1982) and the ways in which offence is both taken ('the way the world organises itself offends me') and given ('the way you express your distress offends us').

Freud's famous phrase that, in the aetiology of melancholia, "the shadow of the object fell upon the ego" (Freud, 1917, p. 258), allows us to understand, at the level of the individual, how 'behavioural' violence (so-called) turned inwards upon the self becomes a reflexive violence – and that this process is neither conscious nor considered nor desired. Yet insult is piled on injury when a societal in-group insists, through its thoughts and proclamations, and by means of its own practices, that people who engage in such reflexive practices 'know what they are doing', and do so *deliberately* in order to 'seek attention', to 'manipulate', antagonise or spite 'us' – and so are told to go away and figuratively to lick their own wounds. This pseudo-formulation is then deployed as a supposedly self-evident rationale for why such annoyances should be excluded, exiled from the mainstream.

The master–slave dialectic: Subjection and emergence

> The Communists disdain to conceal their views and aims. They openly declare that their ends can be attained only by the forcible overthrow of all existing social conditions ... The proletarians have nothing to lose but their chains.
>
> (Marx and Engels, 1872, pp. 120–121)

One way of thinking of what we are calling the Diogenes Paradigm and the relationship between the abject out-group and the excluding in-group from an ideological perspective is to understand it as a perhaps more hopeful political representation of a Hegelian dialectic. According to this view, the *thesis* represented by the Metropolitan city-state encounters, and is engaged by, the *antithesis* of the 'Cosmopolitan' world-view, and as such this encounter may then produce a *synthesis* in which the caesura between out-group and in-group dissolves.

Hegel (1807) charted the dynamics of the relationship between lordship and bondage: the relationship between 'master' and 'slave', and the ways in which their respective 'relatedness' configures their relationship. Their reciprocal relationship makes manifest a structural violence; it also operates to defend both parties from an awareness of this violence. What this means is that both 'master' and 'slave' share an internal sense of what is 'their proper' place: 'the rich man in his castle' and his bondsman, whose societal role is to maintain the uneasy *status quo* that up-keeps his castle – through keeping the *beggar* at the gate. The bondsman is related to the master by his dependency upon him and has little, if any, right to a mind, or indeed a life, of his own.

Because in this book we are also foregrounding the psycho-social realities of colonisation, slavery and racism, we need to emphasise here that our inverted commas, as we address Hegelian theory, are provisional. The master–slave power dynamic is neither a philosophical abstraction nor a thing of the past. Orlando Patterson, the foundational theorist of Afropessimism, developed the concept of 'natal alienation' (Patterson, 1982) to understand the way in which African slaves, at the very moment of birth, were alienated from all the rights that may naturally accrue to the newborn.[3] Ralph Ellison, in *Invisible Man* (Ellison, 1952), vividly expresses this when his protagonist explains that "I am invisible ... because people refuse to see me" (p. 7). He knows that he is a man, and he knows also that he is not recognised as such. He further understands that it is not the colour of his skin that renders him invisible, but rather that his invisibility is inflicted upon him by the perceptual stance of those white 'masters' who decline to recognise him. He also knows that he is caught up in a reciprocal violence located in this profoundly oppressing and negating, white supremacist withholding of the gaze:

> That invisibility to which I refer occurs because of a peculiar disposition of the eyes of those with whom I come in contact ... you're constantly being

bumped against by those of poor vision. Or again, you often doubt if you really exist ... You ache with the need to convince yourself that you do exist in the real world ... you curse and you swear to make them recognize you.

(Ellison, 1952, p. 7)

Building on Du Bois' account of 'double-consciousness' (Du Bois, 1903, p. 7), Fanon (1952) suggested that many Black people's experience is of needing to deny or neglect their own personhood (at least in public) through presenting a 'white mask' in order to manage the violent and discriminatory attitudes of the white 'in-group'. In Stuart Hall's words, the European colonial project "went to great lengths to refashion us, the subjugated colonials, as simulacra of itself. It 'othered' us to ourselves" (Hall, 2018, p. 21). This sense of having (un)consciously to modify and adapt one's identity and presentation to find safety and security is an example of violent re-traumatisation. To proclaim the alternative – being oneself – is to run the very real risk of being driven even further out. Like the lepers in Foucault's account of the origins of psychiatry (Foucault, 1961), these socially constructed out-groups are metaphorically to be quarantined, in sight of, and yet outwith, the city walls – they are 'done away with'; not infrequently, even unto death.

In Hegel's parable, the societal system of feudal slavery was an intermediate step between a primordial fight to the death – a violent state of nature – and the fulfilment of what he thought of as the Spirit of history in mutual recognition. The Lord unquestionably has the easier time of this journey, but his consciousness is as much shackled to the reciprocal relationship of domination as is the bondsman's. The domination of the lord precedes (in Hegel's dialectic, it *necessarily* precedes) the emergence of the bondsman as a separately constituted being:

> [T]he very notion of reflexivity, as an emergent structure of the subject, is the consequence of a 'turning back on itself', a repeated self-beratement [reflexive violence] ... there is no formation of the subject without a passionate attachment to subjection.
>
> (Butler, 1997, p. 67 [our parentheses])

Hall (2018), discussing Patterson's theory of 'natal alienation', suggests that in the mental universe of the plantation, "the slave could not even be *comprehended* without the presence of the master. He or she could not properly exist" (Hall, 2018, p. 70). For the bondsman to exist as a person in his own right, as somebody other than an extension of his master's mind and body, involves what Foucault (1976, p. 81) called the "insurrection of subjugated knowledges", first requiring him to attain a new *reflexive* awareness of himself, a new emergence and reconfiguration of self-consciousness. That this might be no straightforward or painless process is eloquently summed up by Maya Angelou:

> If growing up is painful for the Southern Black girl, being aware of her displacement is the rust on the razor that threatens the throat. It is an unnecessary insult.
>
> (Angelou, 1969, p. 6)

One example of this kind of emancipatory psycho-social phenomenon would be the rise of the survivor movement in the 1960s and 1970s, which gradually brought the prevalence of child sexual abuse back into the public eye – the best part of a century after Freud first uncovered childhood sexual trauma and proclaimed it to be the *"caput Nili* [the source of the Nile] in neuropathology" (Freud, 1896, p. 184).[4] More recent examples include the revisiting of transgressions by powerful predatory men on the bodies of women (and other men) in the #MeToo wave of disclosure and exposure in the 2010s; or the naming of predatory and institutional abuse by wayward clerics and their congregations in Ireland and many other countries (O'Connor, 2019); or the #ClimateStrike movement mobilised by Greta Thunberg taking up residence in her own Diogenesque protest outside the Swedish Parliament in 2018, which brought similar issues of denial and misuse of the *body* of the planet into public consciousness – to name but three. What all these states of affairs hold in common is the ways in which his patriarchal Lordship sought, and still seeks, to dominate, to subjugate and to deny the rights of others to be in charge of the ways in which these personal and socio-political bodies are to be governed.

Our Diogenes Paradigm then offers a means to explore what happens when the contemporary 'bondsman' who harms himself (indeed, anyone who is experienced as not in his proper place) is seen to break the terms of a societal lordship and colonialist control over his body, by having the audacity to imagine that it is *his* body to harm, or to inhabit, and how this stance might be, in itself, an emancipatory act and insurrection, whereby the subjectified individual manifests an embodied mind of his own. Insult is added to injury when a taboo (the taboo that the Lord must not be aware of his own violence) is broken by the injured 'bondsman' (the 'ex-offender' Diogenes, in our paradigm) in asserting that they have their own(ed) body *because* it is injured, whilst the insulter (the 'Lord', or, in our terms, the figure of Alexander), whilst feeling insulted and muddled, has no sense of appreciation of the injury that he had previously perpetrated upon the bondsman.

At a fundamental level, the relations of domination and subjugation that govern the encounter between in-group and out-group at the societal level also work to prohibit the incohesive out-group from thinking its own thoughts about this relatedness and these relationships. These dynamics are often bolstered by specific societal mechanisms, such as 'bread and circuses' in the days of the Roman Empire; Marie Antoinette's apocryphal 'let them eat cake'; or 'the great British bake-off'; and all the other ways in which we are 'amusing ourselves to death' (Postman, 1987). All of these discursive

66 Un-housed minds: The Diogenes Paradigm

moves reveal, in their different ways, the in-group peddling anaesthetics (anti-aesthetics?) as 'opiates' for the people (Marx, 1843), which in turn serve to keep 'man's estate in order' and everyone in their 'proper' place.

Bartleby and the politics of resistance and insurrection

> Nothing so aggravates an earnest person as a passive resistance.
>
> (Melville, 1853, p. 23)

Herman Melville's novella, *Bartleby the Scrivener* (Melville, 1853), offers both a Hegelian (and a Foucauldian) parable for transformation in relations of bondage, resistance and insurrection; and the fictional Bartleby, a lowly but far from humble clerk in a Wall Street office in mid-nineteenth century New York, joins Simeon Stylites and Diogenes as key figures in our analysis of discourses of power at the heart of psycho-social processes of traumatisation and exclusion. In the story, the Master in Chancery, who employs Bartleby as a bonded clerk, asks him to read through his copy. This was a conventional task, well within the job description, and a request (or polite command) with which automatic compliance was entirely taken for granted. But instead of taking up his role in the expected way, Bartleby declares, "I would prefer not to" and continues with his own writing (Melville, 1853, pp. 17–18).

The Master is disturbed and dumbfounded ("I sat awhile in perfect silence, rallying my stunned faculties" (ibid.)) to find himself standing in Alexander's shoes when thus requested to step out of Bartleby's light. He is discombobulated by Bartleby's profoundly disruptive, and potentially transformative, unilateral declaration of autonomy, asserted through his claiming a right to think his own thoughts and to have a preference beyond what is required of him. Later in the story Bartleby asserts his autonomy and renders himself *un-housed* by seemingly refusing offers of accommodation and food, and not merely instructions from his employer. He is interned as a vagrant, where he "lives without dining" for a short while and then pays the ultimate price of his unilateral declaration of independence when he dies in the prison yard. Žižek (2008) has written of 'Bartlebian politics' as the politics of *passive resistance*. For us, this links helpfully to Afuape's observation (2011) that there is always some form of resistance to traumatising forces – that there is no such thing as a wholly passive 'victim of trauma' and that the notion of 'passivity' is itself a violent attribution into the out-group (Afuape, 2011).[5]

Billow (2010) suggests that rebellion, like refusal, functions more on the level of conscious thinking and deliberate action, whereas resistance operates in the realms of a more unconscious and internalised antagonism. However, although these distinctions may or may not remain psychologically significant at the individual, behavioural level, we maintain here that the psycho-social significance of such actions lies in the experience of the *offerer*, when his offer is refused. The object of the offer may or may not have resisted, refused or rebelled against that offer in his manner of not taking it up. All we can say with confidence is that the offer has not been taken up – at least, not on the terms in which it was made – and that toxic psycho-social relations of domination and subjugation have often been, and continue to be, predicated upon the affront experienced by the offerer, who takes offence when his offer has not been gratefully received.

When we previously wrote about Bartleby we tended to take his 'I prefer not to' as an example of refusal. We argue here that the figure of Bartleby stands for the embodied resistance to discourses and relations of domination, even though, in so doing, Bartleby also loses his life. The 'Bartlebian' moment is not the practice itself, not his 'step out of my light, for I prefer not to', but rather the emergent reflexive consciousness of the *power of the practice* within circumstances of apparent powerlessness.

Bartleby's victory is, then, to attain a moment of autonomy. He then resists the force that would drag him away from this moment of self-realisation and self-government back into his proper place. Indeed, at the dénouement of the story, the Master, echoing Alexander's recognition of Diogenes, seems to eventually recognise both the psycho-social power and the tragedy of Bartleby's psycho-social protest when he says of him that, in death, he was sleeping "with kings and counsellors" (Melville, 1853, p. 63).

✱✱✱✱✱✱✱✱✱✱✱✱✱✱✱✱✱

Edward Said wrote that the key process underlying and undermining the pseudo-science of Orientalism is "disregarding, essentialising, denuding the humanity of another culture, people or geographical region" (Said, 1978, p. 108). This is what, for example, Naomi Klein (2016) or Stuart Hall (2018) mean by 'othering'. Societal responses to reflexive violence (within the cycle of reciprocal violence we have already outlined) are generally characterised by the drive to objectify the self-harming subject, to 'turn her into a thing' (Weil, 1939, p. 3); to (insultingly) construct her as 'other' and to condemn her for 'wilfully' (insultingly?) taking up the position constructed by the in-group as 'anti-social'. We have long argued that the violent attribution of conscious, calculated, often malicious intent into the individual – the othering of the out-group – primarily evidences a violent state of mind within the societal in-group that perpetrated this attribution (see, e.g., Richards, 2019). When it comes to what goes on inside Diogenes' barrel, it's always 'they' or 'them', never 'those of us'.

Said (1978) illuminated the way in which 'the Orient' was, and remains, a construction of 'the Occident', of 'the West'. He showed how the West, particularly through the power of the British and French Empires, defined its own imperial self by constructing a feared, exotic and exploited Other – the 'East'. The East was thus dominated and beaten down, not only by means of armies and tax collectors and land laws (for example), but also by the *knowing* of the Orient by the coloniser: by taking control of the language and using it to rewrite its histories so that the Westerners 'knowledge' of the Orient became *the* only knowledge worth knowing.[6]

There are Westerners, and there are Orientals. The former dominate; the latter must be dominated, which usually means having their land occupied, their internal affairs rigidly controlled, their blood and treasure put at the disposal of one or another Western power.

(Said, 1978, p. 36)

This position naturally takes it as a given that the subaltern 'Oriental' may not speak to his own view of the matter (Spivak, 1988), unless to offer suitably deferent appreciation of his 'proper place' in these narratives of domination. Any murmurs of discontent or dissent from the official version must then be the work of the agitator; the malcontent; the criminal or 'the terrorist'; but never the freedom fighter.

In Chapter 1 we set out our hypothesis that the housed need the un-housed, and define themselves in relation to 'them'; sometimes also, in their patronage, *worry* about 'them'. It is only when the distinction starts to break down, when everyone is feeling the cold and no one is in their allocated 'proper place', that trouble (for the housed!) begins to surface. Hall (2018) examines the aftermath of the Windrush migration from the Caribbean to the 'mother country' in exactly this light. He shows how the racism of the 'colour line' projected from London out into 'the colonies' became resurgent in England synchronously and in proportion to its blurring and diminishment in the Caribbean islands. Herein lies the very toxic essence of 'othering'. The homeless, migrant, 'disordered', un-housed 'other' becomes the 'lethargic and suspicious … Oriental' (Said, 1978, p. 39) constructed by that psychiatric imperialism that was established by the Anglo-French bourgeois West during exactly the same time that 'Orientalism' was at the zenith of its power and influence (roughly between the battle of Waterloo and the assassination of Archduke Ferdinand in Sarajevo).

It seems that not only did the 'we' of that civilisation construct ourselves as blessèd, liberal, logical, rational, sceptical, measured, respectable, normal, mature, housed and hard-working; we did so by finding an "irrational, depraved (fallen), childlike, 'different'" other (Said, 1978, p. 40), both without and within: an other which we could construct as perilously exotic and subjugate by knowledge and classification. This is why Fanon needed to argue that decolonisation must be "a programme of complete disorder" (Fanon, 1961, p. 27). There is so much order behind the practice of marking others as disordered. We, the Westerners in possession, became 'alienists', to borrow the old term for a psychiatrist (Littlewood and Lipsedge, 1982), of the dispossessed, Easterner and Westerner alike, constructing them alike as 'other' and 'disordered'. Note this definition of Orientalism offered by Said:

> … so far as the West was concerned during the nineteenth and twentieth centuries, an assumption had been made that the Orient and everything in it was … in need of corrective study by the West. The Orient was

viewed as if framed by the classroom, the criminal court, the prison, the illustrated manual. *Orientalism, then, is knowledge of the Orient that places things Oriental in class, court, prison or manual for scrutiny, study, judgment, discipline or governing.*

(Said, 1978, pp. 40–41 [our italics])

In this view, like Hegel's 'lord' or Melville's 'Master', or like Alexander himself, we in the in-group deny our awareness of the power differentials we exploit, and on which we thrive and prosper, so that we may accede to the outward roles and trappings of power without having to think too much about the experience of those who are subordinate to us. The British tendency to forgetting and disavowal of its own violent imperial past affords a prime example of this. This tendency, perhaps, particularly marks situations where 'we' construct ourselves as being in (public) 'service', in the Victorian tradition, and are then surprised when those we 'serve' decline to be grateful or improved by our *patronising* interventions.

Williams (1958), discussing the tension in the idea of 'culture' between individualist and collective values systems, puts it succinctly:

> … having worked for improvement in the conditions of working people, in the spirit of service, those who are ruled by the idea of service are genuinely dismayed when the workers do not fully respond: when … they don't play the game, are lacking in team-spirit, neglect the national interest … Yet the fact is that working-class people cannot feel that this *is* their community in anything like the sense in which it is felt above them. The idea of service breaks down because while the upper servants have been able to identify themselves with the establishment, the lower servants have not.
>
> (Williams, 1958, p. 432)

In identification with the Master in Chancery, it may be that unless or until the survivor declines to be a recipient of care or patronage in the sense we recognise – unless he engages in the 'Bartlebian politics' (Žižek, 2008, p. 180) of violently preferring to do nothing – we don't notice what sort of doctors or alienists we Alexanders have become, or how much we depend for our very identity upon the continued willingness of Diogenes to offer deferent compliance. However, as we shall discuss further in Part III, this is not to put the onus to drive change upon the membership of the out-group! Creative disruption of the dialectic may depend upon the Master giving up his seat, and not, or not only, upon Bartleby standing his own ground.

Notes

1 A similarly complex dance is played out between Simeon Stylites and the religious authorities of his time. Heliodorus, the abbot of Simeon's monastery, felt he could

live with Simeon's practices of self-starvation but drew the line at his hiding at the bottom of a scorpion-infested well. Later, during his decades on the pillar, the monastic authorities sent a delegation to check on his compliance with his Order, but, finding him holding to his vow of obedience to their authority, took no offence at any of his other extreme ascetic practices and retreated, satisfied, behind their walls (Kociejowski, 2016).

2 Navia (2005) offers an anecdote, reported by Lucian (an Assyrian satirist writing around the second century CE), in which Diogenes is in Corinth when the city comes under attack. All the would-be helpful (and doubtless very anxious) citizens busy themselves with shoring up defences, building fortifications and other preparations for battle. Diogenes starts rolling his pithos up and down the Craneum, in satirical parody of the pointless worldly Metropolitan busyness that has erupted all around him. His explanation when challenged is that he is simply aiming "to make myself look as busy as the rest of you" (Navia, 2005, pp. 37–38). For an analysis of this story, resting in turn upon François Rabelais' extended fictional account of this incident, see Pelletier (2011).

3 In the words of Frank B. Wilderson III (2020), the theory of Afropessimism holds that "Blacks are not Human subjects, but are instead structurally inert props, implements for the execution of White and non-Black fantasies and sadomasochistic pleasures" (Wilderson III, 2020, p. 15 [italics in the original]).

4 Very shortly afterwards, under pressure, Freud abandoned this hard-won ground. He wrote to Fleiss in September 1897 to say that, "surely such widespread perversions against children are not very probable" (Freud, 1897, p. 264). In this way, he adopts a metaphorical 'white mask' (Fanon, 1952) in order to appease the denials and persecution of the Viennese 'in-group' by suggesting that 'it was all in her mind', and privileging the altogether more comfortable notions of unconscious phantasy and the Oedipus Complex (Masson, 1990).

5 An illuminating if altogether toxic example of this kind of violent attribution was provided by the British conservative politician Jacob Rees-Mogg in the aftermath of the catastrophic fire at Grenfell Tower in west London in June 2017. Rees-Mogg suggested that 'common sense' should have dictated, to those caught and ultimately consumed in the smoke and flame, that they exit the building on hearing the alarm sound, rather than obeying explicit fire safety instructions to remain within their flats and await rescue services (Mohdin, 2019). Rees-Mogg here perpetrates the violent offence (for which he was forced into a rare apology) of attributing passivity – and therefore responsibility – to those who died.

6 Closer to home – for some of us – the same could be said of the relationship of the British to the island of Ireland to its west; but we have no argument with the general direction of the needle in Said's compass.

References

Adlam, J., Kluttig, T., and Lee, B.X. (eds) (2018) *Violent states and creative states: From the global to the individual.* London: Jessica Kingsley Publishers.

Adshead, G. (2010) 'Written on the body: Deliberate self-harm as communication', *Psychoanalytic Psychotherapy*, 24 (2), pp. 69–80.

Afuape, T. (2011) *Power, resistance and liberation in therapy with survivors of trauma: To have our hearts broken.* London: Routledge.

Alexander, C.F. (1848) 'All things bright and beautiful', in *Hymns for little children.* Available at: https://archive.org/details/hymnsforlittlech00alex/page/26/mode/2up (Accessed: 2 February 2021).

Angelou, M. (1969) *I know why the caged bird sings*. Reprinted 2007. London: Virago.

Angus, I. (2016) *Facing the Anthropocene: Fossil capitalism and the crisis of the earth system*. New York, NY: Monthly Review Press.

Baldwin, A. and Bettini, G. (eds) (2017) *Life adrift: Climate change, migration, critique*. London: Rowman and Littlefield.

Benjamin, J. (2018) *Beyond doer and done to: Recognition theory, intersubjectivity and the third*. London: Routledge.

Billow, R.M. (2010) *Resistance, rebellion and refusal in groups: The three R's*. New International Library of Group Analysis. London: Karnac.

Bion, W.R. (1961) *Experiences in groups*. London: Tavistock.

Butler, J. (1997) *The psychic life of power: Theories in subjection*. Palo Alto, CA: Stanford University Press.

Dalby, S. (2017) 'On "not being persecuted": Territory, security, climate', in Baldwin, A. and Bettini, G. (eds) *Life adrift: Climate change, migration, critique*. London: Rowman and Littlefield, pp. 41–58.

Danewid, I. (2017) 'White innocence in the Black Mediterranean: Hospitality and the erasure of history', *Third World Quarterly*, 38 (7), pp. 1674–1689.

Dostoyevsky F. (1880) *The brothers Karamazov*. Translated by D. Magarshack, 1982. London: Penguin Classics.

Du Bois, W.E.B. (1903) *The souls of Black folk; with 'The talented tenth' and 'The souls of white folk'*. Reprinted 2018. London: Penguin Classics.

Ellison, R. (1952) *The invisible man*. Reprinted 1965. London: Penguin Twentieth Century Classics.

Fanon, F. (1952) *Black skins, white masks*. Translated by R. Philcox, 2008. New York, NY: Grove Press.

Fanon, F. (1961) *The wretched of the earth*. Translated by C. Farrington, 2001. London: Penguin Modern Classics.

Foucault, M. (1961) *Madness and civilization: A history of insanity in the age of reason*. Translated by R. Howard, 2001. London: Routledge Classics.

Foucault, M. (1975) *Discipline and punish: The birth of the prison*. Translated by A. Sheridan, 1991. London: Penguin Books.

Foucault, M. (1976) 'Two lectures'. Translated by A. Fontana and P. Pasquino, in Gordon, C. (ed.) (1980) *Power/knowledge: Selected interviews and other writings 1972–1977*. New York: Pantheon, pp. 78–108.

Foucault, M. (1983) *Fearless speech*. Reprinted 2001. Los Angeles, CA: Semiotexte.

Foulkes, S.H. (1948) *Introduction to group-analytic psychotherapy: Studies in the social integration of individuals and groups*. London: Heinemann.

Freud, S. (1896) 'Letter of April 26, 1896'. Translated by J.M. Masson, 1985, in Masson, J.M. (ed.) *The complete letters of Sigmund Freud to Wilhelm Fleiss, 1887–1904*. Cambridge, MA: Harvard University Press, pp. 183–185.

Freud, S. (1897) 'Letter of September 21, 1897'. Translated by J.M. Masson, 1985, in Masson, J.M. (ed.) *The complete letters of Sigmund Freud to Wilhelm Fleiss, 1887–1904*. Cambridge, MA: Harvard University Press, pp. 264–267.

Freud, S. (1917) 'Mourning and melancholia'. Translated under editorship of Strachey, J., 1957, in Richards, A. (ed.) (1991) *On Metapsychology*. Penguin Freud Library, Volume 11. London: Penguin, pp. 237–258.

Hall, S. (2018) *Familiar stranger: A life between two islands*. London: Penguin.

72 Un-housed minds: The Diogenes Paradigm

Hegel, G.W.F. (1807) *The phenomenology of spirit*. Translated by A.V. Miller, 1977. Oxford: Oxford University Press.

Herman, J. (1997) *Trauma and recovery: The aftermath of violence – From domestic abuse to political terror*. New York: Basic Books.

Klein, N. (2016) 'Let them drown – the violence of othering in a warming world', *London Review of Books*, 38 (11). Available at: https://www.lrb.co.uk/the-paper/v38/n11/naomi-klein/let-them-drown (Accessed: 1 January 2021).

Kociejowski, M. (2016) *The street philosopher and the holy fool: A Syrian journey*. London: Eland.

Kristeva, J. (1982) *Powers of horror: An essay on abjection*. New York: Columbia University Press.

Lear, J. (2017) *Wisdom won from illness: Essays in philosophy and psychoanalysis*. Cambridge, MA: Harvard University Press.

Lemma, A. (2010) *Under the skin: A psychoanalytic study of body modification*. London: Routledge.

Levi, P. (1986) *The drowned and the saved*. Translated by R. Rosenthal. Reprinted 1989. London: Abacus.

Littlewood, R. and Lipsedge, M. (1982) *Aliens and alienists: Ethnic minorities and psychiatry*. London: Penguin.

Marx, K. (1843) A contribution to the critique of Hegel's philosophy of right. Translator unknown. Available at: https://www.marxists.org/archive/marx/works/1843/critique-hpr/intro.htm (Accessed: 3 January 2021).

Marx, K. and Engels, F. (1872) *The Communist manifesto*. Translated by S. Moore, 1967. London: Pelican.

Masson, J.M. (1990) *Against therapy*. London: Fontana.

Melville, H. (1853) *Bartleby the scrivener*. Reprinted 2010. New York: Melville House.

Mohdin, A. (2019) 'Jacob Rees-Mogg's Grenfell remarks "caused huge distress", admits Tory chairman', *The Guardian*, 6 November. Available at: https://www.theguardian.com/politics/2019/nov/06/jacob-rees-moggs-grenfell-remarks-caused-huge-distress-admits-tory-chairman (Accessed: 3 January 2021).

Motz, A. (2008) *The psychology of female violence: Crimes against the body*. 2nd edition. London: Routledge.

Navia, L. (2005) *Diogenes the Cynic*. New York: Humanity Books.

O'Connor, J. (2019) 'Elective homelessness and the shadow of the institution: Lessons from the lives of survivors of the Irish Industrial School system', in Brown, G. (ed.) *Psychoanalytic thinking on the unhoused mind*. London: Routledge, pp. 80–91.

Patterson, O. (1982) *Slavery and social death: A comparative study*. Cambridge, MA: Harvard University Press.

Pelletier, C. (2011) 'Beating the barrel of inclusion: Cosmopolitanism through Rabelais and Rancière – A response to John Adlam and Chris Scanlon', *Psychodynamic Practice*, 17 (3), pp. 255–272.

Postman, N. (1987) *Amusing ourselves to death: Public discourse in the age of show business*. York: Methuen.

Richards, B. (2019) 'Beyond the angers of populism: A psycho-social inquiry', *Journal of Psychosocial Studies*, 12 (1–2), pp. 171–183.

Said, E. (1978) *Orientalism*. Reprinted 2019. London: Penguin Modern Classics.

Scanlon, C. and Adlam, J. (2013) 'Reflexive violence', *Psychoanalysis, Culture and Society*, 18 (3), pp. 223–241.

Sophocles (442–441) *Antigone*. Translated by E.F. Watling. Reprinted in Sophocles (1947) *The Theban plays*. London: Penguin Classics, pp. 126–162.

Spivak, G.C. (1988) 'Can the subaltern speak?', in Nelson, C. and Grossberg, L. (eds) *Marxism and the interpretation of culture*. Basingstoke: MacMillan Education, pp. 66–111.

Steiner, G. (1986) *Antigones: The Antigone myth in western literature, art, and thought*. Oxford: Clarendon.

Thompson, E.P. (1980) 'Notes on exterminism, the last stage of civilisation', *New Left Review*, 121, pp. 3–31.

Turp, M. (2002) *Hidden self-harm: Narratives from psychotherapy*. London: Jessica Kingsley Publishers.

Weil, S. (1939) 'The Iliad, or the poem of force'. Translated by M. McCarthy, 1945, in Weil, S. and Bespaloff, R. (2005) *War and the Iliad*. New York, NY: New York Review Books, pp. 1–37.

Wilderson III, F.B. (2020) *Afropessimism*. New York, NY: Liveright Publishing Corporation.

Williams, R. (1958) *Culture and Society*. Reprinted 2017. London: Vintage.

Young, J., Lee, B.X., and Lee, G. (2018) 'From human violence to creativity: The structural nature of violence and the spiritual nature of its remedy', in Adlam, J., Kluttig, T., and Lee, B.X. (eds) *Violent states and creative states: From the global to the individual*. Volume 1: Structural violence and creative structures. London: Jessica Kingsley Publishers, pp. 29–44.

Žižek, S. (2008) *Violence*. London: Profile Books.

Chapter 5

Agoraphilia and agoraphobia
Negotiating fraught encounters in open spaces

The ancient *agora* of Athens

> If you hear me defending myself in the same language which it has been my habit to use, *both around the trading-stalls of the market-place* (where many of you have heard me) and elsewhere, do not be surprised …
>
> (Plato, 4th century BCEa, pp. 39–40 [our italics])

In this last chapter of Part I of this book, we intend again to make use of the Diogenes Paradigm to explore the *situated* nature of the psycho-social dynamics of social exclusion and other forms of structural violence that we have been discussing. Not so much a question of when, why or how 'Diogenes met Alexander', but more *where* they met, and where their contemporary counterparts might meet – in what sort of psycho-social spaces and places.

The word 'agora' stems from the Greek word for 'to gather or meet together', and the *agora*[1] of the city-states of ancient Greece was a *marketplace*: "a public open space used for assemblies" (Oxford Dictionary of English, 2005, p. 32). A marketplace in this sense was a place and a space both for the exchange of goods and services and also for the exchange of ideas: the meeting of bodies and the meeting of minds. The sense therefore is of a place where individuals congregate for interactions and transactions of various kinds and where a given community *represents* itself in all its complexity.

The *agora* in ancient Athens was situated at the foot of the Acropolis at a place where several important roads converged. It developed, from the 6th century BCE, as a civic space where judicial, political and religious activities were co-located alongside commercial premises, academies, athletics stadia, museums, theatres and exhibitions of the arts. The *agora* was the heart and soul of the civic community, a gathering place in which citizens could encounter each other and take up their membership of the *commune* in different ways; it was a place and a space in which philosophers and poets rubbed shoulders with merchants and politicians.

The *agora* was also the central point for the oversight of the ethical life of the community. The *Tholos* housed the official weights and measures that

DOI: 10.4324/9781003223115-6

governed commerce in the city, and nearby the *Metröon* contained both the State archives and the temple of the Mother of Gods. Diogenes is supposed to have taken up his abode in his *pithos* just outside the walls of the *Metröon*, and in the *agora* the itinerant and the eccentric were generally afforded a certain degree of liminal hospitality. Here too was where Diogenes' forebear Socrates set about his own self-appointed and ultimately doomed task of making a constructive nuisance and spectacle of himself: a 'stinging fly' to pester the 'large thoroughbred horse' that is the *Metropolis* (Plato, 4th century BCEa, p. 57).

The perimeter of this civic space was marked by marble posts (*pales*), inscribed with the words, "I am the boundary of the Agora", to delineate the *agora* as a public space and to protect it from encroachment by private interests, buildings, gangs (or private security guards), as well as from intrusion from pesky children and (other?) identified criminal elements. The structures of commerce were understood as 'public' and the contrast was with the 'private' spaces within personal and family life. The 'agora' is therefore to be understood, in our contemporary terms, as a negotiated, protected, sacrosanct locus for the mining of what it means to be a citizen member of shared communal spaces; a point of reference and a place of reality orientation, philosophical debate and challenge, and a site of 'commonwealth' psycho-social integration and healing.

We therefore suggest that, by inhabiting the psycho-social agora and setting up their stalls, barrels or pillars there, the historical Diogenes, Socrates and Simeon Stylites, despite their seeming curmudgeonliness, were in significant part *agoraphilic* in tendency and temperament. By 'agoraphilic', we particularly mean to say that these individuals naturally gravitated towards shared spaces and that their seemingly bizarre 'public performances' and fraught but creative encounters, though challenging, were deeply concerned with, and about, the affairs of the people. In that process and by those means, they were essentially expressing the way in which they valued the quality of neighbourly and community-based relationships. Their stance was not about resisting or eschewing human contact. It was much more about efforts to deepen and broaden relationships through encouraging conversation in the psycho-social spaces of community. Under cover of an apparently anti-societal attitude, these men had *de facto* developed a pro-social *praxis*.

In a previous paper (Adlam and Scanlon, 2011), we developed a composite vignette that evoked the figure of a latter-day Diogenes holed up in his bedsit, *agoraphobically* afraid to emerge from his metaphorical barrel; not so much because of a fear of the crowd, as for fear of the havoc he might wreak if he was to tell his truth in these public open spaces. The challenge to us all might be how to feel safe enough to emerge from the intimate, private, enclosed space of our more intimate personal and familial context in order to take in something of the wider social group around us; to internalise a sense of ourselves and to re-member ourselves as a part of, rather than apart from, the social group.

76 Un-housed minds: The Diogenes Paradigm

However, in discussing agoraphobia in these terms our purpose is not to join in with those who would *diagnose*; nor are we proposing some 'quasi-clinical' syndrome of our own.[2] Our purpose here is to explore the psycho-social tension between agoraphobic and agoraphilic tendencies as they are expressed between members of in-groups and out-groups within our paradigm. Here, the complex figure of Alexander the Great is also central. On the one hand, Alexander's agoraphilia leads him to stand in the marketplace, by the opening to Diogenes' barrel, and to engage respectfully with the learned and cantankerous Dog: to step out of his light, when requested to do so and to not turn his back. On the other hand, there is, in our sense of the term, something intrinsically agoraphobic about his cutting of the Gordian knot. Here he shows us his temperamental as well as tactical impatience with negotiation, mutuality and exchange when any such negotiation would obstruct his progress, risk his loss of face and seek to place any limit upon his greatness or his omnipotent claim to divinity.

The agora in the context of our paradigm is therefore to be understood as a particular kind of psycho-social space in which the figure of Diogenes (representing both the out-cast and the out-group) may engage in creative encounters with the figure of Alexander (representing the in-group) so that *truths* may be spoken to the powers in the context of the 'parrhesiastic game' (Foucault, 1983). There is, crucially, an ambivalence in our relatedness to, and our relationships within, this agora-in-the-mind; a tension between an appreciation of its value and of the threat it poses both to the individual and to the polity. This tension is manifested in phenomena of *schwellenangst* (that anxiety at or of the threshold that ripples around the edge of all group experiences) at the borders of the agora.

The evacuation of the agora

> Those who think that they can deal with our present system in this piecemeal way very much underrate the strength of the tremendous organization under which we live, and which appoints to each of us his place ... Nothing but a tremendous force can deal with this force; it will not suffer itself to be dismembered, nor to lose anything which really is its essence without putting forth all its force in resistance; rather than lose anything which it considers of importance, it will pull the roof of the world down upon its head.
>
> (Morris, 1888, Chapter 2)

Bauman (2000) defines the conceptual space of the 'agora' as "that intermediary, public/private site ... where private problems are translated into the language of public issues and public solutions are sought, negotiated and agreed for private troubles" (Bauman, 2000, p. 39). His argument is that there is a gulf or abyss between the condition and constitution of individuals in law, *de jure*, and their possible opportunities to establish their individuality in social reality, *de facto*: "to gain control over their fate and make the choices they truly desire" (ibid.). To put this another way: an agoraphobic distance and alienation has opened up like a chasm, in the 'West', in late modernity, between the potentialities inherent in group membership and citizenship and the practical limits on the agency of the individual who has become more and more constructed as 'consumer' rather than contributor, participant or 'citizen'.

The task of "Politics – with a capital 'P'", argues Bauman (2000, p. 39), is the work of bridging this chasm. However, tragically, contemporary Politics turns out to be more often about blowing up the bridges across which the public might have spoken truth to power, and has more to do with the powerful opening of different kinds of channels for the one-way traffic of speaking lies to the people. We are reminded of Bion's warning:

> ... [i]t is too often forgotten that the gift of speech, so centrally employed, has been elaborated as much for the purpose of concealing thought by dissimulation and lying as for the purpose of elucidating or communicating thought.
>
> (Bion, 1970, p. 3)

In Bauman's view, the problem of not being able to speak the truth or hold others to account has arisen because of "the emptying of public space, and particularly the 'agora'" (Bauman, 2000, p. 39). In the ancient *agora*, as we have seen, Alexander could beard Diogenes in his lair (with potentially frightening consequences for the latter, let us not forget); but so too could Diogenes buttonhole Alexander if he had his wits and courage about him (and in Chapter 2 we recalled a similar story of when Demetrius encountered Vespasian).

Bauman, in contrast, makes the argument that the agora has been emptied out, across two frontiers. The 'interested citizen' has retreated from the agora to the illusory anaesthesia, and very real claustrophobia, of an ideology-free, consumption-driven private life, in retreat from the tensions and fraught encounters of public debate. This retreat then allows the dominant discourses of neo-liberalism and (fossil) capitalism to have free rei(g)n. 'Real power', on the other hand, has escaped from the implicit public scrutiny of the agora into privatised and secluded or secret spaces. Real power deploys resources and wields power in the 'outer spaces' of the world wide web and the will-o'-the-wisp structures of multinational corporations and the inscrutable financial systems that support them.

A contemporary example epitomising this phenomenon (two decades after Bauman made this argument) would be the Cambridge Analytica scandal unearthed by the British journalist Carole Cadwalladr, in which the outcome of the 2016 UK Referendum on membership of the EU was influenced by data abuses and subliminal advertising centred around the Facebook platform (see, e.g., Cadwalladr, 2019). The Cambridge Analytica scandal, then, offers an example of flagrant breaches of laws, which are, to borrow from Swift, "like cobwebs, which may catch small flies, but let wasps and hornets break through" (Swift, 1708, p. 8). The marketplace is now swarming with wasps and hornets, which means that it is easy to understand why the modern citizen might be agoraphobic, even before we contemplate the problems of pandemic (which, as we shall see in Chapter 7, are largely coterminous with the harmful consequences of expansionist 'globalisation minus' (Latour, 2017)).

The 45th President of the United States of America and UK Prime Minister Johnson, those two contemporaries who as populist peas in a pod(cast) (and as perhaps the two key beneficiaries of the projection of extra-territorial power inherent in the Cambridge Analytica story) epitomise the decadence of the modern White Anglo-Saxon Protestant (WASP) democracies provide disconcerting cases. It has been almost impossible to buttonhole either of them in the agora to speak truth to them, or to hear any truthfulness from them. Each man projects almost holographic, chimeric versions of themselves into the agora. Both men like to answer confabulated softball questions on Twitter or Facebook whilst shamelessly evading direct ones put to them by members of the opposition or by the toothless judicial enquiries that fail to hold them to account for their dissembling. Exchanges taking place in public press conferences are stage managed in the quietly privatised territory of the Rose Garden or the White House lawn. In any genuinely impromptu encounter in the agora to which they may be accidentally exposed, through some rare oversight of their minders, both men bumble or harrumph incoherently amidst the mendacious jetsam of their own contradictions.

Big-money capitalism, we might add, scarcely needs a public face any longer; it certainly need not openly set out its stall in the marketplace. There are, by analogy, no publicly held weights and measures, in any latter-day *Tholos*, to govern the secularised yet arcane mysteries of its virtual commerce, its holding companies or its offshore tax havens. Its mechanisms of power involve (il)legal fictions and neologisms, such as 'hedging', 'quantitative easing', 'sub-prime' or 'monetary activism'. These are terms that may mean some things to some bodies but, to all intents and purposes, fall into 'zombie categories' (Beck and Beck-Gernsheim, 2002): concepts which are dead but have the superficial appearance of life, which seem to have 'bodies' and so appear to exist but have no social utility, no liveliness, no beating heart and certainly no soul. Ultimately – and paradoxically – it is only because of the colossal toxicity of the carbon footprint left in Gaia's murky skies and melting snows that we see darkly through the smoke and the mirrors to even know that there is such a thing as big-money capitalism.

Whereas the task of critical theory was once upon a time to give voice to citizens and protect their private autonomy and individual freedom from colonising States, hegemonies and bureaucracies, Bauman suggests that the challenge in liquid modernity is to defend diminishing public spaces and to preserve them from being colonised by inherently selfish and greedy private

Negotiating fraught encounters 79

interests. As Jesus did in the Temple, the task is to overturn the tables of, or to turn the tables upon, the money changers who are in occupation of the sacred spaces and to re-establish those marble pillars that once proclaimed, 'I am the boundary of the Agora'.

Enclosure and the expropriation of the commons

> Enclosure came and trampled on the grave
> Of labour's rights and left the poor a slave.
> (Clare, 182–, p. 89)

To understand the essential precariousness of the contemporary agora in the West from an historical perspective, we need to revisit that period in the history of the UK in the immediate aftermath of the French and American Revolutions, in which those notionally more peaceful revolutions, the Agricultural and the Industrial, and the imperialist expansion they fuelled, were gathering momentum. Thompson (1963) proposed that "the final years of the eighteenth century saw a last desperate effort by the people to reimpose the older moral economy as against the economy of the free market" (Thompson, 1963, p. 73). Their target then, as perhaps it still is now, was the oppressive and dehumanising system of commercialism, rocket-fuelled as it was by industrialisation. "Men are grown mechanical in head and heart, as well as in hand", lamented Thomas Carlyle (1829, p. 67). As the great Romantic poet Shelley (1821) succinctly put it, in terms any present-day psycho-socialist might espouse:

> The rich have become richer, and the poor have become poorer; and the vessel of the state is driven between the Scylla and Charybdis of anarchy and despotism. Such are the effects that must ever flow from an unmitigated exercise of the calculating faculty.
>
> (Shelley, 1821)

There are in fact strong resonances and associations between, on the one hand, psycho-social phenomena of contemporary (post)modern anti-capitalist protest, and, on the other hand, the legend of Ned Ludd and the history of the machine-breaking movement of the early nineteenth century that bore his name (see, e.g., Linebaugh, 2012). A wide range of revolts or rebellions against the enclosure and the ongoing 'plunder' of the commons (Standing, 2019) broke out at the same time (1811–1812) as the Luddite machine-breakers of Yorkshire, Lancashire and Nottinghamshire, and the *saboteurs* in France and the Netherlands were making their respective stands against the relentless onward march of those 'dark Satanic mills' (Blake, 1804, p. 211; for an overview of the economic and social history, see Thompson, 1963; for the cultural and philosophical history, see Williams, 1958).

80 Un-housed minds: The Diogenes Paradigm

The resistance and rebellion of the machine-breakers was immortalised by Byron (in his maiden speech in the House of Lords[3] (Byron, 1812)) and Shelley (in various poetical works, particularly 'Queen Mab' (1813)). The protesters were linked in their adherence to the traditions and practice of a commonage, ownership of shared lands that was enshrined in 1217 in the *Carta de Foresta* and the more famous *Magna Carta* (Standing, 2019). In the terms of Fisher (2009), these protesters, like so many of their latter-day counterparts, were doing what capitalism forbids, by imagining a system other than itself or remembering the customs and practices which preceded it. Hence, we might note, the severity with which their resistance was suppressed: Berry refers to the triumph of 'technological determinism' over Luddism as "the most complete, significant, and lasting victory of modern times" (Berry, 1993, p. 131). It is still felt to be a damning indictment and dismissal to call someone a 'Luddite' (for not wanting to upgrade their smartphone, perhaps ...).

Linebaugh (2012 p. 10) refers to the work of John Clare, the great Romantic 'peasant poet', who wrote in 'The lament of Swordy Well' of how the values of commonage and hospitality allowed a measure of autonomy and safety for all, "till vile enclosure came and made/A parish slave of me" (Clare, 183–, p. 218). We suggest here that for Clare, the commons (meaning the lands held in common, the rights-in-common under which they were worked and the 'commoners' who subsisted in this way) amounted to what we are calling a psycho-social public/private space. Such a space was 'circular' and 'cosmopolitan'[4] in nature (Bate, 2003; citing Barrell, 1972); a space of work, ritual and community which the Enclosure Acts foreclosed (Standing, 2019).

Linebaugh cites John Thelwall, a prominent English Jacobin,[5] who in 1795 spoke of "that system of enclosure by which the rich monopolize to themselves the states, rights and possessions of the poor" (Linebaugh, 2012 p. 10; for more detail on Thelwall's career as a radical, see Thompson, 1963, pp. 171–176). To put this into perspective, from approximately 1760 through 1820 (roughly in the lifetime of the great visionary radical and rebel William Blake (1757–1827), as Williams (1958, p. 49) points out), the British Parliament passed more than three thousand separate Acts of Enclosure. By these devices, more than four million acres of land held in commons were appropriated and transferred into private hands (Williams, 1958, p. 24).

This was an escalation of the wider societal and historical assault upon the 'commons' that emerged in Britain and in Europe in the late Middle Ages (a period which also broadly parallels Foucault's account of the 'Great Confinement' (Foucault, 1961)). As Bate (2003, pp. 46–49) explains, there has been much debate as to the socio-economic consequences of the enclosure of the commons (see, e.g., Hobsbawm, 1969). Some historians point to improved productivity and security of employment under the new 'linear' arrangements of fenced fields and furlongs, while others map the expropriation of the land and the advancement of the interests of the propertied classes at the expense of a rural, and then emergently industrial, proletariat.

Nonetheless, 'structural violence' remains a violence, whatever its intended or unintended consequences.

This then was the epoch, not so much of rebellion as of the great (and perhaps we should say ongoing) counterrevolution of property against liberty (for of course it was the free market economy that won the day); a counterrevolution that actively extended for at least four decades, up to the 1832 Reform Act, and which was spearheaded, at least symbolically, by Pitt the Younger's Draconian 'Two Acts', outlawing a very loosely defined range of 'seditious meetings' or 'treasonable practices', which passed into law in December 1795. This was a time when, as Thompson wryly remarked, "[t]he greatest offence against property was to have none" (Thompson, 1963, p. 66).

Then, as now, the dispossessed were held morally accountable for the depravity signified by their lack of possessions, consequent upon their unwillingness (not incapacity) to work – in this case to work the land. Thompson reports this commentary published in the *Commercial and Agricultural Magazine* in October 1800 (in language readily transferrable to any senior member of the present political Establishment), in which the village poor are held to be,

> designing rogues, who, under various pretences, attempt to cheat the parish ... their whole abilities are exerted in the execution of deceit, which may procure from the parish officers an allowance of money for idle and profligate purposes.
>
> (Cited in Thompson, 1963, p. 243)

The metaphorical boundary stones of the agora crumbled under this onslaught and the spaces they protected were simply confiscated. Linebaugh (2012) charts the way in which enclosure was a colonial mechanism, both literally and dynamically: in Thompson's succinct summary, "a plain enough case of class robbery, played according to the fair rules of property and law laid down by a parliament of property-owners and lawyers" (Thompson, 1963, pp. 237–238). It was the mechanism that drove imperialist expansion in the time of the Industrial Revolution – whole societies were destroyed, and peoples annihilated, 'simply' by forcibly introducing the idea of land ownership and colonising sacred spaces and places. "The loss of the commons entailed, for the poor, a radical sense of displacement", observes Thompson (1963, p. 239).

Moreover, the historical process was not limited to fencing off common land and denying communal rights of pasture and the right to roam. Enclosure also related to, and impacted upon, the distinction between the 'public' sphere of men and the 'private' sphere of women; the emphasis on factory labour at the expense of arts and crafts; the canalisation of the river network and the massive expansion in the construction of prisons, barracks and other 'total institutions' (Goffman, 1961; Linebaugh, 2012; Adlam et al., 2012).

'Public' rights of way, of assembly, and of protest – such as the right to roam protests of 80 years ago[6] – are increasingly tenuous and contingent in urban spaces in the United Kingdom (Monbiot, 2020).

For instance, we might note the muddled response to the 'Occupy' protest camps that 'congregated' outside the doors of St Paul's Cathedral in London in 2011. The protesters were threatened with eviction by an action in the civil courts brought by the Corporation of London that was initially opposed by, though eventually supported by, the Cathedral authorities. Monbiot described the Corporation as like an obscure, unaccountable, Masonic gang (Monbiot, 2011). The Occupy protesters were eventually dislodged (Fraser, 2012) because the supposedly 'public space' in which they were taking up their place in the agora was held to be 'privately' owned and controlled, and was then enclosed and patrolled by 'private' security guards.

Richards (2018) has written powerfully about extremism and its milieux and has explored the phenomenon of multiple shootings understood as acts of terror perpetrated by alienated monadic individuals against the hated public space: hated both for its creativity and for its exclusive quality in the eyes of the outsider. The mass murder perpetrated in 2011 in Norway by Anders Breivik may stand as an extreme example of this, given Breivik's publicly stated ideological position on the 'contamination' of the agora through policies enabling immigration and ethnic diversity.

Jones (2018) focuses in detail on the possibly similar motivations of the Kouachi brothers who perpetrated the *Charlie Hebdo* killings in 2015, and he argues that such attacks upon the agora relate to the framing of the 'bourgeois public sphere' that was proposed by Habermas (1962). By this is meant a distinctively Western post-Enlightenment way of organising society around a particular set of sub-liminal in-group values underpinned by capitalism and empire. This version of the agora may be proudly upheld by advocates of liberal democracy, but it represents a coalescing of multiple discourses of oppression to the excluded out-group.

At the time of writing, the UK is the only European country with no time limit on the detention of immigrants who cannot produce the necessary paperwork to justify their presence within its borders. The UK government also continues to refuse voting rights to prisoners: the former Prime Minister David Cameron once said in the House of Commons:

> it makes me physically ill even to contemplate having to give the vote to anyone who is in prison. Frankly, when people commit a crime and go to prison, they should lose their rights, including the right to vote.
>
> (Mulholland, 2010)[7]

Here, then, is a different example of an agoraphobic position, this time adopted by the in-group rather than the out-group but with the agora similarly constructed as a hated object. Rogue (and not so rogue) States engage in differing forms of violent exclusion, from gerrymandering to ethnic cleansing.

Is it therefore 'disordered' or normative that an individual 'rogue male' such as Breivik might take up arms with possibly equivalent hostile intent against the diversity of the agora?

Anti-societal attacks upon the agora

> Society requires not only that the passions of individuals should be subjected, but that even in the mass and body ... the inclinations of men should frequently be thwarted, their will controlled, and their passions brought into subjection ... the restraints of men, as well as their liberties, are to be reckoned among their rights.
>
> (Burke, 1790, para. 95)

We are able now to see how the 'public/private site' of the agora comes under anti-psycho-societal attack from without and from within: from private individuals and from public interests; from loners and from gangs; from both corporations and States. Agoraphobia finds its ultimate expression not only in the extremist public violence of a Breivik or a McVeigh, but also, and perhaps primarily, in such iconic moments and psycho-social spaces (and State-led massacres) as Peterloo, Asaba, Amritsar, Lidice, Tiananmen Square or the Bogside Massacre, which took place on UK soil on Bloody Sunday.

Whereas Bauman (2000) writes of 'the evacuation of the agora', our focus here is upon destructive, 'enclosing' or annihilatory attacks upon the liminal, transitional and delicately, even precariously, negotiated space that the agora might be understood to represent. This phenomenon comes particularly into focus when we explore the nature of demonstrations, protest camps, certain forms of 'industrial action' and certain types of assembly in public places. In recent times there have been various moves to repopulate the agora, most notably in the domain of environmental activism. Thunberg's school strike would represent, in our terms, a creative rediscovery of an agora in which one can interact with the world from one's *pithos*; and it would be interesting to explore whether there were distinctive qualities of the psycho-social domain and shared spaces in Swedish public life that provided especially fertile ground for the stand she took.

However, our more general observation would be that the agora has not only been evacuated but privatised – paved over, and a parking lot put up instead (to borrow from Joni Mitchell (1970)). The appearance of something like an agora is common enough and is hard to argue with on days, for example, when three hundred thousand people join the People's Climate March in New York in 2014, or when a million or more people march peacefully through London to congregate in Parliament Square, to protest the Iraq War or Brexit. But appearances turn out to be deceptive. Marchers in both cities were corralled and kettled:[8] an ocean of people channelled into narrow canals by State forces that had 'permitted' their assembly. Speeches were made in the square, but there was no audience for them in the corridors of power and the marches became occasions for media manipulation, almost Taylorised;[9] the numbers one could identify as an 'outcome' somehow more important than the cause that had mobilised people to march. The public protests in the wake of the killing of George Floyd, while the COVID-19 pandemic was still at its first peak, show both views of the contemporary agora clearly: the extraordinary coming together of peoples in adversity, and the ruthless neutralising of their ability to influence discourse.

The holographic agora

The adrenaline surge of marching with a mass of people dissipates into disillusion and disappointment when the realisation hits that a million people are speaking only to each other (in the same way that the thrill of membership that can come from social media, such as Twitter or Facebook, dissipates in the face of the realisation that the agora is only holographic and one sits in an echo chamber moulded in one's own image, unable to interact with other bodies of opinion). The metal railings erected to channel the marchers are also thought barriers, preventing the word from spreading or any new minds from being convinced of anything. Scranton (2015) suggests that the People's Climate March ended up as,

> little more than an orgy of democratic emotion ... something that gives you a nice feeling, says you belong in a certain group, and is completely divorced from actual legislation and governance ... it siphoned off organizing energy that could have been more useful elsewhere, made a public display of climate activism's political impotence, and soothed hundreds and thousands of people with a false sense of hope.
>
> (Scranton, 2015, p. 62)

Scranton argues that if power has, as Bauman would have it, evacuated the agora, in large part this is because of the implications of the shift from coal to oil and gas production that accompanied and fuelled the 'Great Acceleration'[10] in the decades following World War Two. Oil and gas production is less labour intensive than coal production, and furthermore the supply and distribution of these fossil fuels is covert or diffuse, and therefore beyond the reach of social democratic movements to obstruct. Scranton quotes from Timothy Mitchell's *Carbon Democracy* (2011) and the passage bears repeating:

> ... whereas the movement of coal tended to follow dendritic networks, with branches at each end but a single main channel creating potential choke points at several junctures, oil flowed along networks that often had the properties of a grid, like an electricity network, where there is

more than one possible path and the flow of energy can switch to avoid blockages or overcome breakdowns.

(Mitchell, 2011, p. 39)

There are exceptions to this trend, such as the Keystone XL pipeline protests (Klein, 2015), but the general point is that power in the agora was to be found in the personal authority of the street philosophers who lectured at the edge of the olive groves; in the standard weights and measures used to mediate trade; or in the temples where the presence of the Gods was felt. In late modernity, the seat of power is usually difficult to find; political power (and force) follows the flow of fuel and energy (and social media) down complex webs of elusive and invisible arteries:

> Protest politics and web-based outrage may send signals to the ruling elites, but these strategies exert no effective pressure. No matter how many people take to the streets in massive marches or in targeted direct actions, they cannot put their hands on the real flows of power, because they do not help produce it. They only consume.
>
> (Scranton, 2015, p. 60)

When the graffiti artist Banksy creates, for example, *trompe l'oeil* bucolic scenes on the barrier wall that Israel has erected to 'enclose' Palestinian land, it is the 'enclosure' of the 'agora' – and the closing down of the possibility of political and philosophical *exchange* across the boundary – that he is protesting and contesting.

> Enlarging the public sphere ... entails struggling against the distribution of the public and the private that shores up the twofold domination of the oligarchy in the State and in society.
>
> (Rancière, 2005, p. 55)

Not only have government leaders of the Global North taken on the quality of holographic projections (on the wall of our Cave (Plato, 4th century BCEb)) on behalf of the covert oligarchical interests they serve, like latter-day Wizards of the Occident; it may also have become the case that the agoras into which they project themselves are also holographic. The transnational economic elite "have invested their lives and loyalties in no locality and in no nation ... [and] are so insulated by wealth and power that they feel no need to care about what happens to any place" (Berry, 1993, p. 81). The passing of modernity into post-modernity "augurs *the end of the era of mutual engagement*", in Bauman's words (Bauman, 2000, p. 11 [italics in the original]). At the macro-political level, there may be no real and clearly demarcated public/ private spaces left within which in-group and out-group could meaningfully have themselves an encounter of engagement (as opposed to a violent confrontation). We should be very clear, though: none of this is to say that there are no such things as agora-like community spaces in which out-group memberships may gather and into which, on occasion, out-reaching in-group representatives may venture, and we return to this theme in Chapter 9 (see also, e.g., Anderson, 2011; discussed in Stopford, 2020).

This conceptualisation, in turn, offers a means with which to critique notionally therapeutic settings, with an eye as to whether the agoraphobic or the agoraphilic impulse dominates. The therapeutic milieu, understood as intermediary agora, is exactly the kind of public/private space that comes under attack from both privatising forces (for being too open and exposing (and potentially egalitarian)) and from 'the public' (for being too closed and secretive). We therefore also note the possibility that the Establishment in the system of care operates no differently than the Establishment in wider society. The fraught quality of 'hostipitality' (Derrida, 1997) in the notional therapeutic milieu within systems of care may also take the form of a 'holographic' agora. It would, then, be not only that real power and meaningful engagement may have quietly drained away, so that the only thing to be said of Diogenes and Alexander is that 'never the twain shall meet', but also that the very space itself would turn out to be illusory.

Notes

1 In what follows, our use of the italicised *agora* is intended to denote the historical phenomenon and the ancient Greek term for it, whereas we use the plain font agora to denote the psycho-social phenomenon in the here and now and in our particular use of the term, following Bauman (2000).

2 Freud, discussing the 'condition' of agoraphobia, first 'classified' by Westphal (1871), proposed that the principal peril of the 'marketplace' was the way in which sexual temptation might present itself (to women, *nota bene*: Freud, 1896). The business that was eventually built upon the 'diagnosis' of 'agoraphobia' is now worth billions of dollars to Big Pharma in medication sales in the United States alone. This is not a chapter about agoraphobia in these narrow and pathologising senses.

3 In February 1812 the Government of the time introduced the Frame Work Bill, which made it a capital offence to break or damage mechanised looms. As many as seventy Luddites were hanged for such offences, although capital penalties in any case existed under existing legislation (and no less than sixty-three capital offences had been introduced into the statute books in the period 1760–1810 (Thompson, 1963, p. 65). Byron protested on behalf of the Luddites that, 'whilst these outrages must be admitted to exist to an alarming extent, it cannot be denied that they have arisen from circumstances of the most unparalleled distress … nothing but absolute want could have driven a large and once honest and industrious body of the people into the commission of excesses so hazardous to themselves, their families, and the community' (Byron, 1812).

He commented privately on his debut speech a week later, saying, 'I spoke very violent sentences with a sort of modest impudence, abused everything and everybody, put the Lord Chancellor very much out of humour, and if I may believe what I hear, have not lost any character in the experiment' (*Ibid.*).

4 In our 'Zeno position' deployment of that term, see Chapter 3.
5 The term 'Democrat' was not part of the political and cultural discourse in Britain, in anything like its contemporary usage, until some while after the end of the Napoleonic Wars. In 1795, if a group of people were referred to as Democrats, this would have denoted 'dangerous and subversive mob agitators' (Williams, 1958, p. 3). The Jacobin Club was a political group that played an active part in the Reign Terror of the French Revolution in the early to mid-1790s; the term 'Jacobin', by derivation, attaches to any radical or extremist political position and was famously reclaimed by C.L.R. James in his polemic history of the Haitian Revolution (James, 1938).
6 After a century of angry confrontations, including the 1932 Mass Trespass on Kinder Scout in the Peak District, the common people were eventually given the 'right to roam' upon England's 'green and pleasant land' (so long as they kept it up year on year!).
7 We also note the initial woeful response of the UK Government to the need to safeguard prison officers and prisoners alike from the ravages of the COVID-19 virus that ripped through those enclosed spaces. Despite a steady increase in cases and deaths, the prison authorities instructed prison officers not to wear personal protective equipment 'for security reasons': instructions that flew in the face of the advice offered by health scientists. As evidence for this attitude, when the news came that the first elderly and vulnerable prisoners were to be vaccinated, the (right-wing) press were outraged that prisoners were to be prioritised over more 'deserving others' living in the community – despite the fact that prisons, like care homes, by dint of their enclosed, unventilated proximity are at high risk of being sites of transmission. When the ink is dry on the eventual investigations into the treatment of vulnerable people in care homes and prisons during the pandemic, there may be an occasion for us all to blush.
8 Mason (2012) tracks the development and spread of the concept of 'kettling' as a form of crowd control. He cites Rowan (2010), who suggests a response to kettling that echoes the dispersal of power in the evacuation of the agora: "A form of protest is needed that places dispersal over concentration, mobility over stasis and perhaps even disruption over symbolism". Rowan argues that the 'kettle' functions both as restraint and incitement, frustrating the valency for mobility in the protesting crowd while generating impulses violently to break out of or evade the kettle. He points out that the kettle "seeks to divide the space of the city into spaces inside and outside the kettle and to isolate and manage disorder within a defined site in order to maintain it elsewhere" (Rowan, 2010): in our terms, it therefore functions as an extension of the enclosure of the agora.
9 Taylorisation is a set of ideas and processes around workforce micro-management, first advanced by Fredrick Winslow Taylor (1856–1915). Two generations of National Health Service, Local Authority and academic staff in the UK have laboured under the dominion of the managerialist false analogy between a hospital or university and a factory. Two foundational maxims of this insidious doctrine are that only numbers count and that everything can be 'outcomed'. For an examination of the consequences of this discourse for those of us caught up in it, see Hoggett (2017).
10 The Great Acceleration is "the dramatic change in magnitude and rate of the human imprint from about 1950 onwards" (Steffen *et al.*, 2015, p. 2), correlated to GDP growth and consumer spending in the Global North, population growth in the Global South, the expansion of domains of human activity, such as communication and tourism, and the destructive impact of all of these changes upon the Earth system (see Chapter 7).

References

Adlam, J. and Scanlon, C. (2011) 'Working with hard-to-reach patients in difficult places: A Democratic Therapeutic Community approach to consultation', in Rubitel, A. and Reiss, D. (eds) *Containment in the community: Supportive frameworks for thinking about antisocial behaviour and mental health*. London: Karnac, pp. 1–22.

Adlam, J., Gill, I., Glackin, S., Kelly, B., Scanlon, C., and MacSuibhne, S. (2012) 'Perspectives on Erving Goffman's "Asylums" fifty years on', *Medicine, Health Care and Philosophy*, 16 (3), pp. 605–613. doi:10.1007/s11019-012-9410-z.

Anderson, E. (2011) *Cosmopolitan canopy: Race and civility in everyday life*. New York, NY: W.W. Norton & Co.

Barrell, J. (1972) *The idea of landscape and the sense of place 1730–1840: An approach to the poetry of John Clare*. Cambridge: Cambridge University Press.

Bate, J. (2003) *John Clare: A biography*. London: Picador.

Bauman, Z. (2000) *Liquid modernity*. Cambridge: Polity Press.

Beck, U. and Beck-Gernsheim, E. (2002) *Individualization: Institutionalized individualism and its social and political consequences*. Translated by P. Camiller. London: Sage.

Berry, W. (1993) *Sex, economy, freedom & community: Eight essays*. Reprinted 2018. Berkeley, CA: Counterpoint.

Bion, W.R. (1970) *Attention and interpretation*. Reprinted 1984. London: Maresfield.

Blake, W. (1804) 'Jerusalem', in Yeats, W.B. (ed.) (1905) *Collected Poems*. Reprinted 2006. London: Routledge Classics, pp. 211–212.

Burke, E. (1790) Reflections on the Revolution in France. Available at: https://www.bartleby.com/24/3/ (Accessed: 3 January 2021).

Byron, G. (1812) Maiden speech in the House of Lords. Available at: http://www.luddites200.org.uk/LordByronspeech.html (Accessed: 3 January 2021).

Cadwalladr, C. (2019) 'Cambridge Analytica a year on: 'A lesson in institutional failure'', *The Guardian*, 17 March. Available at: https://www.theguardian.com/uk-news/2019/mar/17/cambridge-analytica-year-on-lesson-in-institutional-failure-christopher-wylie (Accessed: 3 January 2021).

Carlyle, T. (1829) 'Signs of the times', in Shelston, A. (ed.) (1971) *Thomas Carlyle: Selected writings*. London: Penguin, pp. 50–86.

Clare, J. (182–) 'The moors', in Bate, J. (ed.) (2003) *Selected poems*. London: Faber and Faber, pp. 89–91.

Clare, J. (183–) 'The lament of Swordy Well', in Bate, J. (ed.) (2003) *Selected poems*. London: Faber and Faber, pp. 211–219.

Derrida, J. (1997) 'Hostipitality', *Angelaki*, 5 (3), pp. 3–18. Translated by B. Stocker and F. Morlock, 2000. doi:10.1080/09697250020034706.

Fisher, M. (2009) *Capitalist realism: Is there no alternative?*Ropley: Zero Books.

Foucault, M. (1961) *Madness and civilization: A history of insanity in the age of reason*. Translated by R. Howard, 2001. London: Routledge Classics.

Foucault, M. (1983) *Fearless speech*. Reprinted 2001. Los Angeles, CA: Semiotexte.

Fraser, G. (2012) 'From a colourful camp to a dismal metal fence: The end of Occupy St Paul's', *The Guardian*, 28 February. Available at: https://www.theguardian.com/uk/2012/feb/28/occupy-london-gone-not-forgotten (Accessed: 3 January 2021).

Freud, S. (1896) 'Letter, 17 December', in *The complete letters of Sigmund Freud to Wilhelm Fliess*. Translated by J.M. Masson (ed.), 1985. Cambridge, MA: Harvard University Press.

Goffman, E. (1961) *Asylums*. Reprinted 1991. London: Penguin.

Habermas, J. (1962) *The structural transformation of the public sphere: An inquiry into a category of bourgeois society*. Translated by T. Burger with F. Lawrence, 1989. Cambridge: Polity Press.

Hobsbawm, E.J. (1969) *Industry and empire*. Harmondsworth: Pelican.

Hoggett, P. (2017) 'Shame and performativity: Thoughts on the psychology of neoliberalism', *Psychoanalysis, Culture and Society*, 22 (4), pp. 364–382.

James, C.L.R. (1938) *The Black Jacobins*. Reprinted 2001. London: Penguin.

Jones, D.W. (2018) 'Terror, violence and the public sphere', in Adlam, J., Kluttig, T., and Lee, B.X. (eds) *Violent states and creative states: From the global to the individual. Volume 1: Structural violence and creative structures*. London: Jessica Kingsley Publishers, pp. 147–160.

Klein, N. (2015) *This changes everything*. London: Penguin.

Latour, B. (2017) *Down to Earth – Politics in the new climatic regime*. Translated by C. Porter, 2018. Cambridge: Polity.

Linebaugh, P. (2012) *Ned Ludd and Queen Mab: Machine-breaking, romanticism and the several commons of 1811–12*. Retort Pamphlet No 1. Oakland, CA: PM Press.

Mason, P. (2012) *Why it's kicking off everywhere: The new global revolutions*. London: Verso.

Mitchell, J. (1970) '*Big yellow taxi*', from Ladies of the canyon. LP. Los Angeles, CA: Reprise Records.

Mitchell, T. (2011) *Carbon democracy: Political power in the age of oil*. New York: Verso.

Monbiot, G. (2011) 'Next for protest? The City's medieval, unaccountable defender of the banks', *The Guardian*, 1 November. Available at: https://www.theguardian.com/comm entisfree/2011/oct/31/corporation-london-city-medieval (Accessed: 3 January 2021).

Monbiot, G. (2020) 'The trespass trap: This new law could make us strangers in our own land', *The Guardian*, 15 January. Available at: https://www.theguardian.com/commentisfree/2020/jan/15/tresspass-trap-law-land-travelling-people-rights (Accessed: 3 January 2021).

Morris, W. (1888) Signs of change. Available at: https://www.marxists.org/archive/m orris/works/1888/signs/signs.htm (Accessed: 3 January 2021).

Mulholland, H. (2010) 'David Cameron is leading "government of broken promises", says Ed Milliband', *The Guardian*, 3 November. Available at: https://www.thegua rdian.com/politics/2010/nov/03/david-cameron-broken-promises-ed-miliband (Accessed: 28 March 2021).

Oxford Dictionary of English (2005) Second edition (revised). Soanes, C. and Stevenson, A. (eds). Oxford: Oxford University Press.

Plato (4th century BCEa) *Apology*. Translated by H. Tredennick and H. Tarrant, 2003. Reprinted in *The last days of Socrates*. London: Penguin Classics, pp. 39–70.

Plato (4th Century BCEb) *The Republic*. Translated by D. Lee, 1955. London: Penguin Classics.

Rancière, J. (2005) *Hatred of democracy*. Translated by S. Corcoran, 2014. London: Verso.

Richards, B. (2018) 'Terror in the mind of the terrorist', in Adlam, J., Kluttig, T., and Lee, B.X. (eds) *Violent states and creative states: From the global to the individual. Volume 1: Structural violence and creative structures*. London: Jessica Kingsley Publishers, pp. 191–204.

Rowan, R. (2010) 'Geographies of the kettle: Containment, spectacle and counter-strategy'. Available at: https://criticallegalthinking.com/2010/12/16/geographies-of-the-kettle-containment-spectacle-counter-strategy/ (Accessed: 3 January 2021).

Scranton, R. (2015) *Learning to die in the Anthropocene.* San Francisco: City Lights.

Shelley, P.B. (1813) '*Queen Mab*'. Available at: https://www.marxists.org/archive/shelley/1813/queen-mab.htm (Accessed: 28 March 2021).

Shelley, P.B. (1821) *A defence of poetry and other essays.* Available at: https://www.gutenberg.org/files/5428/5428-h/5428-h.htm (Accessed: 3 January 2021).

Standing, G. (2019) *Plunder of the commons: A manifesto for sharing public wealth.* London: Pelican.

Steffen, W., Broadgate, W., Deutsch, L., Gaffney, O., and Ludwig, C. (2015) 'The trajectory of the Anthropocene: The great acceleration', *The Anthropocene Review*, 2 (1), pp. 81–98.

Stopford, A. (2020) *Trauma and repair: Confronting segregation and violence in America.* Lanham, MD: Lexington Books.

Swift, J. (1708) 'A tritical essay upon the faculties of the mind'. Available at: https://en.wikisource.org/wiki/The_Works_of_the_Rev._Jonathan_Swift/Volume_5/A_Tritical_Essay_Upon_the_Faculties_of_the_Mind (Accessed 22 February 2021).

Thompson, E.P. (1963) *The making of the English working class.* Reprinted 2013. London: Penguin Classics.

Westphal, C. (1871) 'Die agoraphobie: eine neuropathische erscheinung', *Archiv für Psychatrie und Nervenkrankheiten*, 3, pp. 138–161.

Williams, R. (1958) *Culture and Society.* Reprinted 2017. London: Vintage.

Part II

Inhospitable environments

Traumatised and traumatising (dis)organisations

Man is born free, and everywhere he is in chains.
(From *The social contract*, Book One: Jean-Jacques Rousseau, 1762; translated by G.D.H. Cole, 1920)

… I think it is fair to say Europe has done its part, and must send a very clear message – "we are not going to be able to continue to provide refuge and support" – because if we don't deal with the migration issue it will continue to roil the body politic.
(Hilary Clinton, November 2018)

DOI: 10.4324/9781003223115-7

Chapter 6

"Who watches the watchers"?

(Dis)organised responses to psycho-social traumatisation

Brutal cultures and the inhospitable (dis)organisation

> sed quis custodiet ipsos custodes?
>
> (Juvenal, 1st/2nd century CE, ll. 347–348)

In Part I we explored concepts of homelessness and disturbance as metaphors or encrypted ciphers which stand for the reciprocal and reflexive violence that is played out between groupings that hold power in any given 'society' and the most vulnerable of its citizens. We suggested a powerful correlation between 'un-housed' states of mind and the inhospitable socio-political environments in which this violence is perpetrated and perpetuated.

We now wish to explore the spaces and places that the inhospitable State provides to accommodate, contain or detain these un-housed states of mind; places such as psychiatric hospitals, prisons and hostels. We also examine the ways in which 'the streets', considered as institutions without walls (Adlam and Scanlon, 2012), have also become places and spaces where violent encounters and exchanges are played out – especially, but not exclusively, for 'the homeless'.

We are particularly concerned to understand the persistence of 'brutal cultures', characterised by reciprocal processes of shame and shaming, in these institutional settings. Goffman (1961) described many such de-humanising rituals through which 'the outsider' is brought into compliance, and how these institutions deploy their own overt and tacit rules of engagement. Some of these shaming rituals may have changed since Goffman described them sixty years ago, but the requirement that the individual (staff and patient alike) must consciously subjugate themselves to the explicit rules of the 'total institution' has changed little; while the underlying organisational dynamics that support and maintain them have probably not changed at all! One particular example we have in mind is Gilligan's analysis of the instrumentality of the tacit collusion of the system with the prevalence of male rape in the US prison system (Gilligan, 1996).

DOI: 10.4324/9781003223115-8

94   Inhospitable environments

Individual practitioners who are charged with the delivery of health and social care to the socially excluded out-group (whether on behalf of or in dissident opposition to the powerful societal in-group) frequently become themselves (re-)traumatised, stressed, distressed and burned out, while the teams, agencies and organisations in which they work become dis-organised. The psycho-social dynamics played out in these teams and organisations not only inevitably mirror and reproduce wider structural and systemic dis-turbance and dis-organisation, but also condense and amplify the processes of inclusion/exclusion and the (mis)uses of power of these social systems (see, e.g., Cooper and Lousada, 2005; Aiyegbusi and Clarke-Moore, 2009; Armstrong and Rustin, 2017; Hopper, 2012).

In health and social care settings *the self*, with all its myriad cognitions, affects, memories, desires and intuitions, is a key instrument in the process of delivering, and failing to deliver, *ordinary* care. However, a range of other situation-specific concerns must be considered if we are to consider the pre-dicament of the traumatised and disorganised team in such reciprocally vio-lent settings. These include the fear of contagion (of 'mad' and violent states of mind) and the very real difficulties inherent in the need to think one's own thoughts 'under fire' (Adlam et al., 2012). The burden of responsibility to prevent unnecessary death and the related dread of being confronted with the limits of our individual and collective power is an ongoing challenge, as is the risk of being subjected to or (which amounts to the same thing) being witness to acts of violence committed by those to who one is providing care. We should also add that, not infrequently, the acts of violence being witnessed are carried out by one's colleagues – violence and violent states being by no means the exclusive preserves of the out-group, as by now we have hopefully established. The additional dread (common to all such settings) is of being individually blamed for system failures when (not if) things go wrong.

The result of the amplification and condensation of these inhospitable and traumatising dynamics is that even as such organisations themselves become disorganised and psycho-socially traumatised, their task is to continue to prop up these dysfunctional systems. Social defence mechanisms and associated 'basic assumption' group dysfunction (in other words, the dominance of group mentalities that are opposed to learning from experience) replaces the needful work (Menzies, 1959; Bion, 1961; Hopper, 2003; Armstrong and Rustin, 2017). These traumatised and disorganised dynamics are then 'insti-tutionalised' and trans-generationally transmitted through successive cohorts of the ever rotating workforce. The 'moral injury' (see, e.g., Kothari et al., 2020), to which the ruling elite can appear inured, is the only thing that may be genuinely understood to 'trickle down'.

****

In these inhospitable and brutally institutionalised organisational cultures, re-traumatisation is generated by the reality that someone is always pushing someone around; indeed, sometimes it appears that everyone is pushing everyone around. We suggest that the effect of shame, or the contemptuous shaming of others that defends against it, manifests as a *relationally transmitted un-(dis)-ease* or *unsettledness*. This, in turn, subtly permeates and violently contaminates the dangerously intimate relationships within which all parties must work, and live, cheek by jowl with one another. We conceptualise these dangerous and inhospitable places as constituting a microcosm or fractal of the social world in which they are embedded. They also, therefore, offer a laboratory for the study of the nature of the inhospitable environment – and perhaps we might even thereby find a path towards better routes for intervention in such places.

The psycho-socially traumatised (dis)organisation-in-the-mind

> Turning and turning in the widening gyre
> The falcon cannot hear the falconer;
> Things fall apart; the centre cannot hold;
> Mere anarchy is loosed upon the world,
> The blood-dimmed tide is loosed, and everywhere
> The ceremony of innocence is drowned;
> The best lack all conviction, while the worst
> Are full of passionate intensity.
>
> (Yeats, 1920, p. 124)

In this book we are re-mapping the complex reciprocal relationship between those of us who experience ourselves as 'included' and those of us who experience ourselves as 'excluded'; between society's members and those who society dis-members; between the housed and the un-housed. That the members of these sub-out-groups may, in their ambivalence, lack conviction in relation to their 'client' status is entirely understandable – even if the workers themselves are often more passionate in the intensity of their identification with them. As Yeats suggests, neither position is more comfortable than the other. However, notwithstanding this intermittent state of passionate intensity, there is also ambiguity in the position of the workforce. This is not only because there is ambivalence towards the clients in the sub-out-groups but also because the task of 'providing accommodation' is itself intrinsically ambiguous. The allocated task of keeping the out-group at bay is just as significant as the task of bringing 'them' safely in to harbour.

Although we-the-authors are attempting here to eschew the objectification and near sub-speciation of 'the other', we find it near impossible to hold onto the 'we' as we constantly (inevitably?) founder upon the rocks of the jointly imagined, problematic relationship between 'us' and 'them', and especially of the mutual hatred, reciprocal violence and hostile dependency that drives it. In this breaking down of 'we' into 'us' and 'them', battle lines are drawn that run through the whole of society, and all its microcosmic and isomorphic reproductions, and across which hostile projections are directed (Foucault's 'battlefront' (Foucault, 1997, p. 51) or the "wall of life" discussed by Stopford (2020, p. 2)). Those organisations that are 'set-up' (in every sense of this idiom) to work with some of the most vulnerable members of society are understood colloquially to be working at the 'front line'.

The agencies and practitioners who attempt to accommodate the needs of these sub-out-groups are faced daily with members of those sub-out-groups whose relationship to the ambiguously 'including' or 'out-reaching' in-group is understood, by that in-group, as a problematic refusal to take up the 'patient role' (to be in their 'proper place'); and as an implicit or explicit rubbishing or rejecting of that which the out-reaching worker considers to be the 'good' quality of their invitation. This inconvenient and uncomfortable response to their invitation is experienced as aggressive or even violent, and in turn attracts a frustrated, aggressive and sometimes violent response. When the *irresistible force* of the apparatus of the system meets the *immovable object* of the resisting sub-out-group, the latter is often then violently construed by the former as aggressively or violently obstructive – and is then, depending on the primary task of the organisation (and how that gets (re-)constructed under pressure), either forcibly treated or dismissed.

Here, in short, is the locus of our Diogenes Paradigm, in which representatives of the might and greatness of the State find themselves standing in Alexander's shoes when our latter-day Diogenes asks them to step out of their light (or, perhaps equally appositely, not to intrude upon their darkness). They find themselves caught between opposing impulses – the Devil of the impulse to force Diogenes out of his unseemly barrel (and out of the uneasy shadow they cast upon him) and into more appropriate accommodation, and the Deep Blue Sea of the impulse to turn around, walk away and leave him to his fate. Alexander's 'passionately intense' wrath is never far from the surface of his foreign policy. And yet, if there was never any societal bread to begin with, why indeed would we mimic or parody Marie Antoinette's apocryphal error and expect those of *us* who are hungry to devour *her* superficially reparative but nutritionally suspect cake?

What then becomes of us – what state (or State) do we find ourselves in – when, as practitioners, or for that matter as citizens, we experience our *authority* as being thwarted or disrespected by those others whom we imagine we are trying to assist? It is not only the reluctant members of the 'won't-be-helped' out-group who struggle to articulate their feelings. We offer the image of Diogenes' retrenchment in his barrel and the paralysis of we latter-day Alexanders at its threshold to suggest that there are many and varied psycho-social equivalences that are exactly such *places* for people who are un-housed and psycho-socially dis-membered, and who experience being in the shadow of these systems of power.

Incohesive responses to psycho-social re-traumatisation

Institutions of the kind we are examining here struggle to understand the needs of 'outsiders' *and* their own need for there to be such outsiders because concepts like 'cultural integration', 'successful resettlement', 'safe and secure disposal', 'treatment and rehabilitation', 'proper accommodation', 'recovery' and other ideas about what constitutes a 'positive outcome', such as 'punishment and retribution', are predicated upon what the *in-group* defines as 'housed' and what it means to be a *member* of the community.

Whether living in (clients) or working in (staff) these shame-filled, psycho-socially (re)-traumatising contexts, all come to feel a shared sense of helplessness. In these dangerous and endangered states, the capacity of the would-be workers (as well as of the Bartleby-like would-rather-not-be clients) to manage themselves effectively, or to be managed by others, is severely compromised. The demand of the workers that these feelings of helplessness be accommodated by their teams and organisations becomes ever more urgent – although a range of factors, including deference, survivor guilt and vocational idealisation may contribute to these demands not always being directly articulated. A collective sense of helplessness tightens its grip and comes eventually to overwhelm the (dis)organisation's capacity to think about and to manage these tensions and contradictions. The setting becomes a resonant echo chamber and distorting mirror of psycho-socially traumatising experiences in the wider societal system.

Un-housed and dis-membered from their increasingly (dis)organising and inhospitable structural contexts, the workforce collectively breaks down into characteristic and patterned disturbances of *groupishness*. Bion (1961) described these patterns as 'basic assumption' processes – the most 'basic' of which ('dependency') is characterised by the collective wish for a powerful magical leader who will save us without us actually having to do the work of changing anything. Hopper and his associates (Hopper, 2003, 2012), however, have explored what happens to this 'groupish' disturbance when, as a result of an unmitigated re-traumatising experience, the falcon and the falconer lose contact with each other: when leaders and leadership can't be trusted and our dependency upon them fails.

In these circumstances, the location of the traumatic psycho-social disturbance can no longer be *imagined* to be only in the clients (not least because it never was ...!), and these teams and the (re-)traumatised (dis)organisations that have un-housed and dis-membered them oscillate between what Hopper (2003) describes as more *aggregated* or more *massified* patterns of relating within states of incohesion. In aggregated states, individual team members experience themselves as more atomised, monadic and nomadic, increasingly distanced and alienated within themselves, and from their colleagues and from their clients. The team in this state has altogether abandoned what we might call its 'teamishness': its motto is, 'we have nothing really to do with each other at all'. This increased sense of nihilism becomes a socially organised defence against helplessness rooted in their organisations' failure to contain it: in other words, it is an organisational manifestation of *failed dependency* – a fearful incapacity to recognise *precarious interdependence*, which itself becomes an enemy to be annihilated at all costs.

An example of how this aggregation is expressed, when Yeats' 'mere anarchy' is let loose, is the way in which practitioners retreat into what they experience as the *relative* safety of their own 'caseloads', over which they can tell themselves that they have some control. From this position they may then begin to extol the virtues of an individual advocacy for their 'own(ed)' clients, who only they 'really understand'. As 'key workers', they often behave *as if* this notion has come more literally and concretely to mean 'key-holder' or gatekeeper of their own privatised fiefdom: a position that mirrors, mimics and perhaps also parodies the wider problematic psycho-social and political processes of colonisation, appropriation and privatisation that we have already discussed. From this aggregated place, these self-appointed 'Metropolitan'-style gatekeepers unilaterally decide who is to be admitted, who is not to be admitted, who is to be forcibly detained and who is to be forcibly discharged, who is to be chewed over, who is to be incorporated and who is to be vomited out.

Some workers full of 'passionate intensity' are sucked into a social role, born of a powerful identification with the anger of the 'alienated outsider', in which, in their dress and demeanour, their emblematic presentation also mimics, parodies or ventriloquises the vulnerability and aggression of their clients (rather than empathically reflecting or representing it). At the opposite end of these polarising processes, other workers come to be sucked into a complementary social role in which they 'lack conviction', and in this state of mind they exercise a prerogative to avoid all emotional or participative connection with their clients, with their colleagues, and with the life of the organisation as a whole. They become cynically destructive (as opposed to Cynically questioning) in their determination to avoid 'work' and they give an impression of vacancy, laziness or quasi-moral superiority. On each side of the splits that characterise these aggregated patterns of relating, the attitude is one of 'each to their own', every man for himself. In states of aggregation in incohesive systems, there isn't enough social or interpersonal glue to bond the individuals together into a functioning or effective team.

By contrast, in massified states of incohesion, teams are possessed of a kind of *quasi-morale*: a gang-like mentality that serves to shore up the defences. The survival of individual workers in such a system relies upon their 'closing ranks' and directing their shared hostility against an external enemy. A team in this state appears to speak with one voice and its motto is something like this: 'we stick together through thick and thin, because nobody else gives a damn about us, and frankly the feeling is mutual'. Again, there is something essentially *anti-social* and gang-like about the way in which massified teams, like perverse Robin Hoods or 'merry men', *stick together* in order to take from the rich to give to the poor – or, mafia-like, to rob from the poor to feed their own very real sense of inner impoverishment. Either way, there is a pervasive and unspeakable hostility towards a jointly imagined 'persecutory' *system* within which *the team* is inadequately 'housed' and from which it becomes increasingly isolated and dis-connected. These massed gangs, then, come to experience themselves as part of a *special project for special people*, and the rhetoric and language in which they state this position is critical and dismissive of the efforts of others. There are clear parallels here with the gang-like orientation of many in the wider societal system.

In each of these incohesive patterns of relating – aggregation and massification – the possibility of a more empathic understanding of the impact of psychosocial processes of re-traumatisation is replaced by the workers' constant *unconscious* attempts to defend themselves and/or each other against the anxiety that emerges in the face of their clients' grief and grievance. As the irresistible force meets the immovable object, the *organisation* that was established to accommodate traumatised and dis-membered people with un-housed minds becomes itself a traumatised (dis)organisation employing the services of dis-membered staff in correspondingly un-housed states of mind (Hopper, 2003, 2012).

In this dangerous and endangered state, the kinds of agora-like group activities – staff meetings, supervision, reflective practice groups, training and the like – that would usually provide staff members with a sense of cohesion and personal identity become a source of tension, and are attacked or avoided. In this state, any sharing of workers' *experiential* understanding of the pain of 'the would-be-won't-be client' is turned away from or denied, so that both clients and staff teams can then *only* take up conversations within which it is assumed that all knowledge of all distress and dis-ease is *dis-membered* from the body of their shared experience. Professional 'goods and services' are apparently exchanged, but the net result is a *zero-sum game* in which there is no movement, no change. The only game in town becomes the basic assumption objective of *forgetting* the grief and anguish that generated, and so involves, an individual and collective turning away from the primary task of the organisation.

The Panopticon: Contagion and containment

> Morals reformed – health preserved – industry invigorated – instruction diffused – public burthens lightened – Economy seated, as it were, upon a rock – the Gordian knot of the Poor-Laws are not cut, but untied – all by a simple idea in Architecture! ...
>
> (Bentham, 1787, p. 31)

In the late 1780s, the Utilitarian philosopher Jeremy Bentham proposed the implementation of the 'Panopticon' for use in the 'correction' of deviance, anti-social behaviour and criminality (Bentham, 1787). The Panopticon was a design for a form of 'correctional facility' in which the living quarters of the inmates would be sufficiently transparent that the 'deviants' *could* be viewed from all angles at any time by unseen attendants. The watchers were located in a central tower and the inmates were to be placed in conditions of total visibility in peripheral enclosures. The Panopticon, as Foucault points out, separates two experiences that are normally linked – that of seeing and being seen: "in the peripheric ring, one is totally seen, without ever seeing; in the central tower, one sees everything without ever being seen" (Foucault, 1975, p. 202). Bentham's notion was that the Panopticon, as a kind of 'psychologically informed planned environment',[1] would mobilise an unseen *shaming* scrutiny, both actual and imagined, which would *induce* pro-social attitudes in the offenders. Under the improving influence of these new ways of seeing things, the captive subjects would feel impelled to reflect upon their behaviour and come to appreciate the error of their ways. Bentham proclaimed that the Panopticon would provide "a new mode of obtaining power of mind over mind, in a quantity hitherto without example" (Bentham, 1787, p. 31).

Foucault (1961, 1975) widened out the concrete basis of Bentham's proposal to describe and critique modern mechanisms for State regulation and surveillance, deployed as ways of governing, by means of controlling and disciplining the wider citizenry. He used the image of 'plague' as a metaphor for the need of the state to exercise this control in order to protect the population from 'contamination', using the historical analogy of leprosy in Europe (the potential for bodily contamination or infection through leprosy; the isolation of the lazar houses; and the confinement of the sufferer within them). Foucault suggested that madness and criminality (however constructed) likewise brought with them a fear of contagion, but in this case, a contagion of the mind: the idea that social deviance and *indiscipline* was also 'catching', and that therefore 'the mad, the bad and the sad', like so many lepers, also needed to be removed from society and placed under surveillance until they were *seen to be* no longer so disturbing.[2]

In his allegorical novel *La Peste* (1947), Albert Camus examined the problematic dynamics that emerge within enclosed settings, and between that 'enclosure' and the wider society, when bubonic plague breaks out in the (French colonial) Algerian town of Oran, causing the whole town to be quarantined. Camus evokes the fear, within the enclosed setting, of the potential for physical contagion to rapidly spread when the healthy and the contaminated alike are forcibly cast out into an external exile by, and from, the wider society that fears contagion by them. Camus depicts

> ... the lives of the people here who, though they have an instinctive craving for human contacts, can't bring themselves to yield to it, because of the mistrust that keeps them apart. For it's common knowledge that

you can't trust your neighbour; he may pass the dis-ease [our hyphen] to
you without your knowing it ...

(Camus, 1947, pp. 160; see also Chapter 7)

In these circumstances the townspeople must take their chances as they may;
each fearing the dangerousness of the 'dis-ease' of the other. Exiled by the
State, they are forced into a too-intimate and too-dangerous proximity, which
threatens them to the core of their being; longing to turn to one another for
comfort but terrified of the prospect of the plague spreading by these very
means. A peculiar kind of double consciousness (Du Bois, 1903) is theirs, so
long as they survive intact, for they see themselves as healthy and alive, in
contrast to those others who have succumbed to the plague, and yet they must
also hold the perspective of the world outside their walls, a world which sees
them all, without distinction, as lethally compromised, and as dangerous
rather than endangered.

The perverse Panopticon

"Look you, Mr Turnkey," said I, "there is one thing that such fellows
as you are set over us for, and another thing that you are not. You are
to take care we do not escape; but it is no part of your office to call us
names and abuse us."

(Godwin, 1794, pp. 204–205)

In Bentham's imagining of his Panopticon, it was the inmates who were
scrutinised by the unseen but all-seeing eyes of the Warder. However, in the
modern inpatient or residential or custodial planned environment, there has been
a curious reversal in the dynamic of the Panopticon, one which has been brought
about, in part at least, by the contemporary architecture and design of such
accommodation. Staff offices and observation stations, which ostensibly were set
up to enable staff to observe the inmates, have in effect become goldfish bowls
within which staff can also be constantly observed and scrutinised *by* the inmates.

This reciprocal process of observation and scrutiny creates a different version
of the Panopticon, in which all are observed and related to by all. Rather than
'simply' serving as a mechanism for social control to socialise the anti-social (as
Bentham had proposed), the 'perverse Panopticon' that we are describing here
mobilises a kind of anti-social control exercised *upon* the controllers. It provides
a context within which *agents of State* (whether or not directly salaried employ-
ees of the State), acting on behalf of and at the behest of forces constructed as
pro-social, are themselves corrupted and subverted. They become constructed as
contaminated – shamed by association – and as such come to present a clear and
present danger to those whom they watch over – and objects of intense suspicion
to those who watch over them.

The greatest institutional anxiety in residential and custodial care settings, second only perhaps to the death of a resident or a worker in the setting, is the anxiety that attaches to the risk of a sexual assault or sexualised abuse of power. Juvenal's poetic question *'sed quis custodiet ipsos custodes?'* ('but who is to watch those very watchers?' [our translation]) was asked in relation to the imagined impossibility of ensuring that those men whose duty it was to watch over the women of the harem would not be corrupted by, or corrupting in, these duties (an early foreshadowing of what later became manifest in the abuse and exploitation of vulnerable people by institutions of Church and State throughout history and across the world (see, e.g., Ryan, 2009; Royal Commission, 2017; O'Connor, 2019)).

When this reciprocal, vicious cycle of shaming and corruption is transposed into the residential or custodial setting, each is watching the other, on the one hand for any signs of weakness to be exploited, on the other hand, for any signs of the aggression and violence which would put them in harm's way. In the perverse Panopticon, where everyone is staring at everyone and pushing everyone else around, no one will spare your blushes and everyone will hear you scream.

One-to-one or even two-or-more-to-one nursing observations of disturbed patients on contemporary psychiatric inpatient units are informally known as 'special-ing' (although none of the parties to these procedures are likely to end up 'feeling special' in the ordinary sense of the word). Such interventions provide no guarantee that the object of 'therapeutic surveillance' will 'mend' his or her ways. On the contrary, the technique creates a complex and contorted game of hide and seek that can often be exhausting for both parties. Under the conditions of the 'perverse Panopticon', we can notice that it is often the staff who are being 'specialed': given 'special' treatment in the form of the gaze of the invisible Other, and so forced to take up the position formerly occupied, in Bentham's imagination, by the 'miscreant'. In Bentham's Panopticon, it was explicitly the idea that the Warden could see any one prisoner at any time, but the prisoner would not know, at any given moment, that he *was* being watched. It is only the *idea* of constant surveillance that is supposed to be both disciplinary and salutary. Those who work in such settings find themselves unwittingly caught up in the very embodiment of the dream that Bentham had for his prospective prisoners, which Foucault summarises as "the principle that power should be visible and unverifiable" (1975, p. 201).

Foucault (1975) further comments that the major effect of Bentham's pro-social Panopticon was "to induce in the inmate a state of conscious and permanent visibility that assures the automatic functioning of power" (1975, p. 201). Even though they may not be actually under scrutiny at any given moment, the workers too often feel themselves to be constantly watched, not only by the residents but also by the 'management' (Rustin, 2004): there is both hostile and friendly fire, which leaves the fear-filled workers in the position of identifying as 'combatants' and potential casualties. Thus, caught between the ever-present scrutiny of both the patients and 'the establishment', the workers, too, end up in a 'brave new world' (Huxley, 1932) in which they find themselves exercising the persecutory surveillance upon themselves. Watchers are not entirely dispensed with, of course, but neither are they any longer strictly necessary. The simple possibility of being 'caught out' in some way – by either clients, supervisors, colleagues or managers – suffices.

In a microcosm of the 'FitBit Society' (Hoggett, 2017), everyone is pre-occupied by the 'key performance indicators' on which they are being judged – or rather, on which they are *experiencing* themselves as being judged (the surveillance society is usually, and indeed can very well afford to be, rather less efficient than it is presumed to be). The 'residents' have to jump through hoops to get leave; to move to lower security; to get discharged; to get welfare benefits; to get rehoused. The workers have to record their inter-ventions, tick their 'social inclusion' or 'care planning' boxes, meet their tar-gets for 'payment by results'. Thus, does qualitative performance very speedily become alienated and displaced into quantitative 'performance': the performance of performance, for the invisible Warden and his array of elec-tronic eyes.[3]

As in the combat situation, the workers might reasonably expect hosti-lity from one direction but not from the other. Once they realise that even the guns of their own generals are trained upon their positions, the only available solution is to dig ever deeper trenches of defensive practice. This 'friendly fire' from the systems of governance also takes the form of ever greater demands to do more for less. It is coupled with the widespread implementation of technologies in which documented intervention can be monitored by algorithms and by remote and faceless technicians who are required to proceed on the basis that if it is not recorded on the electronic systems, then it did not happen. These are the same faceless algorithmic calculations that enable 'tech' companies to surveil, monitor, influence and control not only the shopping and TV viewing but also the voting habits of the general population.

Whether any of these 'quality control' surveillance measures do in fact have a preventative or remedial effect on potential bad practice, we may leave at least open to question. However, what is beyond doubt is that this managerial surveillance does induce a sense of fear and loathing in many able and experienced practitioners. The effect is to move away from greater relational security, reflective practice and team development in the agora, and inevitably towards an anxious pre-occupation with personal survival, physical security and a retreat into other offensive and defensive practice measures – one consequence of which is that people, staff and clients, get hurt (Pfäfflin and Adshead, 2004; Aiyegbusi and Clarke-Moore, 2009; Scanlon and Adlam, 2009).

The socially excluded workforce in the traumatised (dis)organisation

Hostile environments, understood in these terms, can then be compared to a 'combat zone', where watching and being watched are the weapons of war and of psycho-social trauma, and the projectiles are missiles of shame and humiliation. Like the citizens of Camus' plague-ridden town, workers and their clients (or the clients and their workers?) are cooped up together with the unwelcome shared experience of hostilities on *two* fronts at once. There is the enforced proximity and intimacy inside the 'city' (or ward/wing/street) between the false binary of the 'sick' and the 'well' across a metaphorical 'front line', partitioned by a kind of 'no-man's land' across which workers and residents face each other and across which hostilities and attractions must pass. There is also an awareness of the hostility of the outside world – 'public opinion' (or do we mean the populist press?), government policy, homeland security – that seeks to ensure that the dis-ease is confined and contained and that the staff, damned by association, are also effectively quarantined.

Health and social care services have become increasingly driven by the policies and discourses of austerity and a "market-driven ideology, preoccupied with what is only too aptly called 'the bottom line'" (Armstrong, 2005, p. 54). Almost nowhere in the modern world are there sufficient resources allocated to attend to and appropriately accommodate the most vulnerable members of our communities. What we are left with is "[a] culture focused on doing the system's business – not that of the patients" (Francis, 2013, p. 4) – in much the same way that the UK government may be seen as focused on doing 'party political' business rather than attending to the needs of the people.

We tend to think of our teams, services and wider systems of care – which is to say the ideas of them that we hold and the ideas of us that they hold – as relatively integrated entities that are in good working order most of the time but that have occasional frightening moments of fragmentation and collapse. It is, in fact, more the 'nature of the beast' (unsurprisingly, given the quality of 'combat' which we have been depicting here) that complex systems exist in a baseline state of dis-integration and, perhaps surprisingly, only come together now and again (usually under *emergency* conditions):

> it is a fundamental assumption that dis-integration is the natural, expected state of affairs in any such network, and not a falling away from an idealized collaboration, however much this integrated working may be prescribed or expected.
>
> (Bevington et al., 2017, p. 217)

Services, these authors observe, "are endlessly being transformed, recommissioned, or cut", and they comment that "some workers have been 'transformed' so often it comes as a shock that they remain familiar to themselves"

(Bevington et al., 2017, p. 2). In late capitalism, no senior bureaucrat is worth their managerialist salt unless they have instituted at least one major service 'transformation' in any given two-year period. That livelihoods are involved, the much-diminished trade unions may irritatingly remind them, that the psychic equilibrium of the workforce is thus constantly destabilised, is a psycho-social reality that happens not to be visible on the spreadsheet, and therefore need not concern them.

There is therefore a persistent threat to both psychic and organisational or operational survival, faced both by the would-be workers who provide services and the clients as the would-possibly-prefer-not-to-be 'consumers' of these services.[4] This internalised sense of fear and threat becomes manifest in the dynamic interplay between them within the particular setting. The consequence is that "[a]nxiety and blame are pushed around the system like a pinball" (Evans, 2015, p. 140).

Having said all this, it would manifestly be wrong – misleading, negligent and reinforcing of structural inequalities – not to notice that 'the workforce', considered as a homogenous mass, is also a fictional construct. The burden and threat in health and social care fall unequally upon different sections of the workforce. Frontline workers are exposed to the risk of disempowerment and professional exclusion, of being looked down upon by clients and 'the establishment' alike. Moreover, the occupational demographics of these environments are such that much of the burden of such work falls upon some of the least well paid and least well supported staff (mental health nurses, prison officers, security guards, domestic workers, administrative workers, healthcare assistants, activities workers, hostel project workers).

Many of these colleagues come from marginalised and disadvantaged communities, and we have long held the view as convenors of Reflective Practice Groups[5] across the system of care in the UK over the last two decades that the fact of racial inequality and racial trauma in the workplace is the most important issue to discuss (and is often also the hardest to discuss). The health and social care sectors have their own 'snowy white peaks', and colleagues from Black and minority ethnic groups, immigrant communities and working class white men and women are disproportionately clustered lower down the pay scales and status rankings. They constitute a marginalised and excluded sub-group within those marginalised and excluded services working with marginalised and excluded people. As we shall explore further in Chapters 7 and 8, it is these groupings who, for reasons of these structural inequalities, have been disproportionately impacted (and have died in disproportionate numbers) in the ongoing COVID-19 pandemic.

"Chew them up or spit them out?"

The central endangering psycho-social dynamic at the heart of all such work, as we have argued throughout this book, is that of exclusion – both in its interpersonal and in its social manifestations. The practitioners and teams and (dis-)organisations we are considering here, and the wider society from which it takes its authority and instructions, all inevitably become caught between the conflicting and oscillating impulses described above in the fraught encounter with un-housed, displaced and dis-membered clients. One such impulse is to violently and shamingly exclude or expel the (potential) client from services, out of the practitioners' sight and minds. The alternative move is to forcibly include or incorporate the potential client into a greater compliance with societal norms, to 'twist their arm' or otherwise insist that they 'come in from the cold'. The medico-legal technologies of coercive psychiatry or the hosepipes of outsourced security personnel literally pressure-cleaning street homeless people off of their shopfront perches are, in this regard, two sides of the same 'inclusive' coin.

Levi-Strauss (1955), theorising from an anthropological perspective, developed a categorisation of the societal in-group's responses to the feared difference and otherness of the out-group. One type is the 'anthropophagic' or 'cannibalistic' response, in which difference is abolished through coercive assimilation: devouring, swallowing, ingesting, incorporating. The difference of the feared other is no longer problematic if the feared other has been gobbled up whole by the self-defining in-group, such that its difference can no longer register or be detected. As the American critic Art Buchwald said, "If you attack the establishment long enough and hard enough, they will make you a member of it" (Buchwald, 1989) – and so, by extension, make you once again precariously dependent upon it for your survival in the world.

This is, of course, a very effective and time-honoured method of silencing opposition and dissent, and hence maintaining control of the conversation. The anthropophagic response within systems of care yields to the impulse to induce or coerce the more feared members of the dis-membered out-group to leave their wide-open spaces or their places of refuge and enter into *proper accommodation*. This often involves the over-use of statutory powers, such as mental health legislation and other medico-legal technologies, 'preventative' detention and criminal justice disposal.

The second category of response, conversely – the 'anthropoemic' response – involves the violent 'vomiting out' of difference, in which the self-defined in-group washes its collective hands of those it finds to be problematically 'foreign' or alien to them. The difference of the feared other is no longer problematic if the feared other has been annihilated or otherwise expelled – out of sight and out of mind. Although sometimes just as straightforwardly violent, as many a deportee could attest, it can at other times also wear the cloak of '*laissez-faire*' indifference. This experience is often associated with the *under*-use of statutory powers, such that men and women who are of little or no immediate threat to 'us', except in their 'other'-ness, are 'simply' left un-cared for – the potentially lethal reflexive violence (see Chapter 4) that they visit upon *themselves* goes seemingly unnoticed as they freeze to death in the doorway through which they are unable to enter.

There are some forms of State violence that can fall into either category, such as the establishment of states of exception (Agamben, 2003) that allows some such people to become *disappeared*. They may find themselves either anthropophagically incorporated into the deep dark heart of the machinery of State, or anthropoemically expelled outwith the boundaries of law – or even outwith the boundaries of the human race (into a helicopter, to be flown out over international waters and dropped into the sea; or on a cattle train, destined for a death camp in occupied territory).

All of these potential '(re-)solutions' are rooted in what simplifies the experience or gratifies the desire of the 'in-group', rather than in any real concern for the welfare of 'the other'. The German word *Schwellenangst* – that intense anxiety which is on or at the *threshold* – expresses succinctly the disturbance at the meeting point between two cultures that is sometimes called 'culture shock', and which can lead to the '-agic' or '-oemic' impulses being enacted, as well as to wider and deeper problems of structural racism in systems of care. The quality of hospitality and care delivered by systems riven by such fault-lines, and beset and beleaguered by such anxiety, dread and hostility, is going to be compromised and diminished at very best. Derrida (1997) coined the term 'hostipitality' – a contraction of *hostility* and *hospitality* – to describe this particular phenomenon. That such inhospitable systems, fragmented and fissured as they are, may then often be quick to hold the individuals in their care responsible for processes of 'splitting', as if they were fully integrated and functioning systems before the 'difficult patient' came along to disturb them, affords one further grim example of how insult is piled upon injury in the psycho-social dynamics of reciprocal violence in our systems of (don't) care.

Notes

1 The operation of Psychologically Informed Planned Environments (PIPES) is a contemporary policy and practice in the British prison system. In a PIPE, the milieu is structured in such ways as to promote and enable psycho-social engagement. Although very different to the Panopticon, the PIPE is nonetheless a psychologically informed manipulation of the prison environment by the prison service, "for the benefit of the prisoners" (Turley, Payne and Webster, 2013). Timoclea (2019) notes that the introduction of a PIPE in a women's prison "leaves women extremely vulnerable to having a psy-constructed identity imposed upon them and to accepting the agendas of a coercive prison environment" (Timoclea, 2019, p. 134).

2 Bauman (2000) recognises the force of Foucault's critique but argues that we are now in a 'post-Panoptical' society. Power in the Panoptical society was territorial, its seat was understood to be located in the Warden's control tower or its analogues, and the operation and implementation of power was predicated, at least to some extent, upon engagement between the watchers and the watched. In post-Panoptical

power relations, what is distinctive is that "the people operating the levers of power on which the fate of the less volatile partners in the relationship depends can at any moment escape beyond reach – into sheer inaccessibility" (Bauman, 2000, p. 11). We are not entirely persuaded by this argument: in our observation and experience, the Panopticon has been extended rather than superseded.

3 In our experience, two particularly perverse and perilous sets of consequences may then arise. On the one hand, the symbolic power of being able to shut the door and close the observation window becomes associated with abuses of power, particularly sexual abuse (as in, for example, the case of David Britten (Verita, 2008)). On the other hand, the power of occupying the Warden's seat can become intoxicating, to the point where illicit parallel surveillance can be installed alongside 'above the line' systems.

4 A further layer of structural violence is discernible in the fact that many 'evidence-based' policies, interventions and treatments, developed through trials with less psycho-socially traumatised individuals – for the most part drawn from white populations of the Global North – are then pressed or directly imposed upon people whose lives are more disrupted and precarious. This is done while all the while problematically assuming levels of motivation, pro-social aspiration and reality-oriented engagement that are almost entirely unreasonable to ask of or expect from those towards whom these interventions are targeted. In this way, apparently 'reasonable' and reputable 'three-letter therapies' can still let slip the mask to reveal what Main called "primitive human behaviour disguised as treatment" (Main, 1957, p. 129).

5 For the authors' respective studies of the nature and significance of the Reflective Practice Group within systems of care, see Scanlon, 2012, 2017, 2019; Adlam, 2019.

References

Adlam, J. (2019) '"Scallywag battalions": Reflective practice groups with multi-disciplinary teams in mental health and social care systems', *Organisational and Social Dynamics*, 19 (2), pp. 168–185.

Adlam, J. and Scanlon, C. (2012) 'Beyond these walls: The 'total institution' of homelessness' in Adlam, J., Gill, I., Glackin, S., Kelly, B., Scanlon, C. and Mac-Suibhne, S. (2012) 'Perspectives on Erving Goffman's "Asylums" fifty years on', *Medicine, Health Care and Philosophy*, 16, pp. 605–613.

Adlam, J., Aiyegbusi, A., Kleinot, P., Motz, A., and Scanlon, C. (eds) (2012) *The Therapeutic milieu under fire: Security and insecurity in forensic mental health.* London: Jessica Kingsley Publishers.

Agamben, G. (2003) *State of exception.* Translated by K. Attell, 2005. Chicago: University of Chicago.

Aiyegbusi, A. and Clarke-Moore, J. (2009) (eds) *Relationships with offenders: An introduction to the psychodynamics of forensic mental health nursing.* London: Jessica Kingsley Publishers.

Armstrong, D. (2005) *Organization in the mind: Psychoanalysis, group relations and organizational consultancy.* London: Karnac.

Armstrong, D. and Rustin, M. (eds) (2017) *Social defences against anxiety: Explorations in a paradigm.* London: Karnac.

Bauman, Z. (2000) *Liquid modernity.* Cambridge: Polity Press.

Bentham, J. (1787) 'Panopticon; or The inspection house', in Bentham, J. (1995) *The panopticon writings.* London: Verso, pp. 29–95.

Bevington, D., Fuggle, P., Cracknell, L., and Fonagy, P. (2017) *Adaptive mentalization-based integrative treatment: A guide for teams to develop systems of care.* Oxford: Oxford University Press.

Bion, W.R. (1961) *Experiences in groups.* London: Routledge.

Buchwald, A. (1989) International Herald Tribune, 24 May. Available at: https://en.wikiquote.org/wiki/The_Establishment (Accessed: 2 February 2021).

Camus, A. (1947) *La Peste (The Plague).* Translated by S. Gilbert, 1960. London: Penguin.

Cooper, A. and Lousada, J. (2005) *Borderline welfare: Feeling and fear of feeling in modern welfare.* London: Karnac.

Derrida, J. (1997) 'Hostipitality', *Angelaki,* 5 (3), pp. 3–18. Translated by B. Stocker and F. Morlock, 2000. doi:10.1080/09697250020034706.

Du Bois, W.E.B. (1903) *The souls of Black folk; with 'The talented tenth' and 'The souls of white folk'.* Reprinted 2018. London: Penguin Classics.

Evans, M. (2015) '"I'm beyond caring": A response to the Francis Report', in Armstrong, D. and Rustin, M. (eds) *Social defences against anxiety: Explorations in a paradigm.* London: Karnac.

Foucault, M. (1961) *Madness and civilization: A history of insanity in the age of reason.* Translated by R. Howard, 2001. London: Routledge Classics.

Foucault, M. (1975) *Discipline and punish: The birth of the prison.* Translated by A. Sheridan, 1991. London: Penguin Books.

Foucault, M. (1997) *Society must be defended.* Translated by D. Macey, 2004. London: Penguin Books.

Francis, R. (2013) The report of the Mid Staffordshire NHS Trust public inquiry. Executive Summary. Public Inquiry Chaired by Robert Francis QC. London: HMSO. Available at: https://assets.publishing.service.gov.uk/government/uploads/system/uploads/attachment_data/file/279124/0947.pdf (Accessed: 10 January 2021).

Gilligan, J. (1996) *Violence: Reflections on our deadliest epidemic.* Reprinted 2000. London: Jessica Kingsley Publishers.

Godwin, W. (1794) *Caleb Williams.* Reprinted 1988. London: Penguin Classics.

Goffman, I. (1961) *Asylums: Essays on the condition of the social situation of mental patients and other inmates.* London: Pelican.

Hoggett, P. (2017) 'Shame and performativity: Thoughts on the psychology of neoliberalism', *Psychoanalysis, Culture & Society,* 22 (4), pp. 364–382.

Hopper, E. (2003) *Traumatic experience in the unconscious life of groups: The fourth basic assumption: Incohesion: Aggregation/Massification or (ba) I:A/M.* London: Jessica Kingsley Publishers.

Hopper, E. (ed.) (2012) *Trauma and organizations.* London: Karnac.

Huxley, A. (1932) *Brave new world.* Reprinted 2007. London: Vintage.

Juvenal (1st/2nd century CE) *Satire VI.* Available at: http://www.thelatinlibrary.com/juvenal/6.shtml (Accessed: 31 January 2021).

Kothari, R., Forrester, A., Greenberg, N., Sarkissian, N., and Tracy, D.K. (2020) 'COVID-19 and prisons: Providing mental health care for people in prison, minimising moral injury and psychological distress in mental health staff', *Medicine, Science and the Law,* 60 (3), pp. 165–168. doi:10.1177/0025802420929799.

Levi-Strauss, C. (1955) *Tristes tropiques.* Translated by J. Weightman and D. Weightman, 1973. Reprinted 2011. London: Penguin Classics.

Main, T. (1957) 'The ailment', *Journal of Medical Psychology,* 30, pp. 129–145.

Menzies, I.E.P. (1959) 'The functioning of social systems as a defence against anxiety – a report on a study of the nursing service within a general hospital', *Human Relations*, 13, pp. 95–121.

O'Connor, J. (2019) 'Elective homelessness and the shadow of the institution: Lessons from the lives of survivors of the Irish Industrial School system', in Brown, G. (ed.) *Psychoanalytic thinking on the unhoused mind*. London: Routledge, pp. 80–91.

Pfäfflin, F. and Adshead, G. (eds.) (2004) *A matter of security: The application of attachment theory to forensic psychiatry and psychotherapy*. London: Jessica Kingsley Publishers.

Royal Commission (2017) Royal Commission into institutional responses to child sexual abuse. Final report. Available at: https://www.childabuseroyalcommission.gov.au/final-report (Accessed: 11 February 2021).

Rustin, M.J. (2004) 'Re-thinking audit and inspection', *Soundings*, 64, pp. 86–107.

Ryan, S. (2009) Final report of the Commission to inquire into child abuse. Available at: http://www.childabusecommission.ie/rpt/ (Accessed: 11 February 2021).

Scanlon, C. (2012) 'The traumatised-organisation-in-the-mind: Opening up space for difficult conversations in difficult places', in Adlam, J., Aiyegbusi, A., Kleinot, P., Motz, A., and Scanlon, C. (eds) *The therapeutic milieu under fire: Security and insecurity in forensic mental health*. London: Jessica Kingsley Publishers, pp. 212–228.

Scanlon, C. (2017) 'Working with dilemmas and dis-appointment in difficult places: Towards a psycho-social model for team-focussed reflective practice', in Vaspe, A. (ed.) *Psychoanalysis, the NHS, and mental health work today*. London: Karnac, pp. 115–134.

Scanlon, C. (2019) '"Practising disappointment": From reflective-practice-in-the-organisation to deliberative-practice-in-the-community', in Thornton, C. (ed.) *The art and science of reflective practice in the organisation*. London: Routledge, pp. 76–84.

Scanlon, C. and Adlam, J. (2009) '"Why do you treat me this way?": Reciprocal violence and the mythology of "deliberate self harm"', in Motz, A. (ed.) *Managing self harm: Psychological perspectives*. London: Routledge, pp. 55–81.

Stopford, A. (2020) *Trauma and repair: Confronting segregation and violence in America*. Lanham, MD: Lexington Books.

Timoclea, R. (2019) 'Offensive pathways: The "personality disorder" construct and the over-responsibilisation of incarcerated women', in Watson, J. (ed.) *Drop the disorder! Challenging the culture of psychiatric diagnosis*. Monmouth: PCCS Books.

Turley, C., Payne, C., and Webster, S. (2013) Enabling features of Psychologically Informed Planned Environments. Available at: https://assets.publishing.service.gov.uk/government/uploads/system/uploads/attachment_data/file/211730/enabling-pipe-research-report.pdf (Accessed: 5 March 2021).

Verita (2008) 'An independent investigation into the conduct of David Britten at the Peter Dally clinic: A report for NHS London'. Available at: https://www.verita.net/wp-content/uploads/2017/07/An-independent-investigation-into-the-conduct-of-David-Britten-at-the-Peter-Dally-clinic.pdf (Accessed: 31 January 2021).

Yeats, W.B. (1920) 'The second coming', in Webb, T. (ed.) (2000) *W.B. Yeats: Selected poems*. London: Penguin Modern Classics, p. 124.

Chapter 7

The inhospitable planetary environment

'Climate migration', pandemic and biosphere destruction

> ... a true ecological approach *always* becomes a social approach; it must integrate questions of justice in debates on the environment, so as to hear *both the cry of the earth and the cry of the poor.*
>
> (Pope Francis, 2015, p. 14 [italics in the original])

In Part II of this book, we have looked through the lens of the Diogenes Paradigm at the dynamics of psycho-socially traumatised (dis-)organisations working at the frontline of our systems of care and the fraught encounters that play out between in-groups and out-groups. We have seen how the 'welfare states', as they were imagined in Europe and North America in the aftermath of the Second World War, rather than challenge societal inequalities have, in many ways, replicated them within their structures and in the societal culture of denial of, collusion with, and turning away from the reality of these inequalities.

Since the middle of the 1970s and the advent of what we now recognise as the neoliberal turn,[1] these social systems have been gradually but determinedly reconstituted as hostile environments, deliberately constructed so as to reduce the perceived 'burden' upon the finances of the State, of people perceived as making some claim upon the 'public purse'. We have offered due acknowledgement of the possibility that the days of the Welfare State as an idea or ideal are numbered; not only because powerful forces of reaction are arrayed against it, but also because it contains within it the seeds of its own self-destruction.

In this second chapter of Part II, we develop this theme of what happens to humans in complex systems when 'things fall apart' and 'the centre cannot hold' (Yeats, 1920; Achebe, 1958) by turning our attention to the traumatised planetary system – on the biosphere destruction wrought, in the terms of the Diogenes Paradigm, by the figure of Alexander in his hubris – and on the movement of human populations ('human mobility' (IOM, 2020)) across the surface of the planet in the now increasingly inhospitable environment of the 'Earth system'.

DOI: 10.4324/9781003223115-9

The Great Acceleration and carbon-fuelled capitalism

> ... the characteristic of our age is the contact of European civilization with the world's undeveloped peoples ... War, murder, slavery, extermination, and debauchery, – this has again and again been the result of carrying civilization and the blessed gospel to the isles of the sea and the heathen without the law.
>
> (Du Bois, 1903, p. 123)

Our starting point is the crisis of the global dominance of the post-Industrial Revolution socio-economic model of carbon-fuelled capitalism, or 'fossil capitalism' (Angus, 2016). Chakrabarty (2009) uses the term 'industrial civilization', pointing out that for conservatives, liberals, socialists and communists alike, there was "never any principled difference in their use of fossil fuel" (2009, p. 217). There are, of course, important political differences between these several groupings, related to ownership of the means of production and the distribution of the output and dividends of labour and process. Nonetheless, it is the European socio-economic model built around (and exported by means of) the truly lethal combination of, on the one hand, imperialist-supremacist ideology[2] and, on the other hand, the steam engine and its successor, the internal combustion engine, that has brought humankind to the very edge of an existential precipice. Climate disaster, therefore, is no longer a problem of geology or technology; it is profoundly a *psycho-social* problem:

> Global anthropogenic impacts ... do not just happen but are the consequences, intended or otherwise, of *decisions* taken by human minds ... Humanity is perhaps better described ... as a *geological power*, because we have to consider its ability to make decisions as well as its ability to transform matter. Unlike forces of nature, it is a power that can be withheld as well as exercised.
>
> (Hamilton, 2017, p. 6 [italics in the original])

The Keeling Curve

The Keeling Curve (Scripps Institution of Oceanography, 2020) directly maps the ongoing process of global warming driven by fossil capitalism. It collates measurements of global atmospheric carbon dioxide concentration recorded at the Mauna Loa Observatory in Hawaii, 3400 metres above sea level on the north slope of the largest volcano in the world. They constitute the longest-running continuous carbon dioxide monitoring system on the planet. At the end of April 2021, the Keeling Curve graph was showing 419 particles per million (ppm) atmospheric concentration of carbon dioxide, up from roughly 370 ppm at the turn of the century, and an overall increase of around 100 ppm since the count began in 1958.

The inhospitable planetary environment   113

To put this increase into the context of a much longer timeframe: ten thousand years ago, at approximately the dawn of the 'Holocene' agricultural age in human history, ice-core data points to an atmospheric concentration of around 265 ppm. There has therefore been an increase of roughly 50 ppm *in the previous ten millennia*; and an increase of a further 100 ppm *in the last sixty years*. Carbon dioxide is the most significant of the 'greenhouse gases', and trends and variations in atmospheric concentrations of carbon dioxide closely correlate to trends and variations in near-surface air temperatures. The higher the carbon dioxide concentration in the atmosphere, the hotter it gets in the places where life in the Holocene has mostly thrived, and the more complex and exponential the ripple effects and tipping points thus generated. This is a planetary calamity.

The Keeling Curve allows us to see clearly the extent to which fossil fuel extraction and consumption has colossally accelerated since the 1950s – the 'Great Acceleration'[3] – and how the Curve has consequently risen proportionately steeply. More than half of the carbon dioxide emitted into the atmosphere at ground level is not reabsorbed. The continuing extraction of fossil fuels from the earth – and the reduced capacity of the Earth system to reabsorb carbon from the atmosphere because of the destruction of rain forests and other problematic modern agricultural techniques – means that the carbon balance within the 'Gaian' planetary system is tilted towards the atmosphere. Humankind continues to add carbon to the atmosphere at a rate something of the order of one hundred times faster than at any point in pre-industrial human history (Wallace-Wells, 2019, p. 4 and notes, p. 234).

The Keeling Curve therefore maps the end of the *Holocene*, and marks the onset and development of the *Anthropocene*, a term coined by Dutch Nobel Laureate Paul Crutzen to describe the geological era in which the economic activities of humankind are the most significant determinants of climate. There are many different indicators that we could take up but none that give such a profoundly uncanny sense of watching climate disaster play out on a day-to-day basis. The Curve correlates to a complex range of climate phenomena, including potential 'tipping points' within the Gaia system. It predicts a concentration of more than 700 ppm by 2100 if emissions of carbon dioxide into the atmosphere continue at their present upward rate; whereas 'capped' stability at the present concentration can only be achieved by an immediate and sustainable reduction in carbon emissions to a lower rate than is presently the case (see Scripps Institution of Oceanography, 2020, 'future scenario 1' and 'future scenario 3').

Global warming and climate change therefore represent a real, clear and present man-made danger, and an incontrovertibly established threat to the continuation of life on Earth as we (humans) know it. Significant evidence supports the argument that this is a disaster that has already happened – that tipping points have been passed and that climate disaster now generates its own momentum. Hamilton argues that "we must concede the material possibility of our own extinction, or at least the collapse of civilized ways of life, as a result of our own actions" (2015, p. 37). Bendell (2018), arguing the immediate necessity of 'deep adaptation' to the reality of the civilisation destruction, mass extinction and environmental cataclysm that humankind has already set in motion, is unequivocal:

> ... the evidence before us suggests that we are set for disruptive and uncontrollable levels of climate change, bringing starvation, destruction, migration, disease and war ... in your own life. With the power down, soon you wouldn't have water running out of your tap. You will depend on your neighbours for food and some warmth. You will become malnourished. You won't know whether to stay or go. You will fear being violently killed before starving to death.
>
> (Bendell, 2018, p. 11)

We should have reservations about 'migration' being listed here among Bendell's horsemen of the Apocalypse – as we would see it, migration *per se* is neither 'good' nor 'bad', a point we return to below. Perhaps 'forced migration' would have been a more apt term. However, Bendell's message is clear: "do not [merely] try to *adjust* your sets!" You (*we*) must go further: we must instead learn to live without them.

Exhaustibility and expendability

> The American way of life is not up for negotiations. Period.
> (President George Bush, 1992, quoted in Deen, 2020)

The process mapped by the Keeling Curve has been generated and driven by the "insatiable appetite of oligarchs" (Rancière, 2005, p. 73) and the consumerist value system (and its concomitant disregard for alternative value systems based around respect and sustainability), which those oligarchs have encouraged and exploited. Bear in mind that President Bush Senior, quoted above, who was no more or less than a frontman for the oligarchs Rancière has in mind, was seen in some quarters as, relatively speaking, a stand-up guy, by 'Grand Old Party' (Republican) standards, when it came to climate change.

These oligarchs are also exposed to the hostility of the environment they have thus despoiled; though they fancy themselves well enough insulated to its short-term threats and have plans (which it would be complacent to dismiss as fanciful) for accessing other biospheres via space travel or cryogenics, so they are not worrying too much about their grandchildren's futures either. They are certainly not worrying about anyone else's future. Their 'plan B' allows them to contemplate burning the planetary house for the technological insurance payback. "They ruin things on earth. And now they go to disturb

God in his realm", as the character Muturi says of the nature of the white colonialist in *Petals of Blood* (wa Thiong'o, 1977, p. 97); C.L.R. James succinctly dismisses European imperialists as "insatiable gangsters" (James, 1938, p. 220). If there is perhaps in the wider populace any tendency to imagine that someone, somewhere, possessed of the wealth and power to make a difference, is planning something that will get us all through, rather than leave us all behind, then this is a tendency for which some vigorous and fast-acting corrective is urgently required.

Nonetheless, and having said all this, the psycho-social reality is that "[t]he problem is that the problem is us" (Scranton, 2015, p. 68). It is 'us' who have embraced those consumerist values and turned blind eyes to the telescopes of the globalised gaze – it is all our appetites that are now so destructively in play:

> The world is being destroyed, no doubt about it, by the greed of the rich and powerful. It is also being destroyed by popular demand. ... We acquiesce in the wastefulness and destructiveness of the national and global economics by acquiescing in the wastefulness and destructiveness of our own households and communities.
>
> (Berry, 1993, p. 32)

It is 'us' who have ridden the fantasy of the inexhaustibility of resources so hard, and now find that exhaustibility is a limit which we have already passed, and perhaps can never again retreat behind. It is 'us' who are responsible for the present reality that there is now more human-made or 'anthropogenic' mass on the planet than there is living biomass (Elhacham et al., 2020). It is our 'doublethink'[4] that is destructively operative in the fact that climate disaster, consequent upon known and avoidable causes, is clearly understood to be unfolding and yet at the same time is still mostly considered not to be a factor that needs taking into anything more than superficial and disconnected account in our present-day decision-making.

Chakrabarty states that "the crisis of climate change has been necessitated by the high-energy consuming models of society that capitalist industrialization has created and promoted" (Chakrabarty, 2009, p. 217). The *relative* peace and prosperity of Western Europe and North America since the immediate aftermath of the Second World War – particularly the 'golden' period from the end of rationing around 1950 to the 'oil price' crises of 1973 (the longest continuous economic boom in capitalist history, taken all in all, if you were lucky enough to be one of its beneficiaries (Angus, 2016, p. 153)) – was a 'peace' that came at a terrible cost to the rest of the world and to the planet as a whole.

Sacrificial zones and sacrificed peoples are always the hidden export, the 'expendable' waste product of the drive for economic growth. This point becomes immediately clear when we consider that the period of the 'Great

Acceleration' is marked by the first atom bomb detonation in the New Mexican desert in July 1945. The American military may have considered that 'desert' to be a zone worth sacrificing to serve a higher purpose, but the radioactive isotopes spread across the globe by the explosion have left a worldwide geological marker of the moment when humankind (or the Western white man, more precisely) became an agent of lasting change in the Gaian system. A mushroom cloud heralded the dawn of the Anthropocene.[5]

Žižek, in his analysis of what he calls the primarily ecologically driven 'apocalyptic zero-point' of the global capitalist system, observes:

> the limitation of our freedom that becomes palpable with global warming is the paradoxical outcome of the very exponential growth of our freedom and power, that is, of our growing ability to transform nature around us, up to and including destabilizing the very framework for life.
>
> (Žižek, 2011, p. 333)

For most of the Holocene epoch, in which language has emerged and spread across the globe, humankind has regarded geological and ecological change as a process so slow as to be invisible to history, and so the preserve of something called 'nature' as to be outside the remit of human decision-making. The Great Acceleration has propelled us into a position where belatedly we can glimpse the interconnectedness of things and begin to grasp the possibility of conceptualising our world as the Earth system:

> the current crisis has brought into view certain other conditions for the existence of life in the human form ... connected rather to the history of life on this planet, the way different life-forms connect to one another, and the way the mass extinction of one species could spell danger for another.
>
> (Chakrabarty, 2009, p. 217)

We began this book by setting out a psycho-social model of unhousedness. The idea that the planetary environment on Earth (so often referred to as 'our home, the Earth') is now a hostile one requires us to think carefully about what we mean and how we think it. We do not mean by this that the sea was always a friendly environment to humans and is no longer so, or that mountains at high altitude were ever safe for humans to climb. However, it is clear that the global State of fossil capitalism, which 'we' Europeans first instigated, has created an environment hostile to the survival of all of us (human and animal alike, as Diogenes would have reminded us):

> You forget that in those days the land was not for buying. It was for use. ... The land was also covered with forests. The trees called rain. They also cast a shadow on the land. But the forest was eaten by the railway.

You remember they used to come for wood as far as here – to feed the iron thing. Aah, they only knew how to eat, how to take away everything. But then, those were Foreigners – white people.

(wa Thiong'o, 1977, p. 99)

Therefore, we have done this by means of active hostility *to* our environment – to that Earth system of which we, though possessed of intellect and awareness, have been thus far unwitting – as well as through passive indifference. We have hated 'nature' under cover of idealising it from a distance, in much the same way that in the United Kingdom we seem, as a culture, to hate childhood – and perhaps for very similar reasons. It is now as though the environment is replete with the hostility we have projected into it.[6] Regarding such matters as radioactive isotopes, micro-plastics and carbon particles, this is in all sorts of ways literally and concretely the case. The maintenance of active doublethink on a societal or even global scale is necessary in order to keep this awareness of human destructiveness at bay.

None of this is to suggest that any 'intentional' hostility should be imputed to the Earth system itself. Although some accounts do tend to personalise or anthropomorphise 'Gaia', this is misleading. Gaia doesn't do 'reciprocal violence': it 'simply' self-regulates. Chakraborty points out that "the crisis of climate change ... is not a crisis for the inorganic planet in any meaningful sense" (2009, p. 217). If the human element within the Gaian system pollutes and despoils itself into extinction as the ice melts, the sea level rises and the storms blow ever fiercer, this will not be evidence of Gaian 'revenge' (Lovelock, 2007). It will simply show that the complex fluctuating equilibrium of the Gaian system does not depend upon the human element for its continuation. We are a part of it but it *is* – independently of us – in ways beyond our comprehension.

Securitisation and the contested category of 'climate migration'

There has been a tragic rise in the number of migrants seeking to flee from the growing poverty caused by environmental degradation ... Our lack of response to these tragedies involving our brothers and sisters points to the loss of that sense of responsibility for our fellow men and women upon which all civil society is founded.

(Pope Francis, 2015, p. 8)

In 2019 the number of international migrants[7] as estimated by the United Nations was just under 272 million (about 3.5 percent of the world population, or one in thirty people); up from 150 million in 2000 (IOM, 2020). The recent report of the Institute for Economics and Peace suggested as many as 1.2 billion people could be displaced by 2050 (Henley, 2020). These figures correlate to multiple complex factors, mostly consequent upon the ravages of

fossil capitalism, such as the increased accessibility and reach (if not afford-
ability) of global travel networks; processes of globalisation (especially globalisation of the workforce and of the means of capitalist production); wars
fought over access to and control of fossil fuel and other resources, especially
water;[8] political unrest and State instability; and environmental or climate
migration. An average of 26.4 million people yearly have been displaced by
weather events since 2008 (Lancet, 2020):

> As a real, tangible anthropogenic climate crisis starts to alter centuries of
> patterns of human behaviour, migration is beginning to take on a differ-
> ent shape. Extreme weather events are becoming more common, con-
> tributing to pre-existing drivers of migration … The world is unprepared
> to deal with a population movement on this scale, particularly with
> regard to migrant health.
>
> (Lancet, 2020)

The UN International Organization for Migration (IOM, 2019) offers the
following definition of 'climate migration':

> The movement of a person or groups of persons who, predominantly for
> reasons of sudden or progressive change in the environment due to cli-
> mate change, are obliged to leave their habitual place of residence, or
> choose to do so, either temporarily or permanently, within a State or
> across an international border.
>
> (IOM, 2019, p. 29)

This is presented as a subcategory of environmental migration in which the
cause of the migratory movement is given the wider definition of "reasons of
sudden or progressive changes in the environment that adversely affect their
lives or living conditions" (IOM, 2019, p. 63).

Ghosh (2017, p. 3) writes that his ancestors "were ecological refugees long
before the term was invented": their village in what is now Bangladesh was
washed away when the Padma River suddenly changed its course in the
1850s.[9] The Mississippi delta is another example of a vulnerable low-lying
area at the mercy of extreme weather events. The State of Louisiana, on the
coast of the Gulf of Mexico, loses an area the size of Manhattan each year to
the sea. Since 1955, Isle de Jean Charles in Terrebone Parish, south-south-east
of New Orleans, has lost 98% of its 22,000 acres to saltwater intrusion and
subsidence. In 2016 members of the Band of Biloxi-Chitimacha-Choctaw
Indians who inhabited Isle de Jean Charles became the first Federally-funded
'climate refugees'.

There is therefore evidence and testimony to suggest that 'climate migrant'
is a recognisable category, encompassing a range of alternative terminologies
with which one might variously identify, or by which one might be identified

The inhospitable planetary environment 119

in local or international legislation and regulations (although it is important to note that 'climate migrants' are not protected by any international treaty, nor by any specific international body).[10] In the 1990s and beyond (see e.g. Myers, 1993), a body of theory emerged to identify 'climate migrants' as a distinct category of study and as presenting a distinctive set of problems to be solved. Since at least the mid-1970s, a wave of populist politicians has actively preyed upon the fears aroused by such constructs in pursuit of power.

'Climate migration', empire and racism

> The conquest of the earth, which mostly means the taking it away from those who have a different complexion or slightly flatter noses than ourselves, is not a pretty thing when you look into it too much. What redeems it is the idea only.
>
> (Conrad, 1902, pp. 31–32)

The hostility towards the environment of the proponents and propagators of fossil capitalism is matched only by its hostility towards those directly or indirectly displaced by its pillage and plunder. 'Climate migrants' are the new 'barbarians at the gate', laying claim to 'our' lands and 'our' opportunities, for 'theirs' have been (or are about to be) either eroded or washed away. 'They' – migratory human beings – are often dismissed by means of the mysteriously pejorative term 'economic migrants', or simply branded as 'illegal migrants' ("[a] lot of people coming to Europe are ... economic migrants and they want to enter Britain illegally" (UK Prime Minister David Cameron, quoted in Dearden, 2015). Reference has already been made to the rise of neoliberalism and the following definitive statement from one of its foremost frontpersons suggests strongly that climate migration in consequence of fossil capitalism was being foreseen and politically pre-empted back in the late 1970s (in the same way that Big Tobacco was aware of the health science around lung cancer long before the whistle was blown and the story broke):

> ... if we went on as we are then by the end of the century there would be four million people of the new Commonwealth or Pakistan here. Now, that is an awful lot and I think it means that people are really rather afraid that this country might be rather swamped by people with a different culture and, you know, the British character has done so much for democracy, for law and done so much throughout the world that if there is any fear that it might be swamped people are going to react and be rather hostile to those coming in ...
>
> It is not as if we have great wide open spaces or great natural resources; we have not. So, either you go on taking in 40 or 50,000 a year, which is far too many, or you say we must hold out the prospect of a clear end to immigration and that is the view we have taken ...

> We are a British nation with British characteristics. Every country can take some small minorities and in many ways they add to the richness and variety of this country. The moment the minority threatens to become a big one, people get frightened.
>
> (Thatcher, 1978)

Institutional racism in the British Home Office and the protracted and ongoing *Windrush* scandal are by now very well documented (Gentleman, 2019; Goodfellow, 2019). When Government is in the violent state of considering plans to deploy Heath Robinson-style contrivances for the sabotage of small boats making the Channel crossing (Grierson, 2020), or to recommission former ferry boats as offshore detention centres, or construct concentration camps on Saint Helena or Ascension Island (Walker and Murray, 2020), then the hostility towards those of us who are understood to be migrants is not difficult to infer.

There is, in short, a fixed idea, now deeply entrenched in neoliberal discourse, that there is a migratory horde 'out there somewhere' which is an unnatural phenomenon 'headed our way' and which therefore 'should go elsewhere'. The Global North 'securitises' the 'problem' of flows of displaced peoples – constructs it as a threat to 'our' housedness, one to be guarded against and repelled by force – but would prefer to turn a blind eye to the history of colonialist and imperialist, military and economic domination that caused or contributed to the displacement of so many of our fellow human beings.

Ghosh reminds us (lest we forget) that "we live in a world that has been profoundly shaped by empire and its disparities" (Ghosh, 2017, p. 146). Not the least of the consequences that flow from this truth is that 'climate migration', a phenomenon originating (thus far) primarily among the displaced peoples of the Global South, is researched and commented upon (for the most part) by the likes of we-the-authors, embedded as we are in the discourses of the Global North. While we all stand at the intersections between globalisation and climate disaster, hitherto and on an ongoing basis, it is the poor, the excluded and the Black and minority ethnic displaced who suffer the most. More than 20,000 migrants have died attempting the Mediterranean Crossing since 2014 (The Migrant Project, 2020). The 'Black Mediterranean' has represented "an ongoing crisis for black people" (Saucier and Woods, 2014, 2015) for many centuries now. This slaughter on the seas of migrants from Africa and the Middle East is but one more horrendous episode or sequence in an ongoing saga of racial subordination and exploitation – "slavery's afterlife", in the words of Saucier and Woods (2015; see also Danewid, 2017).

Reframing human mobility

> The idea that most people do not move or are fixed at a specific location might be appealing but it is wrong. Mobility is an inherent

characteristic of all populations unless specific policies or other factors are in place that limit or control that mobility.

(IOM, 2020, p. 5)

It is crucial to note the *negative* framing (generated by the 'settled' in-group) of the construct of climate migration. Racism and the neoliberal cover-up of racism plays a large part in this framing. When Hurricane Katrina, which devastated New Orleans and its surrounding area in 2005 and internally displaced over a million people, is instead presented 'simply' as an extreme weather event that just happened to be generative of 'climate migration':

a judgement is made concerning the relative value accorded to the hurricane as opposed to American racism in explaining this displacement ... the undeniable eventfulness of the hurricane is oftentimes mobilized as a fact which is then used to sustain the belief that climate change is a problem of migration ...

(Baldwin and Bettini, 2017, p. 5)[11]

The negative framings of 'climate migration' are not only located in moves to 'securitise' the threat thus constructed (IOM, 2020). The 'protection' agenda sees 'climate migrants' only as vulnerable victims of forces beyond their control (and therefore turns a blind eye to anthropogenic climate factors that are in the power of this same agenda to influence). High vulnerability in 'climate migration' stems from a combination of high exposure to climate disaster effects, high coercion, poor crisis management and low adaptive capacity. Yet it is also fundamentally the case that "migration can also be a form of adaptation to environmental stressors, helping to build resilience of affected individuals and communities" (IOM, 2019, p. 29). Migration in search of new loci for sustainable practices and ways of being, and in response to environmental changes, seasonal or otherwise, has always been the human way:

[h]uman mobility in times of changing environments historically has always been an important adaptation measure, and generally, migration is a normal societal process and not an exception.

(Klepp, 2017)

In many islands of Oceania immediately threatened by rising sea levels, the ethos is to 'migrate with dignity' – in others, the watchword is 'we are not drowning, we are fighting'. Adaptation models of understanding climate migration thus foreground the agency and decision-making of the human beings involved. The decision to stand one's ground is well expressed by the Arabic word '*sumud*', which Klein, referring to Said's (1994) usage, describes as "that steadfast refusal to leave one's land despite the most desperate eviction attempts and even when surrounded by continuous danger" (Klein,

2016). The *Foresight* Report (Foresight, 2011) shows how climate change can, on the other hand, cause some communities to be 'trapped' and rendered *less* likely to make an adaptive migratory move. Multiple socioeconomic and cultural variables influence and inform the differing reactions of different sections of 'a society' under threat of climate disaster. For that matter, a similarly broad range of variables contributes to different reactions to the 'migrant threat' in the Global North, both at local and national level.[12] In the analysis of patterns and practices of human mobility and immobility, complexity is the keynote.

Contagion, quarantine and biosphere destruction

The socio-political idea of a centre with a controlled perimeter has been perhaps the defining construct of the Holocene age: one in which relative climatic stability for ten millennia framed and enabled that phenomenon which began with the first agricultural settlements and encompassed what we now think of as human civilisation. As Rancière (2005) notes, the idea of a controlled border contains in it the idea of how controls can be lifted as well as imposed, in the power of lowering as well as raising the drawbridge:

> The same States that surrender their privileges to the exigencies of freely circulating capital rediscover them straight away in order to close their borders to the freely circulating poor of the planet in search of work.
>
> (Rancière, 2005, p. 82)

The Global North, for the most part, pursues policies of both anthropophagic (cannibalistic) coercive social inclusion and anthropoemic (vomiting out) coercive social exclusion (the 'hostile environment', both inward- and outward-facing) (Levi-Strauss, 1955). We can observe, following Foucault (1961), that the practice of 'quarantine', originating (in its recognisably modern form) in the Adriatic ports during the time of bubonic plague,[13] has to do with many kinds of contagion other than the biological; and includes aspects of both anthropophagic and anthropoemic positions (see also Chapter 6). Whether the in-group identifies the feared contagion to be plague, difference, discontent, madness, disorder, socialism, migration or simply fear itself, quarantine is, in effect, the technology now always reached for. Fear of climate disaster and 'climate migration' drives what Parenti (2011) calls 'the politics of the armed lifeboat', in which the only strategy in town is "arming, excluding, forgetting, repressing, policing, and killing" (2011, p. 11).

In this position, 'we' the in-groups of Fortress Britain, Fortress Australia, Fortress America or the transnational super-rich intend to "get rid of all the burdens of solidarity as quickly as possible" (Latour, 2017, p. 18). You can only come on board 'our' lifeboat (or island, or space station) if you score enough 'usefulness to us' points to count as 'one of us' – because then there's

The inhospitable planetary environment 123

no longer anything threatening about you – *and/or* if you look like the 'right stuff' to serve us by helping us fend off the 'horde' (and/or helping us to high-tail out of here to a new planetary environment altogether). This is because the mindset here is that *'we're* not planning to be the ones drowning (or starving) as the waters rise'. This is the profound fallacy that inheres in the bromide, 'we're all in the same boat'.

However, neither migrations nor carbon particles nor micro-plastics recognise borders to be boundaries, as we already noted in Chapter 3 – and nor do viruses. "Even if you seal the frontiers against two-legged refugees, you cannot prevent these others from crossing over", Latour observes (Latour, 2017, p. 10) – and he was writing a few short years before the COVID-19 pandemic forced its way to the top of this list. At the time of going to press, the world is still in the throes of successive waves of this zoonotic contagion and its mutations, and more than five million human beings have lost their lives.

In Camus' plague-ridden North African town in his allegorical novel *La Peste*, "it's common knowledge that you can't trust your neighbour; he may pass the disease to you without your knowing it ..." (Camus, 1947, p. 160). We contemporary readers now find ourselves perhaps in uneasy identification with the novel's characters Tarrou and Cottard, when Tarrou comments in his journal:

> [o]ne can have fellow-feelings towards people who are haunted by the idea that when they least expect it plague may lay its cold hand on their shoulders ... Like all of us who have not yet died of plague he [Cottard] fully realises that his freedom and his life may be snatched from him at any moment.
>
> (Camus, 1947, p. 161)

We cannot hold perspective or say anything definitive while the storm still rages and arousal is still so high. However, it seems reasonably clear that COVID-19 marked a new clarity of intersection between capitalism and its excesses, globalisation, and biosphere destruction. The 'securitised' figure of the (climate) migrant risks becoming further conflated than is already the case with biological perils and 'enemies at the gate' – as vividly demonstrated in the grammatical confusion (or deliberate misrepresentation) inherent in this extraordinary statement of a UK Home Office 'source': "*[a]nyone who slips through could be a new mutant strain*, hence the need for *blanket measures*" (Elgot and Davis, 2021 [our italics]). It has held up a powerful magnifying glass to pre-existing structural inequalities and to the harm that these inequalities cause. If we turn to the simple definition of structural violence offered by Gilligan ("the increased rates of death and disability suffered by those who occupy the bottom rungs of society" (Gilligan, 1996, p. 192)), then the lethal rampages of this pandemic at the intersection of race and class and health inequalities have (or should have) left no room for debate. Everyone is impacted but there is no equality of impact. We are not 'all in the same boat': some of us imagine ourselves safe on some latter-day Ark; some of us are falling out of or desperately scrabbling to get into overcrowded dinghies. It may be that it is part of human nature and group mentalities of different kinds to wish for an equal or privileged share of the protections and an unequal distribution of the harm:

> ... plague ... exacerbated the sense of injustice rankling in men's hearts. They were assured, of course, of the inerrable equality of death – but *nobody wanted that kind of equality.*
>
> (Camus, 1947, p. 194 [our italics])

The pandemic has also afforded us a glimpse of the limit of neo-liberal 'free-trader' *jouissance*. As Latour (2020) observes:

> The first lesson the coronavirus has taught us is also the most astounding: we have actually proven that it is possible, in a few weeks, to put an economic system on hold everywhere in the world and at the same time, a system that we were told it was impossible to slow down or redirect.
>
> (Latour, 2020)

Lear proposes that "[a]t a time of cultural devastation, the reality a courageous person has to face up to is that one has to face up to reality in new ways" (Lear, 2008, pp. 118–119). Latour (2017) offers a glimpse of this with his new binaries for a new politics, distinguishing globalisation *plus* (the recognition and celebration of diversity) from globalisation *minus* (the fundamentally imperialist projection of homogeneity). Likewise, he points to the tension between localisation *minus* (nationalism, parochialism, xenophobia, Brexit) and localisation *plus* (hospitable communities operating open systems, attaching to a particular patch of soil – "living together in a place and wishing to continue to do so" (Berry, 1993, p. 119) – and declining to be called 'backward' for wishing it).

There are other lessons which we cannot right now perceive, and that may well be long in the learning (and at the time of going to press, the exact origins of the COVID-19 contagion are not yet definitively settled); but some of the learning is surely already clear enough. First, we need to stop encroaching upon animal habitats as though 'no one lived there' (the quintessence of the imperialist project). It is these encroachments that create the locus for zoonotic infection. In Berry's words, "[i]f we speak of a healthy community, we cannot be speaking of a community that is merely human" (Berry, 1993, p. 14). Secondly, we need to stop eating meat, for it is the demand for meat that mostly propels the encroachments and it is the practice of eating meat that opens the channel for zoonotic infections to spread among humans. Thirdly, we need to stop flying (Gössling and Humpe, 2020), for it is the practice of international air travel that generated the phenomenon of pandemic at such speed. We of the Global North need to stop securitising the migrant and divert those energies into addressing health inequalities. Lastly (for now!), we need to attend to our own predictive models ('1.5° to stay alive'!) and take anticipatory action while the going is good. These several imperatives apply equally to climate disaster as to pandemic: on both climate disaster and pandemic, and as to their intersection, all the warnings were there in plenty of time – and yet we have fundamentally disregarded them (Lancet, 2021).

Latour proposes that "[e]ven Diogenes has the right to a barrel, as does a nomad to his tent, a refugee to her asylum" (Latour, 2017, pp. 10–11). Whether barrel-dwelling comes down to a question of rights is perhaps a matter for debate. As the Keeling Curve maintains its upward trajectory, everything now feels up for grabs. Unless the out-group can successfully insist upon radical change, or the in-group can somehow find its own way towards dismantling its own power structures, then "we are headed for a whole world of people searching for a home that no longer exists" (Klein, 2016). If necrophilia and death cults are keynotes of the decadent culture of the 'West', then perhaps it is deeply apt to contemplate a civilization dying, like Thomas Mann's von Aschenbach in deserted and cholera-ridden Venice (Mann, 1912), of impossible unsated desire and nostalgia.

Notes

1 The accession to power of Thatcher in the UK in May 1979 and Reagan in the USA in January 1980, and the waves of privatisation and deregulation that followed, might be understood to mark the first full flowering of the neoliberal project incubated in think tanks and policy institutes from the late 1960s onwards, and brought to term by the 'oil crises' of 1973 and 1979 (perhaps the Islamic Revolution in Iran of 1978–1979 was by way of being its Caesarian section). Because the privatisation of distress and individualisation of responsibility for adversity are signature features of the neoliberal world view, it is important to make the connection that 1980 also marks the first appearance of that pejorative and stigmatising, nonexistent illness entity, 'borderline personality disorder', in the Diagnostic and Statistical Manual of the American Psychiatric Association (APA, 1980). It will also be the Reagan and Thatcher administrations who 'empty the asylums' but withhold community care or Federal responsibility for those who fall through the safety nets thus widened. We should also note that authorities from varying perspectives agree that racism in the West was somewhat in decline (albeit still very much in evidence, as we shall see in Chapter 8) from the 1930s until the early to mid-1970s (Davis, 1981, p. 177; Dorling, 2010, p. 145). The rise of neoliberalism marched alongside the resurgence of racism and can therefore succinctly be understood as a racist counter-revolution – and in so far as the Republican Party in the USA is the vanguard political wing of neoliberalism, this has been explicitly the case since their 'Southern strategy' of appealing directly to racist sentiment brought Nixon into power in 1969 (Gilligan, 2011, p. 76).

2 One formulation of this ideology is the idea of 'Manifest Destiny' that emerged in the United States in the mid-nineteenth century. The journalist John L. O'Sullivan coined the term in an article published in 1845 in which he was arguing for the

126 Inhospitable environments

annexation of Texas to the Union, in pursuit of "the fulfillment of our manifest destiny to overspread the continent allotted by Providence for the free development of our yearly multiplying millions" (O'Sullivan, 1845).

3 The Great Acceleration ("the dramatic change in magnitude and rate of the human imprint from about 1950 onwards" (Steffen et al., 2015, p. 2)) is not only about carbon emissions. It is evidenced as a distinct phenomenon by a sequence of graphs, twelve showing features of the Earth system (such as methane concentration, ocean acidification and surface temperature) and twelve showing domains of human enterprise (such as GDP, urbanisation, water use and tourism) – initially mapped from 1750 to 2000 (Steffen et al., 2004). These were subsequently updated to 2010, with some variations in methodology (most significantly, regarding the socio-economic domains, to ask equity-oriented questions of the data and thus to differentiate factors such as population growth and consumption as between wealthy nations and poorer nations: see Steffen et al., 2015). Most of these graphs show 'hockey-stick' upticks in the trajectory of the curve from 1950 onwards, similar in kind to that shown by the Keeling Curve.

4 'Doublethink', in psychoanalytical terms, refers to perverse internal structures and processes in the internal world of the individual whereby an external or a psychic reality can be both known and not known at the same time. The term comes from George Orwell's 1984, where it is defined as: '... the power of holding two contradictory beliefs in one's mind simultaneously, and accepting both of them. The Party intellectual knows in which direction his memories must be altered; he therefore knows that he is playing tricks with reality; but by the exercise of doublethink he also satisfies himself that reality is not violated' (Orwell, 1949, p. 223 [italics in the original]).

5 There is some debate as to whether the Great Acceleration precedes and precipitates the advent of the Anthropocene (and therefore the end of the Holocene) – or whether the Anthropocene should be dated back to the Industrial Revolution (and Watt's design of the steam engine in 1784 – see, e.g., Crutzen, 2002) and the Great Acceleration is an escalatory phase within it. However, most authorities now accept the mid-point of the twentieth century as the marker: '[i]t is only beyond the mid-20th century that there is clear evidence for fundamental shifts in the state and functioning of the Earth System that are (1) beyond the range of variability of the Holocene, and (2) driven by human activities and not by natural variability' (Steffen et al., 2015, p. 13; see also Angus, 2016; Hamilton, 2017).

6 Naomi Klein (2015) has gathered a mass of evidence of such hostility: "the best thing about the Earth is if you poke holes in it oil and gas come out" (the aptly named Republican Congressman Stockman, tweeting in 2013 (Klein, 2015, p. 161)); "what good is a mountain just to have a mountain?" (this from the Vice President of the West Virginia Coal Association in 2011 (*ibid.*, p. 337)); or Sarah Palin, also in 2011, on the 'Tea Party' warpath, unconsciously channelling Robert Duvall's Lieutenant Colonel Kilgore in Apocalypse Now (1979; a film in turn based upon Conrad's story Heart of Darkness (Conrad, 1902)) when she proclaimed, "I love that smell of the emissions" (Klein, 2015, p. 1).

7 Defined as, 'the midyear (1 July) estimate of the number of people living in a country or area other than that in which they were born. Where the number of foreign-born was not available, the estimate refers to the number of people living in a country other than that of their citizenship' (United Nations, 2019).

8 There is much controversy surrounding the origins of the Syrian upheavals. However, two overarching realities dominate the biopolitics of the Middle East and North Africa (MENA) region and therefore the continuing toxicity of imperialist domination over the region: these are the abundance of oil and the scarcity of

The inhospitable planetary environment 127

water. Gleick (2014) explores the complex interplay between water shortage, water resource mismanagement and internal displacement in the early stages of the political unrest. The Water Conflict Chronology (Pacific Institute, 2019) has tracked more than five hundred water-related conflicts since 1900, two thirds of which have occurred since 2000. The town of Dara'a (historically the 'bread basket' of Syria), where the conflict first erupted, is on the 'aridity line' inside which average annual rainfall drops below 200 ml. Klein (2016) shows how war and violent upheaval (and drone strikes by Western powers) can be closely correlated to points on that border line between sufficiency and scarcity as it stretches all the way across from southern India to the Atlantic coast.

9 Almost as many people live in and around the confluence of the Ganges and Brahmaputra rivers that disperse into the Bay of Bengal as there are international migrants worldwide today. The area as a whole is threatened by rising sea levels; by the melting of the Hindu Kush-Himalaya icecap (the greatest concentration of ice outside of the two poles (Carrington, 2019; Wester *et al.*, 2019)); by salinisation and riverbank erosion; and by the increased frequency of destructive cyclones sweeping up the Bay of Bengal. Two thirds of Bangladesh is less than five metres above sea level. In the next thirty years, with a projected 50 cm rise in sea level, Bangladesh alone may lose approximately 11% of its land, affecting an estimated 15 million people living in its low-lying coastal region (Environmental Justice Foundation, 2019; see also Ghosh, 2017; Wallace-Wells, 2019).

10 For a recent UN Human Rights Committee ruling, finding that there were at least possible pathways to protection under Article 6 (the right to life) of the International Covenant on Civil and Political Rights for individuals claiming refugee status because their homeland was threatened by impending climate disaster, see UNHRC, 2020.

11 For a report on the various issues of structural racism pertaining to Hurricane Katrina, see Harden, Walker and Akuno (2007). These authors cite a Republican Congressman from Louisiana, one Richard Baker, who commented: "We finally cleaned up public housing in New Orleans. We couldn't do it, but God did" (Harden, Walker and Akuno, 2007, p. 1).

12 While the British political 'elite' was fulminating about 'hordes of illegals' in 2015 and 2016, Germany alone accommodated 1.3 million refugees of the Syrian upheavals (Lancet, 2020).

13 The term 'quarantine' is derived from the Italian word *quarantena* or *quarantino*, signifying the forty days and forty nights of isolation imposed by the Venetian Senate in 1448 in order to combat bubonic plague. Visitors by ship suspected of carrying the plague would have to spend that amount of time in one of two outlying islands in the Venetian lagoon, Lazzaretto Vecchio and Lazzaretto Nuovo. This early public health measure extended the *trentino* or thirty-day isolation imposed seventy years earlier by the Venetian authorities who controlled the port of Ragusa, now Dubrovnik in Croatia. In those days the germ theory of disease infection was unknown and it was therefore a happy circumstance that modern estimates of the span of bubonic plague from infection to death suggest a thirty-seven-day period of threat (Sehdev, 2002; Drews, 2013).

References

Achebe, C. (1958) *Things fall apart*. Reprinted 2010. London: Penguin.

Angus, I. (2016) *Facing the Anthropocene: Fossil capitalism and the crisis of the earth system*. New York, NY: Monthly Review Press.

APA (1980) *Diagnostic and statistical manual of mental disorders (DSM-III)*. 3rd edition. Washington, DC: American Psychiatric Association.

Apocalypse now (1979) Directed by Francis Ford Coppola [Film]. Beverley Hills, CA: United Artists.

Baldwin, A. and Bettini, G. (eds) (2017) *Life adrift: Climate change, migration, critique*. London: Rowman and Littlefield.

Bendell, J. (2018) 'Deep adaptation: A map for navigating climate tragedy'. IFLAS Occasional Paper 2. Available at: http://www.lifeworth.com/deepadaptation.pdf (Accessed 4 January 2021).

Berry, W. (1993) *Sex, economy, freedom & community: Eight essays*. Reprinted 2018. Berkeley, CA: Counterpoint.

Camus, A. (1947) *The plague*. Translated by S. Gilbert, 1960. London: Penguin.

Carrington, D. (2019) 'A third of Himalayan ice cap doomed, finds report', *The Guardian*, February 4. Available at: https://www.theguardian.com/environment/2019/feb/04/a-third-of-himalayan-ice-cap-doomed-finds-shocking-report (Accessed: 4 January 2021).

Chakrabarty, D. (2009) 'The climate of history: Four theses', *Critical Inquiry*, 35, pp. 197–222.

Conrad, J. (1902) *Heart of darkness*. Reprinted 1985. London: Penguin Classics.

Crutzen, P.J. (2002) 'Geology of mankind', *Nature*, 415, p. 23.

Danewid, I. (2017) 'White innocence in the Black Mediterranean: Hospitality and the erasure of history', *Third World Quarterly*, 38 (7), pp. 1674–1689.

Davis, A.Y. (1981) *Women, race and class*. Reprinted 2019. London: Penguin Modern Classics.

Dearden, L. (2015) 'David Cameron says he did not dehumanise migrants with "swarms" comment', *The Independent*, 15 August. Available at: https://www.independent.co.uk/news/uk/politics/david-cameron-says-he-did-not-dehumanise-migrants-swarms-comment-10456984.html (Accessed: 1 January 2021).

Deen, T. (2020) 'U.S. lifestyle is not up for negotiation', Inter Press Service News Agency, 28 November. Available at: http://www.ipsnews.net/2012/05/us-lifestyle-is-not-up-for-negotiation/ (Accessed: 4 January 2021).

Dorling, D. (2010) *Injustice: Why social inequality persists*. Bristol: Policy Press.

Drews, K. (2013) 'A brief history of quarantine', *The Virginia Tech Undergraduate Historical Review*, 2. doi:10.21061/vtuhr.v2i0.16.

Du Bois, W.E.B. (1903) *The souls of Black folk; with 'The talented tenth' and 'The souls of white folk'*. Reprinted 2018. London: Penguin Classics.

Elgot, J. and Davis, N. (2021) 'Johnson being urged to impose blanket Covid border controls', *The Guardian*, 24 January. Available at: https://www.theguardian.com/world/2021/jan/24/boris-johnson-urged-blanket-covid-border-controls-uk (Accessed: 10 February 2021).

Elhacham, E., Ben-Uri, L., Grovoski, J., Bar-On, Y.M., and Milo, R. (2020) 'Global human-made mass exceeds all living biomass', *Nature*, 2020. doi:10.1038/s41586-020-3010-5.

Environmental Justice Foundation (2019) 'Climate displacement in Bangladesh'. Available at: https://ejfoundation.org/reports/climate-displacement-in-bangladesh (Accessed: 4 January 2021).

Foresight (2011) 'Foresight: Migration and global environmental change'. Final Project Report. London: The Government Office for Science. Available at: https://assets.

publishing.service.gov.uk/government/uploads/system/uploads/attachment_data/file/287717/11-1116-migration-and-global-environmental-change.pdf (Accessed: 15 January 2021).

Foucault, M. (1961) *Madness and civilization: A history of insanity in the age of reason*. Translated by R. Howard, 2001. London: Routledge Classics.

Gentleman, A. (2019) *The Windrush betrayal: Exposing the hostile environment*. London: Faber and Faber.

Ghosh, A. (2017) *The great derangement: Climate change and the unthinkable*. Chicago: University of Chicago.

Gilligan, J. (1996) *Violence: Reflections on our deadliest epidemic*. Reprinted 2000. London: Jessica Kingsley Publishers.

Gilligan, J. (2011) *Why some politicians are more dangerous than others*. Cambridge: Polity.

Gleick, P.H. (2014) 'Water, drought, climate change, and conflict in Syria', *Weather, Climate and Society*, 6, pp. 331–340.

Goodfellow, M. (2019) *Hostile environment: How immigrants became scapegoats*. London: Verso.

Gössling, S. and Humpe, A. (2020) 'The global scale, distribution and growth of aviation: Implications for climate change', *Global Environmental Change*, 65, 102194. doi:10.1016/j.gloenvcha.2020.102194.

Grierson, J. (2020) 'Home Office may use nets to stop migrant boats crossing Channel', *The Guardian*, 11 October. Available at: https://www.theguardian.com/world/2020/oct/11/home-office-considers-using-nets-to-stop-migrant-boats-crossing-channel (Accessed: 4 January 2021).

Hamilton, C. (2017) *Defiant Earth: The fate of humans in the Anthropocene*. Cambridge: Polity.

Harden, M., Walker, N., and Akuno, K. (2007) 'Racial discrimination and ethnic cleansing in the United States in the aftermath of Hurricane Katrina: A report to the United Nations' committee for the elimination of racial discrimination'. Available at: https://www2.ohchr.org/english/bodies/cerd/docs/ngos/usa/USHRN23.doc (Accessed: 4 January 2021).

Henley, J. (2020) 'Climate crisis could displace 1.2bn people by 2050, report warns', *The Guardian*, 9 September. Available at: https://www.theguardian.com/environment/2020/sep/09/climate-crisis-could-displace-12bn-people-by-2050-report-warns?ref=hvper.com (Accessed 4 January 2021).

IOM (2019) Glossary on Migration. International Migration Law No. 34. IOM: Geneva. Available at: https://publications.iom.int/system/files/pdf/iml_34_glossary.pdf (Accessed: 5 January 2021).

IOM (2020) World Migration Report 2020. Available at: https://publications.iom.int/system/files/pdf/wmr_2020.pdf (Accessed: 5 January 2021).

James, C.L.R. (1938) *The Black Jacobins*. Reprinted 2001. London: Penguin.

Klein, N. (2015) *This changes everything*. London: Penguin.

Klein, N. (2016) 'Let them drown – the violence of othering in a warming world', *London Review of Books*, 38 (11). Available at: https://www.lrb.co.uk/the-paper/v38/n11/naomi-klein/let-them-drown (Accessed: 1 January 2021).

Klepp, S. (2017) 'Climate change and migration', *Oxford Research Encyclopedias: Climate Science*. doi:10.1093/acrefore/9780190228620.013.42.

Lancet (2020) 'Editorial: Climate migration requires a global response', *Lancet*, 395, p. 839, March 14, 2020. doi:10.1016/S0140-6736(20)30571-7.

Lancet (2021) 'Editorial: Climate and COVID-19: Converging crises', *Lancet*, 397, p. 71, January 9, 2021. doi:10.1016/S0140-6736(20)32579-4.

Latour, B. (2017) *Down to Earth – Politics in the new climatic regime*. Translated by C. Porter, 2018. Cambridge: Polity.

Latour, B. (2020) 'What protective measures can you think of so we don't go back to the pre-crisis production model?' Translated by Stephen Muecke. Available at: http://www.bruno-latour.fr/sites/default/files/P-202-AOC-ENGLISH.pdf (Accessed: 5 January 2021).

Lear, J. (2008) *Radical hope: Ethics in the face of cultural devastation*. Cambridge, MA: Harvard University Press.

Levi-Strauss, C. (1955) *Tristes tropiques*. Translated by J. Weightman and D. Weightman, 1973. Reprinted 2011. London: Penguin Classics.

Lovelock, J. (2007) *The revenge of Gaia*. London: Penguin.

Mann, T. (1912) *Death in Venice*. Translated by H.T. Lowe-Porter, 1928. Reprinted 1983. London: Penguin Modern Classics, pp. 7–83.

Migrant Project, The (2020) 'Migrant deaths in the Mediterranean exceed 20,000 since 2014'. Available at: https://www.themigrantproject.org/mediterranean-deaths-2/ (Accessed: 5 January 2021).

Myers, N. (1993) *Ultimate security: The environment basis of political security*. New York, NY: W.W. Norton.

Orwell, G. (1949) *1984*. Reprinted 2000. London: Penguin Classics.

O'Sullivan, J.L. (1845) 'Annexation', *The United States Magazine and Democratic Review*, 17, pp. 5–10. Available at: http://web.grinnell.edu/courses/HIS/f01/HIS202-01/Documents/OSullivan.html (Accessed: 5 January 2021).

Pacific Institute (2019) 'The water conflict chronology'. Available at: http://www.worldwater.org/water-conflict/ (Accessed: 5 January 2021).

Parenti, C. (2011) *Topic of chaos*. New York: Nation Books.

Pope Francis (2015) Encyclical letter Laudato Si' of the Holy Father Francis on care of our common home. Available at: https://laudatosi.com/watch (Accessed: 2 January 2021).

Rancière, J. (2005) *Hatred of democracy*. Translated by S. Corcoran, 2014. London: Verso.

Said, E. (1994) *Culture and imperialism*. London: Vintage.

Saucier, P.K. and Woods, P.T. (2014) 'Ex Aqua: The Mediterranean basin, Africans on the move, and the politics of policing', *Theoria*, 61 (141), pp. 55–75.

Saucier, P.K. and Woods, P.T. (2015) 'Slavery's afterlife in the Euro-Mediterranean basin'. Available at: https://www.opendemocracy.net/en/beyond-trafficking-and-slavery/slaverys-afterlife-in-euromediterranean-basin/ (Accessed: 5 January 2021).

Scranton, R. (2015) *Learning to die in the Anthropocene*. San Francisco: City Lights.

Scripps Institution of Oceanography (2020) 'The Keeling Curve'. Available at: https://sioweb.ucsd.edu/programs/keelingcurve/ (Accessed: 5 January 2021).

Sehdev, P.S. (2002). 'The origin of quarantine', *Clinical Infectious Diseases*, 35 (9), pp. 1071–1072. doi:10.1086/344062.

Steffen, W., Broadgate, W., Deutsch, L., Gaffney, O., and Ludwig, C. (2015) 'The trajectory of the Anthropocene: The Great Acceleration', *The Anthropocene Review*, 2 (1), pp. 81–98.

Steffen, W., Sanderson, A., Tyson, P.D., Jäger, J., Matson, P.A., MooreIII, B., Oldfield, F., Richardson, K., Schellnhuber, H.-J., Turner, B.L., and Wasson, R.J. (2004) *Global change and the earth system: A planet under pressure*. Berlin: Springer-Verlag.

Thatcher, M. (1978) 'TV Interview for Granada World in Action ("rather swamped")'. Margaret Thatcher Foundation. Available at: https://www.margaretthatcher.org/document/103485 (Accessed: 5 January 2021).

UNHRC (2020) 'Views adopted by the Committee under article 5(4) of the Optional Protocol, concerning communication No. 2728/2016'. Available at: https://tbinter net.ohchr.org/_layouts/15/treatybodyexternal/Download.aspx?symbolno=CCPR/C/127/D/2728/2016&Lang=en (Accessed: 5 January 2021).

United Nations (2019) International Migration 2019. Wallchart. UN Department of Economic and Social Affairs – Population Division. Available at: https://www.un.org/en/development/desa/population/migration/publications/wallchart/docs/Migra tionStock2019_Wallchart.pdf (Accessed: 5 January 2021).

wa Thiong'o, Ngũgĩ (1977) *Petals of blood.* Reprinted 2018. London: Vintage.

Walker, P. and Murray, J. (2020) 'Priti Patel looked at idea of sending asylum seekers to South Atlantic', *The Guardian*, 30 September. Available at: https://www.thegua rdian.com/politics/2020/sep/30/priti-patel-looked-at-idea-of-sending-asylum-seekers-to-south-atlantic (Accessed: 5 January 2021).

Wallace-Wells, D. (2019) *The uninhabitable earth: A story of the future.* London: Allen Lane.

Wester, P., Mishra, A., Mukherji, A., and Shrestha, A.B. (eds) (2019) *The Hindu Kush Himalaya assessment – mountains, climate change, sustainability and people.* Cham: Springer Nature Switzerland AG.

Yeats, W.B. (1920) 'The second coming', in Webb, T. (ed.) (2000) *W.B. Yeats: Selected poems.* London: Penguin Modern Classics, p. 124.

Žižek, S. (2011) *Living in the end times.* London: Verso.

Part III

Reclaiming the agora
Activist research and anti-oppressive practice

If not us, then who? If not now, then when?
(John Lewis, Freedom Rider 1961)

10. We Want Land, Bread, Housing, Education, Clothing, Justice And Peace.
(Huey P. Newton and Bobby Seale, from The Black Panther Party for Self-Defense Ten-Point Platform and Program 1967)

Chapter 8

Racial (re-)traumatisation and practices of equality

Social exclusion and racial inequality

> Between me and the other world there is ever an unasked question ... They approach me in a half-hesitant sort of way, eye me curiously or compassionately, and then, instead of saying directly, How does it feel to be a problem? they say, I know an excellent colored man in my town; or, I fought at Mechanicsville; or, Do not these Southern outrages make your blood boil? ... To the real question, How does it feel to be a problem? I answer seldom a word.
>   And yet, being a problem is a strange experience ...
>
> (Du Bois, 1903, pp. 5–6)

At the centre of the Diogenes Paradigm lies a colossal and yet paradoxical power differential. The most powerful man in the world invites a homeless mendicant ex-offender to his table and finds his invitation declined; a street philosopher, a manic street preacher (an (un)holy fool(?)) commands a God-King to step out of his light. Our purpose in much of our work has been to explore the curious push-me/pull-you ambiguities and ambivalences that emerge whilst trying simultaneously both to accept and also to reject the stranger. We also remind health and social care practitioners that if our Paradigm applies, then they are appointed to read Alexander's lines in this drama, and therefore might reflect upon their own hospitality before grumbling about the real or perceived hostility to their good int(erv)entions of those allocated the part of Diogenes. Audre Lorde (1979a) succinctly nails this tendency on the part of the membership of the in-group to feel misunderstood and hard done by: "Oppressors always expect the oppressed to extend to them the understanding so lacking in themselves" (Lorde, 1979a, p. 63).

We have emphasised, in our re-telling of the Diogenes and Alexander story, that which the two men held in common across the power difference: the strange(r) affinity they may have felt for each other even as they confronted each other in the agora. We have also noted the unwritten conventions according to which Diogenes is afforded a kind of carnival licence to take a verbal swing at Alexander; whilst Alexander, in his 'accepting' of the verbal

DOI: 10.4324/9781003223115-11

136 Reclaiming the agora

barrage without retaliation, has the opportunity to show just how much power he holds in reserve.

However, the reader may still be left with a sense of inevitability that the 'business as usual' of the reciprocal violence and psycho-social processes of traumatisation which we have been mapping throughout this book will resume at the end of the allocated time of the temporary suspension of hierarchies (if not of hostilities). Thus runs the familiar narrative in which the emancipatory moment is yet again met with a reactionary force, and so the 'insurrection' of the 'subjugated knowledge' (Foucault, 1976, p. 81) will have been but fleeting.[1]

Butler (1990) observes how different versions of 'we' hold themselves in precarious coherence by excluding, or constituting as 'excess', '*et cetera*', some part of their potential constituency:

> [T]he theories of feminist identity that elaborate predicates of colour, sexuality, ethnicity, class, and able-bodiedness invariably close with an embarrassed etc. at the end of the list. Through this horizontal trajectory of adjectives, these positions strive to encompass a situated subject, but invariably fail to complete.
>
> (Butler, 1990, p. 196; see also Pelletier, 2009, p. 269)

If the reader by this stage is minded to allow our own equivalent hypothesis – that projects for social inclusion exclude, by definition, and, moreover, perpetuate relations of domination between in-group and out-group (even as they seem to seek to take the edge off of those apparently unintended consequences) – then it would also be bizarre to imagine that projects that aim for the creative temporary suspension of inequality could be let off the very similar conceptual and ethical petard upon which they hoist themselves.

We therefore propose now to extend this critique, from practices that purport to be in pursuit of social inclusion (propelled towards an imaginary and ever-receding vanishing point on the horizon beyond which everyone would be included) to practices apparently in pursuit of equality. These likewise have tended to be aimed in the direction of an ever-receding horizon, beyond which, if we could ever somehow get to the other side of it, we really might, *in practice*, 'hold these truths to be self-evident, that all men are created equal' – as Thomas Jefferson and his colleagues so eloquently and yet so equivocally and ambiguously proclaimed two and a half centuries ago (Declaration of Independence, 1776).[2]

'Approximation', gradualism, reformism and reaction

Abraham Lincoln, in his 1858 debate (with Judge Douglas) specifically convened to establish whether the word 'men' in the Declaration was intended to bring slaves under the protection of its provisions, argued that the authors, intended to include all men, but they did not mean to declare all men equal in all respects. They did not mean to say all men were equal in color, size, intellect, moral development, or social capacity. They defined with tolerable distinctness in what they did consider all men created equal – equal in "certain inalienable rights, among which are life, liberty, and the pursuit of happiness." ... They meant simply to declare the right, *so that the enforcement of it might follow as fast as circumstances should permit.* They meant to set up a standard maxim for free society which should be familiar to all, constantly looked to, constantly labored for, *and even, though never perfectly attained, constantly approximated* ...

(Lincoln, 1858 [our italics])

We argue here that, 'circumstances' having evidently not yet permitted the 'enforcement' of equality 'in certain inalienable rights', a century and a half after Lincoln's dictum, it would seem that a new approach is required. Such an approach should not be predicated upon the principle and the methodology of 'approximation', which is equivalent to the project of exclusion by inclusion already discussed. We take as our motto Jean-Paul Sartre's words from his great anti-colonialist polemic in support of Frantz Fanon:

... we only become what we are by the radical and deep-seated refusal of that which others have made of us.

(Sartre, 1961, p. 15)

One can no more achieve equality by approximation than one can achieve social inclusion by twiddling or fiddling with Butler's '*et cetera*'. 'Approximation', in this sense, is a practice of *in*equality – that is to say, a practice that projects 'equality' into an apparently longed-for but, in reality, endlessly (?) deferred future and, in so doing, upholds, maintains and perpetuates present-day inequalities.

Approximation has had and continues to have its place and to play its part – it must in some sense be better than doing nothing (or is it?). The reforms that are part of its practice of conservatism must at least in themselves be welcome. We are not, after all, arguing that, as a society, we should actively pursue social exclusion as a policy. We-the-authors are also certainly not presuming to prescribe to anti-racist movements and organisations what their politics should be (we note that the #BlackLivesMatter website (2020) proclaims a mixture of both the gradualist or reformist and the revolutionary positions).

The Obama presidency and its aftermath in the United States perhaps affords a vivid example of what we *are* trying to say. That a Black man became President in that country is a phenomenon we would want to celebrate, and we join with those who did and still do celebrate it (see, for example, Anne Aiyegbusi's Prologue to this volume). That Obama was succeeded by the 45th President, an unabashedly racist white man; a man who came to political prominence, even directly to power, by denying that Obama was an American citizen, by declaring him a non-citizen; a man who, when in power, notoriously refused to condemn or even criticise self-declared 'white supremacists' marching in opposition to #Black Lives Matter demonstrations, and whose last move in office was to bring upon himself a second impeachment for inciting those same white supremacists to march on the Capitol in an attempted *coup d'état* – is compelling evidence of the continuing and perhaps even escalating perils of policies and practices of approximation.

The point is made even more strongly by Wilderson III (2020), developing the 'Afropessimist' critique that understands Black people as subjected on a continuing basis to the annihilatory violence of 'social death':

> The changes that begin to occur after the Civil War and up through the Civil Rights Movement, Black Power, and the American election of a Black president are merely changes in the weather. Despite the fact that the sadism is no longer played out in the open as it was in 1840, nothing essential has changed.
>
> (Wilderson III, 2020, p. 96)

If others, therefore, have 'made of us' (to borrow Sartre's phrase) mere approximators, then we must take a deep breath and clear our minds of that pervasive and pernicious fogginess,[3] and consider what a practice of equality might look like.

Equality, common humanity and racial inequality

It might at this point be objected that we have not yet defined equality, nor yet made the case for why it is a good to be pursued. As MacIntyre (1981) compellingly argues, if virtues and values can no longer be agreed in the post-Enlightenment (western) world, then no substantial or lasting consensus may be expected to cohere around pursuit of any one particular 'good'.

It is beyond the scope of this book to analyse that long tradition of philosophical, ethical and political debates around the idea of equality, whose lineage can be traced back to Aristotle (350 BCE), nor around the perception of tensions between the competing goods of equality, liberty and justice in political systems (see e.g. Rawls, 1971). Our rationale for bypassing what would otherwise be a very long preliminary exposition is that *our primary concern here is with the structural violence coterminous with societal inequalities, specifically racism and racial inequality, and the manifest and demonstrable harm this violence does.* The case for this has been clearly and conclusively made (James, 1938; Davis, 1981; Gilligan, 1996, 2011; Wilkinson and Pickett, 2009; Olusoga, 2016; Gentleman, 2019; Akala, 2019).

Our argument here is predicated upon the contention (one that is neither Metropolitan nor Cosmopolitan) that *we are all equal in our common humanity* and that practices of inequality are therefore taken up in defensive or hostile denial of that common humanity. This fundamental equality is a fact and a given; it is not some potential good, the merits of which we might debate, and then aspire, approximately or otherwise, to establish at some future date. Nor is it merely a right, to be accorded, upheld, eroded or removed, as the political winds change direction, whether locally or globally.

Our focus here is upon the specific inequalities of racism and, therefore, upon practices of equality as central to anti-racist practice. This focus, let us be clear, does not detract from the harm or significance of other intersecting structural inequalities such as (for example, and mindful of Butler's '*et cetera*') gender, class, sexuality, age and psycho-social disability. We defer here to Audre Lorde, who as we understand it was identifying not 'simply' as Black, but as a Black, gay, feminist socialist, and as a woman, daughter, mother and partner, when she wrote:

> I simply do not believe that one aspect of myself can possibly profit from the oppression of any other part of my identity.
>
> (Lorde, 1983, p. 219)[4]

However, we trust that the application to all issues of structural inequality, and to all relations and practices of domination, of the line of thought which we will set out here, will be readily apparent.[5]

Our own stance as two similar/different *white* men is that we intend *to try* to stand alongside our different/similar brothers and sisters everywhere, yet at the same time know, in our human frailty, that we will fail to achieve this: we will not get it right. When we do fail, we must undertake, as the great Irishman Samuel Beckett puts it, to "[t]ry again. Fail again. Fail better" (Beckett, 1983, p. 81).

'Race', racism, racialisation and racial trauma

> A belief in humanity is a belief in colored men [*sic*]. If the uplift of mankind must be done by men, then the destinies of this world will rest ultimately in the hands of darker nations.
> (Du Bois, 1903, p. 240 [our parenthesis, to acknowledge the gendered text])

Racism in its fully fledged modern form can be traced back to the middle third of the eighteenth century, in the wake of the scientific revolution and (paradoxically?) at the zenith of the Enlightenment, and as part of "a revolution in the way in which the human body was studied and observed in order to formulate scientific conclusions relating to human variability" (Bancel, David and Thomas, 2019, p. 11). The ideology (and the violence to body and

140 Reclaiming the agora

psyche) of modern racism emerged, we therefore suggest, out of commercial and political self-interest, enhanced and amplified along the way by the various threads of pseudo-science (such as phrenology and social Darwinism) that came to prominence at the height of Victorian imperialism in the second half of the nineteenth century (Olusoga, 2016) – and which therefore coincides with the rise to power of European medical-model psychiatry (Littlewood and Lipsedge, 1982).

This ideology holds to be axiomatic the claim that 'race'[6] is a scientifically established category located in biology – rather than merely a social construct. It further proclaims that perceived or imagined differences between one 'race' and another are a meaningful and legitimate basis for asserting superiority of one 'race' over another (or all others), and establishing relations of domination over that 'race' or those 'races' thus constructed as inferior (Dalal, 2002). The second claim cannot logically exist independently of the first, although the axiomatic claim could, in theory, exist without the second following from it.

> ... the term 'race' has no biological basis but continues to operate within a social-political context ... Race needs to be understood not as a biological difference with biological consequences, but as a categorisation of people, which has social consequences.
>
> (British Psychological Society, 2020, p. 4)

Lorde (1978) specifies, "the belief in the inherent superiority of one race over all others and thereby the right to dominance" (Lorde, 1978, p. 45). Carter and Scheuermann (2020) use the definition first offered by Jones and Carter (1996):

> Racism is the exercise of power against a racial group defined as inferior by individuals and institutions with the intentional and unintentional support of the entire (race or) culture.
>
> (Jones and Carter, 1996, p. 3; Carter and Scheuermann, 2020, p. 1)

The structural violence of racism and the prevalence of racist beliefs, attitudes and practices constitute an inescapably hostile environment for those subjected to its manifest and latent ordinances, embedded in Empire and the colonialist project, and manifesting in different ways and with differing degrees of severity at both local and global levels. This is the hostile environment in which people who are not racialised as white[7] have to live and make their way in the world. At the core of the ideology that underpins this hostility is the conviction that our common humanity within the species *homo sapiens* is not a given; that the stranger is not only frightening but has a lesser or an invalid claim upon membership. It constitutes a sub-speciation of those 'others'. It is the starting point from which stems and flows everything from day-to-day micro-aggressions

Practices of equality 141

through the denial of the legitimacy of indigenous languages to race hate crime, structural violence, imperialism, chattel slavery, lynching,[8] ethnic cleansing, genocide and other crimes against humanity.[9]

Du Bois (1903) proclaimed, "the problem of the Twentieth Century is the problem of the color-line" (p. 3), by which he meant, "the relation of the darker to the lighter races of men in Asia and Africa, in America and the islands of the sea" (ibid., p. 14). For Du Bois, the 'color-line' was a high wall across the top of which neither 'side' could truly perceive the experience of the other, but which created for Black people (and othered-others) a 'double-consciousness' in which was internalised and entrenched a set of harrowing and toxic ideas about the experience of being viewed by the white 'Other': "of measuring one's soul by the tape of a world that looks on in amused contempt and pity" (ibid., p. 7).

Stuart Hall (2018), in turn, reflecting on his experience growing up in Jamaica in the 1930s and 1940s, wrote of how colonialism, "bequeathed that most soul-destroying of legacies ... [i]t 'othered' us to ourselves" (ibid., p. 21). He further observed:

> Class discrimination and racialized differentiation were ubiquitous. I won't speculate here on what it does to a young person's head to have the mind furnished in this bizarre, pathological way.
>
> (Hall, 2018, p. 65)

James Baldwin concisely captures something of the hostile environment of racism in his novel *Another Country*, in which his two protagonists, Ida and Vivaldo, walk through the streets of New York – a Black woman with a white man – and "their passage raised small clouds of male and female hostility which blew into their faces like dust" (Baldwin, 1962, p. 147). And Maya Angelou, who met Du Bois in Ghana just before his death in 1963, gives her own direct testimony of what it was like for her to be one side of the 'color-line' in Arkansas, in the southern United States of the 1930s:

> In Stamps the segregation was so complete that most Black children didn't really, absolutely know what whites looked like. Other than that they were different, to be dreaded, and in that dread was included the hostility of the powerless against the powerful, the poor against the rich, the worker against the worked for and the ragged against the well dressed.
>
> I remember never believing that whites were really real.
>
> (Angelou, 1969, p. 27)

Whiteness

We have already seen in Part I of this book how the 'housed' came, over time, to define themselves more sharply in relation to the constructed category of 'the un-housed'. In the same way, the emergence (in the eighteenth century) of skin colour as a primary (supposed) determinant of identity and worth and the construction of Black-ness as equivalent to dangerousness, worthlessness and Other-ness (an inferior or even sub-human otherness) has led, among other disastrous consequences, to the emergence of a mostly (but not always) subliminally-held and self-reinforcing belief system built around the assumption of the 'good' of whiteness. As Du Bois drily observed, "[t]he discovery of personal whiteness among the world's peoples is a very modern thing" (Du Bois, 1903, p. 227).

'Race' is the creation of white people and whiteness is an offshoot of 'race'. The term 'race' in this usage may have originated in the Spanish word *raza*, used to differentiate animal breeds and then applied in the Middle Ages to Moorish and to Jewish populations (Fernando, 2017, p. 11). Although the Portuguese had started taking African people into slavery in the fifteenth century[10] (and although the practice of enslavement in various forms – not all of them as harsh and annihilatory as was Black chattel slavery in the Americas – goes back to ancient times), Black people were not exposed to '*racialised*' prejudice (notwithstanding manifest violence driven by superstition and xenophobia) until *ideological justification* for the slave trade was felt to be needed (a century or more after the trade itself had been established). The historical moment in which racism, in what would become the modern sense, is first enshrined in law arrives with the Barbados Slave Code of 1661:

> The Atlantic slave trade had taken Africans from numerous and widely differing cultures and ethnic groups and defined them en masse as 'negroes'. Now the pioneers of English plantation slavery ... ushered all Europeans, irrespective of their ethnic or social backgrounds, into the new category of 'white'; a term that had to be explained to newly arriving Europeans who were unfamiliar with the working of the new slave society.
>
> (Olusoga, 2016, p. 71)

On this view, nascent white European capitalism and imperialism (and the profits to be made from sugar, cotton and tobacco if labour costs were minimised) begat the Atlantic slave trade ("the fatal encounter of black sweat and white imperialism", in the words of Ngũgĩ wa Thiong'o (1977, p. 131)); the slave trade (gradually) begat 'race';[11] and 'race' (almost at once) begat whiteness (Kinouani, 2019), which then in turn generated anti-Blackness and intensified structural violence against 'blackened' bodies: "[o]n such a soil as San Domingo slavery, only a vicious society could flourish" (James, 1938, p. 22).

Kinouani (2019) defines whiteness as "the production and reproduction of the dominance, and privileges of people racialized as white" (Kinouani, 2019, p. 62). She goes on to add:

Whiteness holds its power by the ways in which it has become woven into the fabric of 'western' (and former colonized) societies, so that all aspects of 'our' culture, norms, and values centre and privilege white people ... Whiteness is not consciously known to white people who generally are not socialized to see it nor to understand they are racialized beings ...

(Kinouani, 2019, pp. 62–63)

Whiteness, therefore, reproduces power differentials and relations of domination and psycho-social traumatisation in the same way that 'free trade', capitalism or neo-liberalism does: by appearing not to be an ideology at all, by hiding in plain view, dressed up as the 'natural order of things'. The matter is incisively put by the character Gilbert Joseph when he confronts his landlord Bernard Bligh at the climax of Andrea Levy's *Small Island*:

"You know what your trouble is, man?" he said. "Your white skin. You think it makes you better than me ... But you know what it make you? ... It make you white. That is all, man. White ... Am I to be the servant and you the master for all time?"

(Levy, 2004, p. 525)

This supposed 'natural order of things' continues to obtain despite the observable phenomenon, also commented upon by many Black writers and leaders (see Lebron, 2019), that "the souls of white folk" (Du Bois, 1903) receive harm from racism and the maintenance of those power differentials – in much the same way that the consumer society is diminished and eroded by its own greed and ecocidal tendencies. Lebron (2019) shows, for example, how Martin Luther King Jr saw racism as "tragically destroying and warping the characters" of white people and "corrupt[ing] their moral sensibilities" (Lebron, 2019, p. 122). Carter and Scheuermann (2020) state that racism "harms both the perpetrator and the target, the oppressed as well as the oppressor" – although of course this harm is not evenly distributed (2020, p. 11). As Frederick Douglass wrote, in an open letter to his former slaveowner Thomas Auld:

Born and brought up in the presence and under the influence of a system which at once strikes at the very foundation of morals ... it is almost impossible that one so environed can greatly grow in virtuous rectitude.

(Douglass, 1849, p. 144, cited in Lebron, 2019, p. 19)

It should be clear that no shame whatsoever *need intrinsically* attach to the anatomical and literally superficial happenstance of having paler or darker skin (or any other supposed 'racial' signifier). Humankind could just as easily and just as randomly have got itself into a tangled knot of toxicity and violence about eye colour or height. But shame has nonetheless been generated down through the centuries, and it is there for white people in the 'race thinking' (Barzun, 1937); in the status of being accessory after the fact of slavery; in the complicity with the advantages of structural racism and the inheritance of privilege; in the often subliminal but never entirely unconscious awareness of those day-to-day micro-aggressions. This kind of shame, when it doesn't transmute into shameless and disinhibited violence, usually leads to 'white fragility' (DiAngelo, 2018) and the denial inherent in the idea that only *other* white people (less sophisticated, less educated, less civilised, less human whites) are racist; or that 'some of my best friends are Black'; or in the defensive, 'yes, but *all* lives matter' response to the #BlackLivesMatter movement.

The problem with this version of 'we're all in the same boat (but [in silent parenthesis] just on different decks)' was poignantly captured by Baldwin (1962) in the following conversation between Vivaldo and Cass, as they take a taxicab into Harlem to attend Rufus's funeral:

> "They're coloured and I'm white but the same things have happened, really the *same* things, and how can I make them know that?"
> "But they didn't", she said, "happen to you *because* you were white. They just happened. But what happens up here ... happens because they are coloured. And that makes a difference ... You'll be kissing a long time, my friend, before you kiss any of this away."
>
> (Baldwin, 1962, p. 117)

Racial trauma

James Joyce, addressing the colonial oppression of the Irish (a different example of racism from the main theme of this chapter but nonetheless evidencing the same kind of in-group colonial oppression), wrote that, "[w]hen the soul of a man is born in this country there are nets flung at it to hold it back from flight" (Joyce, 1916, p. 220). The contemporary, structurally violent state of racism is just such a net. It constitutes (as we have already noted) a hostile environment that provides a central example of processes of psychosocial (re-)traumatisation. To reiterate part of our definition from Chapter 1, this specifically means that the 'remedy', if one may be found, does not lie in the Clinic, for the 'ailment' is not located in the individual psyche. As Fanon (1952) states, "[s]ince the racial drama is played out in the open, the black man has no time to 'unconsciousnessize' it" (Fanon, 1952, p. 129).

In the United States, 20% of Black Americans live in poverty, compared to 8% of white Americans (and 22% of Native American peoples) (Resler, 2019, p. 4). More African American adults are under legal coercion within the criminal justice system than were enslaved in 1850, and one in nine African American children has a parent in prison, against one in 56 white children (Resler, 2019, p. 5) – this is why activist researchers now speak of the 'school-to-prison pipeline':

Baltimore put more of its focus into building things down town instead of building communities around town ... they don't want certain people down there, poor people, so it just shows the city would rather build a new prison or jail than open up the rec centers, *so it's alright for your child to go from middle school to elementary school to prison rather than to college.*

(Gardnel Carter, interviewed in Stopford, 2020, p. 49 [our italics])

In a survey of 800 African American people (NPR, 2017), 40% reported experiences of people being afraid of them because of their skin colour (this figure includes 57% of Black men); 51% had been subjected to racial slurs; 60% reported having been unfairly stopped by police (down to 49% in urban areas, but rising to 67% in suburban areas); and 42% of all Black respondents had been subjected to racial violence (NPR, 2017).

Among 16- to 24-year-olds in the UK, unemployment rates from 2018–2019 were twice as high for people from a Black background (20%) as from a white background (House of Commons Library, 2020). Black women are five times more likely than white women to die in childbirth in the UK (House of Commons/House of Lords, 2020); Black men are five times more likely than white men to be murdered (Kumar, Sherman and Strang 2020). Ethnic inequalities in mental health care generally are now well documented (Synergi Collaborative Centre, 2018). From 2017–2018, Black or Black British people (in the terms in which this data is collected) were more than four times more likely than white people to be detained under the Mental Health Act; and Community Treatment Orders (for coercive mental health treatment plans for patients released from hospital) were used on eight times as many 'Black or Black British' as on white patients (NHS Digital, 2018). More than three quarters of Black people in the UK do not believe their human rights enjoy equal protection with those of white people and 85% do not believe they would receive equal treatment from the police force (House of Commons/House of Lords, 2020).

The COVID-19 pandemic has acted as a magnifying glass to these, as to many other, structural fault lines in our society. Black and other minority ethnic people in the UK have been found to be at increased risk of acquiring the infection (because they are more likely to live in urban areas, in over-crowded households,[12] in deprived areas, and be in jobs that expose them to higher risk, especially higher viral load) and increased risk of poor outcomes consequent upon becoming infected (for example, because of the prevalence of pre-morbid conditions such as hyper-tension) (Public Health England, 2020, p. 40; Lawrence, 2020).

In recent times greater attention has started to be paid, within the clinic and beyond, to identifying and assessing the particular impact of different kinds of overt and covert racism upon people who are exposed to the hostile environment they generate: the micro-aggressions and day-to-day hostilities of

Baldwin's constant 'dust in the face', the structural disadvantages and discrimination that follows upon it, and also the impact of particular eruptions of racist violence against the person. Carter (2007) and Williams, Printz and DeLapp (2018) have both offered rating scales for assessing this newly cohering concept of racial trauma (also referred to as 'race-based trauma' or 'race-based traumatic stress'). Carter's model explores reactions to 'race'-based events that are experienced as "sudden, out of one's control, and emotionally painful" (Carter, 2007, p. 3; see also Carter and Scheuermann, 2020). Williams and her colleagues define racial trauma as "a traumatic response to an accumulation of negative race-related experiences" (Williams, Printz and DeLapp, 2018, p. 2):

> As race is a social construct, these experiences are always linked to racism (as opposed to a natural disaster or random violence), where racism can be defined as prejudice, discrimination, and violence against a subordinate racial group based on attitudes of superiority by the dominant group.[13]
>
> (Ibid.)

Racism, therefore, generates processes of psycho-social (re-)traumatisation, individually and collectively, as daily insult is added to profound bodily injury. We are talking here of continuous traumatisation, in which there is yet to be a moment in time in which the 'post-traumatic' impact can be reflected back upon: the (re-)traumatisation is ongoing (see, e.g., Goldhill, 2019). These recent developments and refinements in the way that racial trauma is thought about and evaluated illuminate the responsibility of all white people to change their habits and patterns and practices. There is no room for manoeuvre left in which to deny the traumatising and re-traumatising impact of all of our ways of being in the world, or the necessity of sharing that world on terms of equality and respect with our fellow human beings.

Equality, empowerment and emancipation

> Must we blame God because He made of one blood all people that dwell on earth but went to sleep during the firing when some millions were tanned yellow, some brown, and some even black … The concept of Equality as it is the genuine product of the idea of inherent value in the individual derived from the essential worth of Humanity must be before all else unquestionably of universal application.
>
> (Cooper, 1925, pp. 296–297)

In division 49 of the vast Parisian necropolis of Père Lachaise, visitors may pass along the rows of stones and monuments without particularly noticing the tomb of Joseph Jacotot (1770–1840). The inscription, now somewhat faded, reads as follows: "*Je crois que Dieu a créé l'âme humaine capable de s'instruire seule et sans maître*" ("I believe that God created the human soul capable of learning by itself, without a teacher" [our translation]).

Jacotot's story is inventively retold and re-imagined by the contemporary French philosopher Jacques Rancière (1987). Jacotot was a teacher and administrator who had served in the French Republican armies in 1792 and as a deputy in Dijon in the last year of Napoleon's rule. The return of the Bourbon monarchy in 1815 meant that Jacotot had to go into exile, and thus he found himself, in 1818, in the city of Louvain, near Brussels, lecturing in French at the university there. He may perhaps have hoped for the quiet academic life: a gentle sinecure. However, Jacotot's lectures were so popular that many students who spoke only Flemish clamoured to study under him – and yet he spoke only French.

Jacotot decided to conduct an experiment. He came across a bilingual French/Flemish edition of a late seventeenth century account of the travels of Telemachus, the son of Odysseus (Homer, 8th Century BCE), and his guide Mentor (Fénelon, 1699). Here, then, was common ground upon which to build a project of learning. Jacotot discovered, to his surprise, that not only was it thus possible for the Flemish-speaking students to understand the text of *Télémaque* in French, by deriving it from the Flemish, but that they could then write, in Fénelon's immaculate French, about their understanding of the text.

Jacotot had thus accidentally discovered that if he discarded the value which he had been attaching to the power differential between himself and his pupils, he could enable them to learn French, even though he spoke no Flemish. More precisely, he could help them to emancipate themselves from the subjugation that flows from the idea that they could not learn French without a Master's learned explication and expert methodology.

> Experience forces Jacotot to acknowledge, against everything he has been taught, that learning does not require explanations, that it can take place without teaching. What is more, as his students learned French without his teaching it, Jacotot guesses that anyone can teach things he or she does not know.
>
> (Morlock, 1997, p. 109)

Jacotot's experience and authority as a professional teacher had been irrelevant to the quality and extent of the learning that had ensued. The only concepts that had mattered turned out to be the ideas inscribed by Fénelon and his translator upon the pages of the edition of *Télémaque*. He concluded that one can teach what one does not know, that the role of the 'master' in relation to the 'pupil' needed to be rethought (although not abolished: his was not a doctrine of autodidacticism (Morlock, 1997)), and that he had stumbled upon a discovery – specifically, in Jacotot's thinking, the equality of intelligences – that could change the world.

148 Reclaiming the agora

Rancière develops Jacotot's argument that all of humankind is born with an equal intelligence that is vested in our common humanity. He argues that equality "cannot be demonstrated through induction or deduction; it can only be verified locally and problematically in *practice*" (Deranty and Ross, 2012, p. 1 [our italics]). A remedy is needed for the "juiceless, abstract intellectuality of the universities" (Berry, 1993, p. 35) and the tendency to stultify or stupefy (*abrutir*, in French) that is inherent in the Master's appropriation of the alienating role of explication (in order to cement his own position of authority and power). This remedy, we are arguing, lies in processes of (intellectual) *emancipation* realised and established in a shared *praxis* centred upon the idea of 'radical equality' (Deranty and Ross, 2012). In Rancière's words, the potentiality here is "that every common person might conceive his human dignity, take the measure of his intellectual capacity, and decide how to use it" (Rancière, 1987, p. 17).

Following Jacotot, Rancière critiques, by extension, processes of social inclusion predicated upon the ideology of (pedagogical) *empowerment*, in which equality is constructed as a goal to be worked towards. He dismisses these various projects of empowerment across the power differential as self-serving variants of what the contemporary reader might recognise as 'trickle-down theory': "[W]hoever teaches without emancipating stultifies" (Rancière, 1987, p. 18). Whatever may have been the good intentions of the different parties involved in the gradualist projects of social inclusion we have been examining, we therefore suggest that the outcome of such projects is the reinforcement of hierarchies of oppression in which the subaltern may not speak (Spivak, 1988) and not even the Master may meaningfully think his own thoughts. Projects of 'empowerment' ultimately only empower those who are already powerful. Paolo Freire (1970), who was himself highly influenced by the writings of Frantz Fanon, approached a similar paradox from a slightly different angle when he asked, "How can the oppressed … participate in developing the pedagogy of their liberation?" (Freire, 1970, p. 30). He goes on to suggest, "As long as they live in the duality in which *to be* is *to be like*, and *to be like* is *to be like the oppressor*, this contribution is impossible" (ibid.).

We therefore propose to bring Rancière's philosophical and political perspective to bear upon the problem of racism and racial trauma, and what Lamming identifies as the opposition between "White instruction and Black imagination" (Lamming, 1953, p. xi). Rather than endlessly engage in 'empowering' projects to *reduce* racial inequality or to mitigate its deleterious consequences, what is indicated (*if* one is to eschew revolutionary violence – a point to which we shall return) is to make an *emancipatory* move (we shall come back directly to the question of who might make it). "Unequal society does not carry any equal society in its womb" (Rancière, 2005, p. 96): on this view, there's no merit or mileage in waiting around for society to give birth to it.

There are no madmen except those who insist on inequality and domination ... Reason begins when discourses organized with the goal of being right cease, begins where equality is recognized: not an equality decreed by law or force, not a passively received equality, but an equality in act ...

(Rancière, 1987, p. 72)

Anti-racism and practices of radical equality

We hold these truths to be self-evident ... That *whenever any Form of Government becomes destructive of these ends, it is the Right of the People to alter or to abolish it* ...

(Declaration of Independence, 1776 [our italics])

It's time to stop singing and start swinging.

(Malcolm X, 1964)

It is, therefore, open to us (we would say, incumbent upon us) to assume equality from the outset, as Diogenes did when he asked Alexander to step out of his light; to make equality our starting point and not know our destination (rather than to construe equality as our destination but not know how to get there from here). It is open to us to turn the "practical verification of equality" (Deranty and Ross, 2012, p. 1) into the foundation stone of our practice; and then to observe both how our practice develops from being thus reconstituted and also how that practice may then differently impact upon the world around us.

Rancière (2005) offers, as an example of such moves ("singular and precarious acts", as he describes them (ibid., p. 97)), a pivotal moment in the American civil rights movement. This was the moment on December 1st, 1955, when Rosa Parks, riding a Montgomery bus in the days of Jim Crow segregation, refused to move to the back section of the bus (to make way for a white man) after the bus driver instructed her to do so. Parks had recognised the driver (whose name was James Blake) as the very same white man who had cynically prevented her boarding a similar bus back in 1943. Parks was arrested after she told Blake that she didn't think she should have to make way. This was, in effect, her 'Bartleby' moment (see Chapter 4). She was asked to move and 'preferred not to'; she preferred instead to assume and proceed from equal terms with everyone else on the bus. Parks later rejected the (racist) imputation that she had been too tired to move, saying that "the only tired I was, was tired of giving in" (Parks and Haskins, 1992, p. 116).

Parks was at the time of her act of resistance already an experienced and seasoned activist, and earlier that year she had attended a workshop on race relations and, specifically, on racial equality at the Highlander Folk School in

150 Reclaiming the agora

Tennessee: she was well aware of the creative possibilities of civil disobedience. Of her experience at the Highlander workshop, she said that this was "the first time in my life I had lived in *an atmosphere of complete equality* with the members of the other race" (Williams, 2002, p. 66 [our italics]). The Montgomery city ordinances, and the racist practices that had developed there (and elsewhere) in their wake, enshrined a socio-political inequality and imposed a pervasive lived experience of oppression and exclusion. However, Parks, in that moment, by publicly adopting and performing an anti-racist practice of equality in the agora – as we would wish to put it here – catalysed a radical shift in those previously established socio-political 'realities'.

****

Rosa Parks was a woman of greatness whose name shall not be forgotten. At the same time, the example of how she embraced and embodied a practice of radical equality is only one among many. In terms of our Diogenes Paradigm, the happenstance of the subsequent fame and historical significance of her 'Bartlebian' moment of resistance stems not only from the moral courage of her particular deed but from the way her case was taken up in the courts by the burgeoning civil rights movement. Practices of radical equality are crucially important, whatever the sequel. We should also remember that although the episode is famous for leading to a change in the law, this does not mean that practices of *inequality* in this specific domain were thereby abolished. This is what Rancière (1987) is getting at when he emphasises equality in act over equality in law.

Moreover, although her story illuminates the argument we are making here, and many contemporary Rosa Parks are similarly declining to go along with micro- and macro- aggressions of different kinds, we need to alter the perspective by imagining what might be the consequence if our contemporary James Blakes and the in-group they serve were to decide that they would no longer, in effect, uphold the structural inequality from which they have so long benefitted. In other words, we-the-authors need to be clear that the moral responsibility to change and the challenge to practice equality must lie with we-the-oppressors and not be projected on to those we subjugate (who will take their own view, and not need *our* help to do so).

A better plan by far would be to challenge ourselves to dismantle inequality by relinquishing our own power – as the figure of Jacotot does in our reading of the story when he recognises that the technologies he would instinctively bring to bear upon the task in fact obstruct it (although the historical Jacotot did not relinquish his post). Light pours out into the night from the doorway of Equality: but there are doormen in the shadows to either side, and a sign above the lintel which still says 'Members Only'.[14] *We need actively to make equality the ground and premise of all our encounters.*

Fanon averred that "[d]ecolonization, which sets out to change the order of the world, is, obviously, a programme of complete disorder" (Fanon, 1961, p. 27), and we can conceive of no more conclusive retort to the ethos of 'approximation' and gradualism. Order demands to be disordered and, of course, contains the seeds of disorder within it. Empires fall as well as rise. #BlackLivesMatter proclaim by way of strategy the "ongoing fight to end State-sanctioned violence, liberate Black people, and end white supremacy forever" (Black Lives Matter, 2020). And we might also recall these words of Haile Selassie (1963) in his speech to the United Nations; words which were famously recaptured in the track 'War' by Bob Marley and the Wailers (Marley, 1976), iterating this fundamental reality:

> [t]hat until the philosophy which holds one race superior and another inferior is finally and permanently discredited and abandoned; … That until the color of a man's skin is of no more significance than the color of his eyes; That until the basic human rights are equally guaranteed to all without regard to race; That until that day, the dream of lasting peace and world citizenship and the rule of international morality will remain but a fleeting illusion, to be pursued but never attained.
>
> (Selassie, 1963)

Confronted with these authorities, we can only say that we must listen closely to and learn from what the strategy or tactics of our Black comrades might be. At the same time, the question for us is what *our* strategy should be (allies we might be, but white European male middle-class professionals we nonetheless are). We understand that *"the master's tools will never dismantle the master's house"*, as Audre Lorde taught (Lorde, 1979b, p. 112 [italics in the original]). The 'British' gradualist or reformist model of turning Empire into Commonwealth while continuing to plunder and to diminish is clearly no model to follow. Neither will it suffice 'merely' to sit on committees, to call out structural violence and to 'no-platform' conferences where only white speakers are on the programme, to pull down the statues of the slavers; meaningful though these kinds of move may be in their own way. Toni Morrison cogently remarked that the world "will not become unracialised by assertion" (cited in Baird, 2021). We (this same white 'we') must acknowledge the ways in which our own moral sensibilities have been corrupted, to borrow again from Lebron (2019), by the way in which we have stood or trampled upon the shoulders of our fellow human beings who are Black.

James Joyce's Dedalus (Joyce, 1916) affirms that "I will not serve that in which I no longer believe", and that he will defend his practice with "silence, exile, and cunning" (Joyce, 1916, pp. 268–269). We take this first part of what he says to mean that we must first of all own and then repudiate our own racism – and therefore also embrace and uphold a practice of equality in all our doings. As we will explore further in Chapter 9, we urgently need to 'go along with stuff less and get out more' – as Rosa Parks did; but in our case, this move would be made from positions of relative power and privilege rather than adversity and oppression. We

152 Reclaiming the agora

are not limited to 'silence, exile, and cunning': other moves are open to us. This is a responsibility we must not duck.

However, the in-group does not give up power, although it is adept at appearing to do so. It relies heavily upon "the patience and forbearance of the poor" (James, 1938, p. 299). We-the-authors are sufficiently implicated in its manoeuvring to know that it will not go against its own prime functioning – which, as we have argued throughout this book, is to hold onto power by defining, excluding and oppressing the out-group – no matter how many people take to the streets of its capital cities to protest.

White people, in short, don't seem to be any hurry to give up their (our) power. This is a truth that C.L.R. James knew when he drew the links between the radical revolutionary Jacobins of the 1790s in Paris and Toussaint L'Ouverture in Haiti:

> The monarchy in France had to be torn up by the roots. Those in power never give way, and admit defeat only to plot and scheme to regain their lost power and privilege.
>
> (James, 1938, p. 104)

If we don't give up our power – and if the Haitian and Cuban Revolutions are the pertinent precedents – and if Fanon was right to urge 'complete disorder' – and if Malcolm X was right to suggest that it's more than past 'time to start swinging' – then it may be that we must prepare ourselves to see power taken *necessarily* and more or less violently from us. "Scorched earth and some replanting, in the hope something good might grow", as Steve McQueen has it in the closing scenes of *Red, White and Blue* (2020). We can't be bystanders, keeping our fingers crossed that some Rosa Parks will hold fast and not surrender her ground: we need to stop pushing her around in the first place.

Notes

1 The recent report from the (UK) Commission on Race and Ethnic Disparities (2021) spectacularly suggested that there is "a new story about the Caribbean experience which speaks to *the slave period not only being about profit and suffering but how culturally African people transformed themselves into a re-modelled African/Britain*" (2021, p. 8 [our italics]); and concluded that "we no longer see a Britain where the system is deliberately rigged against ethnic minorities" (*ibid.*). A violent and provocative disavowal of the lived experience of multitudes, therefore – and a concise and conclusive demonstration of the argument against pervasive and pernicious reformism, if ever one were needed. In the face of a storm of protest, the Commission amended the line about slavery with a 'clarifying' footnote (Mohdin, 2021).
2 In validation of that concern, we have, here and elsewhere, acknowledged both our own personal and professional investment in the Democratic Therapeutic Community (DTC) project in the UK, in which we both participated around the turn of the century – and our recognition, not only that the DTCs were shut down, and

Practices of equality 153

then forgotten, but also that there was something self-inflicted around their demise that predicted exactly this oblivion.

3 By the time that the US Constitution was drafted, a decade after Independence, much of that ambiguity had congealed. When the population of a given State came to be calculated, a slave was counted as three fifths of a (free) person, and a Native American did not count at all: 'Representatives and direct Taxes shall be apportioned among the several States which may be included within this Union, *according to their respective Numbers, which shall be determined by adding to the whole Number of free Persons, including those bound to Service for a Term of Years, and excluding Indians not taxed, three fifths of all other Persons*' (Constitution of the United States (1789) Article 1 Section 2 [our italics]).

   Similar 'calculations' were applied to the maintenance and labour costs and relative 'productivity' of slaves considered as 'chattel' (Davis, 1981, p. 3) in much the same way as were beasts of the field, constructed as "a herd of subhuman labor units" (*ibid.*, p. 12). It is important for context also to note that in the early 1770s, slaves made up fully one fifth of the entire population of the American colonies (Olusoga, 2016, p. 145).

4 See also the following extract from the mission statement of #BlackLivesMatter: 'We are a collective of liberators who believe in an inclusive and spacious movement. We also believe that in order to win and bring as many people with us along the way, we must move beyond the narrow nationalism that is all too prevalent in Black communities. We must ensure we are building a movement that brings all of us to the front' (Black Lives Matter, 2020). For intersections of gender, 'race' and class in the United States, see Davis (1981).

5 Mention must here be made of the structural inequalities in the 'psy' professions – psychiatry, psychology and psychotherapy – and their impact upon the provision of health and social care. There are longstanding issues in terms of access to these professions and the invisible 'glass ceilings' or 'snowy white peaks' blocking advancement, as well as the maintenance of and collusion with structural racism and inequalities of different kinds in service user access to health and social care. For discussions of racism in the 'psy' professions, see Tate, 1996; Fernando, 2017; Stopford, 2020. For the recent statement of apology of the American Psychiatric Association (APA) for its active support of structural racism, see APA (2021).

6 To foreground and underpin this understanding, in this book we use the word 'race' in inverted commas, except where quoting from a text. In this usage we follow the example and authority of many other commentators before us (see, e.g., Gilroy, 1987; Lewis, 2000; Fernando, 2017).

7 Our focus in this chapter is on racism as it arises out of ideologies of white supremacy. We should here acknowledge, as many other commentators do, that it is not only white people and white societies who get caught up in the toxicity of racism. Much of what we have to say pertains to all kinds of racisms – and racists – but our primary concern here is with the depredations which are perpetrated, to borrow from Viet Thanh Nguyen (2016), by "the most dangerous creature in the history of the world, the white man in a suit" (Nguyen, 2016, p. 326). We also acknowledge the 'Afropessimist' argument put forward by Wilderson III, which cuts through both Lorde's intersectionality and Butler's '*et cetera*' by stating flatly that "Blacks are the sentient beings *against which Humanity is defined*" (Wilderson III, 2020, p. 167 [italics in the original]).

8 Lebron (2019) suggests that more than 3400 Black Americans were murdered by means of the practice of lynching between 1862 (when the Emancipation Proclamation was signed) and 1968 (shortly after Black Americans were finally released in law, in 1964 and 1965, from the tyrannies of 'Jim Crow' segregation and disenfranchisement) (Lebron, 2019, p. 3; see also Davis, 1981). The sequence of violent

deaths of Black Americans at the hands of US police forces, which led to the emergence of the Black Lives Matter movement, can be understood as continuing to add to that grim tally of what Lebron calls "horrific acts of violence in the form of racial resentment and terror masquerading as justice" (*ibid.*); although an important counter-argument holds that the unique horrors of lynching should not be diluted by being used as an analogy.

9 Here we are reminded of Douglas's (2002) link to notions of 'dirt' – which is matter that is not in its proper place and so faces the ever-present danger of being tidied away: cleaned – or perhaps even cleansed. For a compelling legal discussion of the relationship between genocide and crimes against humanity in the context of racial/ethnic cleansing, see Sands (2016).

10 Wilderson III (2020) gives 625 CE as the beginning of the Arab slave trade and 1452 as the start date for the European slave trade; therefore, for more than 1200 years, "everyone south of the Sahara had to negotiate captivity" (Wilderson III, 2020, p. 302). The English didn't begin to muscle their way into the slave trade until the second half of the sixteenth century, after Henry VIII's excommunication in 1538 had rendered irrelevant the continuing Papal protection of the Portuguese traders. It wasn't until the first quarter of the seventeenth century that the demand for labour in the sugar plantations of Britain's new Caribbean colonies generated a sustainable 'market' for slaves. It wasn't until the accession to the throne of Charles II in 1660 and his creation in 1672 of the Royal African Company that the British royal family formalised the 'triangular' slave trade (Olusoga, 2016).

11 In 1858, the year of the Lincoln-Douglas debate on slavery, equality and the Constitution, the following argument in 'justification' of the intersection between free trade economics and slavery was offered in the Senate by the slaveowner James Henry Hammond: 'In all social systems there must be a class to do the menial duties, to perform the drudgery of life … Such a class you must have, or you would not have that other class which leads progress, civilization and refinement. It constitutes the very mud-sill of society … Fortunately for the South, she found a race adapted to that purpose to her hand. A race inferior to her own, but eminently qualified … to answer all her purposes. We use them for our purpose, and call them slaves'(Rodriguez, 2007, p. 666; cited in Olusoga, 2016, p. 346).

12 Black households accounted for 26% of all overcrowded households in the UK between 2016 and 2019, and a further 22% were identified as of either white/Black African or white/Black Caribbean mixed heritage; only 2% of all overcrowded households were classified as White British (Cabinet Office, 2020). For the impact of housing policies driven by the pursuit of racial segregation in the United States, see Stopford, 2020.

13 The 'Race-Based Traumatic Stress Symptom Scale' categorises traumatised responses under the headings of depression, intrusive thoughts, anger, hypervigilance, physical health issues, low self-esteem and avoidant behaviour (Carter, 2007, p. 6). The 'Trauma Symptoms of Discrimination Scale' assesses "uncontrollable distress and hyperarousal, feelings of alienation from others, worries about bad things happening in the future, and perceptions that others are dangerous" (Williams, Printz and DeLapp, 2018, p. 10).

14 George Lamming (1953), in the final crescendo of his classic novel, *In the castle of my skin*, has the character Trumper dissect and denounce the particularly English way of running a racist empire (the 'great administrators'): 'There be clubs which you an' me can't go to, an' none o' my people here, no matter who they be, but they don't tell us we can't. They put up a sign, "Members Only," knowin' full well you ain't got no chance o' becomin' a member. An' although we know from the start why we can't go, we got the consolation we can't 'cause we ain't members' (Lamming, 1953, p. 332).

References

Akala (2019) *Natives: Race and class in the ruins of empire.* London: John Murray Press.

APA (2021) 'APA's apology to Black, Indigenous and People of Color for its support of structural racism in psychiatry'. Available at: https://www.psychiatry.org/news room/apa-apology-for-its-support-of-structural-racism-in-psychiatry (Accessed: 23 January 2021).

Angelou, M. (1969) *I know why the caged bird sings.* Reprinted 2007. London: Virago.

Aristotle (350 BCE) *Ethics.* Translated by J.A.K. Thomson, 1955. London: Penguin Classics.

Baird, R.P. (2021) 'The invention of whiteness: The long history of a dangerous idea', *The Guardian*, 20 April. Available at: https://www.theguardian.com/news/2021/apr/20/the-invention-of-whiteness-long-history-dangerous-idea (Accessed: 25 April 2021).

Baldwin, J. (1962) *Another country.* Reprinted 1990. London: Penguin Modern Classics.

Bancel, N., David, T., and Thomas, D. (eds) (2019) *The invention of race: Scientific and popular representations.* London: Routledge.

Barzun, J. (1937) *Race: A study in modern superstition.* New York: Harcourt, Brace, and Company.

Beckett, S. (1983) 'Worstward ho', in Van Hulle, D. (ed.) (2009) *Company; Ill seen, ill said; Worstward ho; Stirrings still.* London: Faber and Faber, pp. 79–103.

Berry, W. (1993) *Sex, economy, freedom & community: Eight essays.* Reprinted 2018. Berkeley, CA: Counterpoint.

Black Lives Matter (2020) Available at: https://blacklivesmatter.com/ (Accessed: 6 January 2021).

British Psychological Society (2020) 'Racial and social inequalities: Taking the conversations forward'. Division of Clinical Psychology. Available at: https://www.bps.org.uk/sites/www.bps.org.uk/files/Member%20Networks/Divisions/DCP/Racial%20and%20Social%20Inequalities%20in%20the%20times%20of%20Covid-19.pdf (Accessed: 6 January 2021).

Butler, J. (1990) *Gender trouble.* Reprinted 2006. London: Routledge Classics.

Cabinet Office (2020) 'Overcrowded households'. Available at: https://www.ethnicity-facts-figures.service.gov.uk/housing/housing-conditions/overcrowded-households/latest (Accessed: 6 January 2021).

Carter, R.T. (2007) 'Racism and psychological and emotional injury: Recognizing and assessing race-based traumatic stress', *The Counseling Psychologist*, 35, pp. 13–105.

Carter, R.T. and Scheuermann, T.D. (2020) *Confronting racism: Integrating mental health research into legal strategies and reforms.* New York, NY: Routledge.

Commission on Race and Ethnic Disparities (2021) 'The report of the commission on race and ethnic disparities'. Available at: https://www.gov.uk/government/publications/the-report-of-the-commission-on-race-and-ethnic-disparities (Accessed: 15 April 2021).

Constitution of the United States (1789) Available at: https://constitution.congress.gov/constitution/ (Accessed: 6 January 2021).

Cooper, A.J. (1925) 'Equality of race and the democratic movement', in Lemert, C. and Bahan, E. (eds) (1988) *The voice of Anna Julia Cooper.* New York, NY: Rowman and Littlefield, pp. 291–298.

Dalal, F. (2002) *Race, colour and the processes of racialisation.* London: Routledge.

Davis, A.Y. (1981) *Women, race and class*. Reprinted 2019. London: Penguin Modern Classics.

Declaration of Independence (1776) 'The unanimous declaration of the thirteen United States of America'. Declaration Resources Project, Harvard University. Available at: https://declaration.fas.harvard.edu/resources/text (Accessed: 9 January 2021).

Deranty, J.-P. and Ross, A. (eds) (2012) *Jacques Rancière and the contemporary scene: The philosophy of radical equality*. London: Continuum.

DiAngelo, R. (2018) *White fragility*. London: Penguin.

Douglas, M. (2002) *Purity and danger*. London: Routledge.

Douglass, F. (1849) 'To Capt. Thomas Auld, formerly my master', in Foner, R.S. (ed.) (1975) *Frederick Douglass: Selected speeches and writings*. Chicago: Lawrence Hill Books, pp. 143–145.

Du Bois, W.E.B. (1903) *The souls of Black folk; with 'The talented tenth' and 'The souls of white folk'*. Reprinted 2018. London: Penguin Classics.

Fanon, F. (1952) *Black skins, white masks*. Translated by R. Philcox, 2008. New York, NY: Grove Press.

Fanon, F. (1961) *The wretched of the earth*. Translated by C. Farrington, 2001. London: Penguin Modern Classics.

Fénelon, F. (1699) 'Les aventures de Télémaque suivies des aventures d'Aritonoüs'. Available at: http://www.gutenberg.org/files/30779/30779-h/30779-h.htm (Accessed: 6 January 2021).

Fernando, S. (2017) *Institutional racism in psychiatry and clinical psychology*. London: Palgrave Macmillan.

Foucault, M. (1976) 'Two lectures'. Translated by A. Fontana and P. Pasquino, in Gordon, C. (ed.) (1980) *Power/knowledge: Selected interviews and other writings 1972–1977*. New York: Pantheon, pp. 78–108.

Freire, P. (1970) *Pedagogy of the oppressed*. Translated by M.B. Ramos, 1996. London: Penguin.

Gentleman, A. (2019) *The Windrush betrayal: Exposing the hostile environment*. London: Faber and Faber.

Gilligan, J. (1996) *Violence: Reflections on our deadliest epidemic*. Reprinted 2000. London: Jessica Kingsley Publishers.

Gilligan, J. (2011) *Why some politicians are more dangerous than others*. Cambridge: Polity.

Gilroy, P. (1987) *There ain't no black in the Union Jack*. Reprinted 2002. London: Routledge Classics.

Goldhill, O. (2019) 'Palestine's head of mental health services says PTSD is a western concept', *Quartz*, 13 January. Available at: https://qz.com/1521806/palestines-head-of-mental-health-services-says-ptsd-is-a-western-concept/ (Accessed: 10 February 2021).

Hall, S. (2018) *Familiar stranger: A life between two islands*. London: Penguin.

Homer (8th Century BCE) *The Odyssey*. Translated by E.V. Rieu, 1946. Reprinted 1959. London: Penguin Classics.

House of Commons Library (2020) 'Unemployment by ethnic background'. Briefing Paper Number 6385, 19 February 2020. Available at: https://dera.ioe.ac.uk//35096/1/SN06385.pdf (Accessed: 6 January 2021).

House of Commons/House of Lords Joint Committee on Human Rights (2020) 'Black people, racism and human rights'. Eleventh Report of Session 2019–2021. HC 559;

HL Paper 165. Available at: https://committees.parliament.uk/work/409/black-peop le-racism-and-human-rights/ (Accessed: 6 January 2021).

James, C.L.R. (1938) *The Black Jacobins*. Reprinted 2001. London: Penguin.

Jones, J. and Carter, R.T. (1996) 'Racism and racial identity: Merging realities', in Bowser, B.P. and Hunt, R.G. (eds) *Impacts of racism on White Americans*. 2nd edition. Newbury, CA: Sage, pp. 1–24.

Joyce, J. (1916) *A portrait of the artist as a young man*. Reprinted 2000. London: Penguin Classics.

Kinouani, G. (2019) 'Difference, whiteness and the group analytic matrix: An integrated formulation', *Group Analysis*, 53 (1), pp. 60–74.

Kumar, S., Sherman, L.W., and Strang, H. (2020) 'Racial disparities in homicide victimisation rates: How to improve transparency by the Office of National Statistics in England and Wales', *Cambridge Journal of Evidence-Based Policing*, 2020. doi:10.1007/s41887-020-00055-y.

Lamming, G. (1953) *In the castle of my skin*. Reprinted 2016. London: Penguin Modern Classics.

Lawrence, D. (2020) 'An avoidable crisis: The disproportionate impact of covid-19 on Black, Asian and minority ethnic communities'. The Doreen Lawrence Review. Available at: https://www.lawrencereview.co.uk/ (Accessed: 6 January 2021).

Lebron, C.J. (2019) *The making of Black Lives Matter: A brief history of an idea*. New York, NY: Oxford University Press.

Levy, A. (2004) *Small island*. Reprinted 2017. London: Tinder.

Lewis, G. (2000) *'Race', gender, social welfare: Encounters in a postcolonial society*. Cambridge: Polity.

Lincoln, A. (1858) 'Abraham Lincoln (1809–1865): Political debates between Lincoln and Douglas 1897'. Available at: https://www.bartleby.com/251/pages/page415.html (Accessed: 6 January 2021).

Littlewood, R. and Lipsedge, M. (1982) *Aliens and alienists: Ethnic minorities and psychiatry*. London: Penguin.

Lorde, A. (1978) 'Scratching the surface: Some notes on barriers to women and loving', in Lorde, A. and Boreano, N. (eds) *Sister Outsider: Essays and speeches*. Berkeley: Crossing Press, pp. 45–52.

Lorde, A. (1979a) 'Sexism: An American disease in blackface', in Lorde, A. and Boreano, N. (eds) *Sister Outsider: Essays and speeches*. Berkeley: Crossing Press, pp. 60–65.

Lorde, A. (1979b) 'The master's tools will never dismantle the master's house', in Lorde, A. and Boreano, N. (eds) *Sister Outsider: Essays and speeches*. Berkeley: Crossing Press, pp. 110–113.

Lorde, A. (1983) 'There is no hierarchy of oppressions', in Bird, R., Cole, J.B., and Guy-Sheftall, B. (eds) (2009) *I am your Sister: Collected and unpublished writings of Audre Lorde*. New York: Oxford University Press, pp. 219–220.

MacIntyre, A. (1981) *After virtue*. Reprinted 2014. London: Bloomsbury.

Marley, B. (1976) 'War', from Rastaman vibration. LP. New York, NY: Island Records.

Mohdin (2021) 'UK race commission amends line on slave trade after criticism', *The Guardian*, 30 April. Available at: https://www.theguardian.com/world/2021/apr/30/uk-ra ce-commission-amends-line-on-slave-trade-after-criticism (Accessed: 30 April 2021).

Morlock, F. (1997) 'The story of the ignorant schoolmaster', *Oxford Literary Review*, 19 (1/2), pp. 105–132.

Nguyen, V.T. (2016) *The sympathiser*. London: Corsair.

NHS Digital (2018) 'Mental Health Act statistics, Annual figures 2017–18'. Available at: https://digital.nhs.uk/data-and-information/publications/statistical/mental-health-act-statistics-annual-figures/2017-18-annual-figures (Accessed: 6 January 2021).

NPR [National Public Radio, Robert Wood Johnson Foundation, and Harvard T.H. Chan School of Public Health] (2017) 'Discrimination in America: Experiences and views of African Americans'. Available at: https://media.npr.org/assets/img/2017/10/23/discriminationpoll-african-americans.pdf (Accessed: 6 January 2021).

Olusoga, D. (2016) *Black and British: A forgotten history*. London: Pan Macmillan.

Parks, R. and Haskins, J. (1992) *Rosa Parks: My story*. New York: Dial Books.

Pelletier, C. (2009) 'Rancière and the poetics of the social sciences', *International Journal of Research & Method in Education*, 32 (3), pp. 267–284.

Public Health England (2020) 'Disparities in the risk and outcomes of Covid-19'. London: Crown Copyright. Available at: https://www.gov.uk/government/publications/covid-19-review-of-disparities-in-risks-and-outcomes (Accessed: 6 January 2021).

Rancière, J. (1987) *The ignorant schoolmaster: Five lessons in intellectual emancipation*. Translated by K. Ross, 1991. Stanford, CA: Stanford University Press.

Rancière, J. (2005) *Hatred of democracy*. Translated by S. Corcoran, 2014. London: Verso.

Rawls, J. (1971) *A theory of justice*. Cambridge, MA: Harvard University Press.

Red, White and Blue (2020) BBC TV. 29 November, 21.00.

Resler, M. (2019) 'Systems of trauma: Racial trauma'. Issue brief. Available at: http://www.fact.virginia.gov/wp-content/uploads/2019/05/Racial-Trauma-Issue-Brief.pdf (Accessed: 6 January 2021).

Rodriguez, J.P. (2007) *Slavery in the United States: A social, political, and historical encyclopedia*. Volume 1. Santa Barbara, CA: ABC-Clio.

Sands, P. (2016) *East West Street*. London: Orion Publishing.

Sartre, J.-P. (1961) 'Preface', in Fanon, F., *The wretched of the earth*. Translated by C. Farrington, 2001. London: Penguin Modern Classics, pp. 7–26.

Selassie, H. (1963) 'Address to the United Nations'. Available at: https://en.wikisource.org/wiki/Haile_Selassie%27s_address_to_the_United_Nations,_1963 (Accessed: 6 January 2021).

Spivak, G.C. (1988) 'Can the subaltern speak?', in Nelson, C. and Grossberg, L. (eds) *Marxism and the interpretation of culture*. Basingstoke: MacMillan Education, pp. 66–111.

Stopford, A. (2020) *Trauma and repair: Confronting segregation and violence in America*. Lanham, MD: Lexington Books.

Synergi Collaborative Centre (2018) 'The impact of racism on mental health'. Available at: https://synergicollaborativecentre.co.uk/wp-content/uploads/2017/11/The-impact-of-racism-on-mental-health-briefing-paper-1.pdf (Accessed 6 January 2021).

Tate, C. (1996) 'Freud and his "Negro": Psychoanalysis as ally and enemy of African Americans', *Journal for the Psychoanalysis of Culture and Society*, 1 (1), 53–62.

wa Thiong'o, Ngũgĩ (1977) *Petals of blood*. Reprinted 2018. London: Vintage.

WildersonIII, F.B. (2020) *Afropessimism*. New York, NY: Liveright Publishing Corporation.

Wilkinson, R.G. and Pickett, K.E. (2009) *The spirit level: Why more equal societies almost always do better*. London: Allen Lane.

Williams, J. (2002) *Eyes on the prize: America's civil rights years, 1954–1965*. London: Penguin.

Williams, M.T., Printz, D.M.B., and DeLapp, R.C.T. (2018) 'Assessing racial trauma with the trauma symptoms of discrimination scale', *Psychology of Violence*, 8 (6), pp. 735–747.

X, Malcolm (1964) 'The ballot or the bullet'. Available at: http://malcolmxfiles.blogsp ot.com/2013/06/the-ballot-or-bullet-april-12-1964.html (Accessed: 6 January 2021).

Chapter 9

Practices of disappointment
Going along with stuff less and getting out more

> Put not your trust in princes, nor in the son of man, in whom there is no help.
> (Psalms 146:3: King James Bible, 1611)

Imperfect systems

> *'Caveat emptor'* ['let the buyer beware'].
> (C16 CE maxim in English common law)

To be disappointed is to be human; to be disappointing is also to be human. To endure, engage with, and then reach beyond 'disappointment' in our internal relatedness, and in interpersonal and social relationships, *may* enable us to re-connect with our own humanity and with the humanity of others. If we do not grapple with disappointment in these kinds of ways, we *certainly* risk becoming and remaining aggrieved and resentful; locked into cycles of humiliating, reciprocal self-and-other destructive violence and recrimination. At the level of the individual sufferer, it is not enough (though the inadequate offer is too often made) merely (and insultingly) to prescribe 'getting past one's disappointment' to the excluded, psycho-socially (re-)traumatised peoples whose fraught relationship with and treatment at the hands of the in-group it has been the project of this book to understand more deeply.

Our purpose in picking out the theme of disappointment is not to recirculate bromides of that kind. Instead, it feels incumbent upon us (we-the-authors), as psycho-social practitioners as well as theorists, to wrestle with our own angels and demons here. We have in mind to re-imagine different narratives for the experience of being disappointed (in ourselves, in others, in each other) and disappointing (to each other, to others, to ourselves); to understand both disappointed-ness and disappointing-ness as existential threats and as impediments to our creativity that need to be urgently re-thought. These two related states can be understood as violent states that pervade that societal system of care which operates to press upon us an invitation to lose ourselves in endless unproductive and fundamentally acquiescent disappointed-ness that things are as they are. At

DOI: 10.4324/9781003223115-12

the same time, the same system presses us to address our presumed and assumed disappointing-ness with ceaseless and equally futile striving to meet and exceed performance targets and output monitoring. These discourse-bound pressures combine to tunnel for us a colossal rabbit-hole, down which any possibility of creative challenge and meaningful emancipatory change to 'the way things are' is endlessly dissipated.

In his 'Choruses', written for the pageant play *The Rock*, T.S. Eliot (1934) pinpoints the avoidant and illusory pursuit of systems that are so perfectly constructed that the ordinary moral and ethical challenges assembled under the heading of 'being good' can be quietly and conveniently set aside. His observation was that the 'establishment' – in his case the established Church (Eliot had converted to Anglicanism in 1927 and had also become a British citizen later that same year) – was in a terrible collusion with its congregation to provide simple, institutionalised solutions to the profoundly testing moral and ethical, historical and contemporary problems in which the Church was, and had been, implicated.

Here we use Eliot's text to discuss the ways in which, through our personal and collective failure to address violent states, we are in danger of sleep-walking into psycho-social and ecological catastrophe by repeatedly dreaming up social institutions and systems that allow us *not* to engage in emotional thinking about what the 'good' might look like. We (the societal 'we') have thus been dis-abling ourselves from (re)-thinking what needs to be done to address those psycho-socially traumatising darknesses that have been charted in this book, at the centre as well as at the edges of the societal structures we have co-created.

Part of the challenge would then be to articulate the need for psycho-social practitioners of all kinds – perhaps especially psychological therapists and academics – to leave our psycho-social retreats (our clinics, consulting rooms, libraries, classrooms; our professional guilds and our disciplinary silos; our artefacts, relics, totems, fetishes and theoretical models *within*) and, once again, to join with un-'like-minded' (and particularly, we might add, un-'psychologically-minded') others and engage more deliberatively with conversations in 'public spheres' (Habermas, 1962; Jones, 2018). In short, we might need to consider how to go along with things less and to *get out more* (Scanlon, 2019; see also Russell, 2020). Stopford (2020), writing with particular reference to racial (re-)traumatisation in the United States, puts it clearly:

> Breaking down segregation necessitates getting out of our offices, conferences, and seminars in exclusive neighbourhoods and academic institutions, at least some of the time, and directly connecting with community-based projects. *It is not enough to theorise from a distance.*
>
> (Stopford, 2020, p. 16 [our italics])

Here, again, we note the inspirational example that Rosa Parks has handed down to us, and how essentially it was exactly her resolve to go along with things less and get out more – to be determined, and undaunted – that catalysed a disruptive moment of true emancipation. We cannot all stand in the shoes of a Rosa Parks, Diogenes or Bartleby – it can be very endangering to attempt to do so, and untold multitudes have foundered on the rocks of such subversion. At the same time, as we have also already observed, it would scarcely be ethical – although regrettably commonplace – for those of us associated with the discomfited in-group to sit on our hands and hope that someone else with exceptional moral courage and authority might come along, peacefully, to challenge our dominion – and in so doing to 'let them' do 'our' work for us in ways that perpetuate the dynamic.

However, if we are to have any hope of dis-appointing those who occupy and assume positions of power and privilege, it will be necessary to take up a psycho-social position that is necessarily subversive and disruptive – not only an action research project but a consciously targeted project of activist research. It may even be, if we follow Fanon (1952, 1961), that such modes of subversion will involve forms of civil disobedience, perhaps even violent revolt. In order to take up this social appointment in more thoughtful ways, we suggest that we must first engage with our own current states of dis-appointment. If 'we' are to seek to question, challenge, subvert and dis-appoint those who wield Metropolitan power in the established order, we also must engage with the many and varied ways in which 'we' are necessarily and inevitably dis-appointing to others, and so, very much part of the problem that we are seeking to address.

Parks spoke truth to power. In refusing or declining to go along with the ideas of others as to what should be her 'proper place' at the back of the bus, she stood firm and insisted that *this* was her proper place. She did this even though she surely knew that she ran the risk of being forcibly unseated, or of being thrown off the bus altogether; that expressions of racial hatred would be thrown at her; that she would be prosecuted for her 'presumption'. Indeed, she was not the first to take such a stand and undergo such an ordeal, and she was in fact very aware of the precedent, for she had previously met with Claudette Colvin, who had been prosecuted for a similar act of resistance nine months earlier (Laughland, 2021), and whose name we also take the opportunity to honour here. Nonetheless, these were deeds, disruptive moves and acts of resistance that *had to be done*.

Frantz Fanon (1961) proposed that *self-appointed* colonial in-groups, most of whom have become the entitled inheritors of this colonial wealth in modern times, for the most part, have had no interest in civil conversations that might lead to giving up willingly any of this appropriated wealth, or the social position, power and privilege that it buys. For Fanon, the most important issue was that newly emancipated peoples should neither imitate, nor concern themselves with catching up with, the old colonial powers, but should instead look to invent "new forms of social organisation" (Fanon, 1961, p. 254). He also earlier proposed that,

> [t]o induce man to be *actional*, by maintaining in his circularity the respect of the fundamental values that make the world human, that is the task of utmost urgency for he who, after careful reflection, prepares to act.
>
> (Fanon, 1952, p. 197)

We suggest that Fanon is also inviting us all to concern ourselves with forms of profound historical or contemporary disappointment.

Dreaming in imperfect systems

> Pity would be no more,
> If we did not make somebody poor,
> And Mercy no more could be
> If all were as happy as we.
> (Blake, 1794, p. 77)

To struggle with disappointment is *necessary*, therefore, if we are to live and work together in these good-less societal institutions and systems. We must then engage with our sleeping and waking daydreams and nightmares; to rouse ourselves up from and out of these psycho-social states of dis-connectedness and dis-memberment – to 'smell the coffee'. If we accept that a human being may be understood as "a group animal who is constantly at war, not only with the group, but also with himself [sic] for being a group animal" (Bion, 1961, p. 131), then we can perceive that disappointment at the boundary or threshold of group membership (the German word for which is *Schwellenangst*) is an existential given. Our desire or drive to belong exposes us to both an inevitable disappointment in the hospitality of the group and a disappointment with our own need of the inhospitable environment that the group has presented in response. On the other hand, but at the same time, our pursuit of individual autonomy constantly draws attention to and exposes our dependency upon others – and it is then difficult not to be 'at war with' these others. This inter-dependency also reminds us of the limits of our indivi-duality, and it is in this sense that we are always existentially and dis-appointingly at war with ourselves.

Clancy, Vince and Gabriel (2011) discuss how organisations, and by impli-cation all other social institutions, frequently become arenas of disappoint-ment where emotions such as shame and guilt prevail, and a consequent sense of failure is followed by defensive blame and recrimination. Craib (1994) observes that this existential disappointment is about both needing to and failing to recognise our frailty and vulnerability – and the frailty and vulner-ability of others. The failure to grieve and mourn these cumulative separations and losses accumulates in socio-political matrices where disappointment, like all other psycho-social as well as material resources (or de-privations), is not equally distributed. As we have seen throughout this book, we inhabit and have organised ourselves in a social world which, at its roots and branches, is characterised by the marked psycho-social differentials between those who are understandably extremely disappointed and those others who, though doubtless wrestling with their own disappointment, are also extremely disappointing.

Craib goes on to suggest that to consider disappointment in these terms is to see it not only as inevitable or desirable, but also as a necessary aspect of the human condition: one which demands that we be in a complex and ambivalent relationship with something that *doesn't happen* – or hasn't yet happened. He argues that the more we deny the extent of our individual and collective disappointment, the more we become involved in breaking the links and connections between people, and within ourselves: between *relationships* and *relatedness* respectively. Disappointment, on this view, contains a painful interplay between intense longing and profound unrequited sadness: a painful bipolarity of regressive and progressive forces that demands a necessarily disappointing relinquishing or subversion of 'some things' in order to make space for 'some things' else.

Disappointment, disrespect and disillusion

Gilligan (1996) explores the intersection of disappointment with experiences of being *disrespected*. He suggests, as we have seen above, that to be 'dissed' is also to be humiliated, and that the unbearable experience of feeling (a) shamed is at the core of much of the re-traumatising interpersonal and structural violence that characterises modern society. To take disappointment seriously is to revisit our individual and shared experience of feeling 'dissed' in oh so many ways, and to explore how this experience shapes the shaky foundations of all the organisations and social institutions that we co-construct. It is also to explore disappointment – existentially, relationally, affectively and performatively – as a psycho-social phenomenon that forms the substrate of family, neighbourhood and community matrices, where there are no lasting solutions to everyday social conflicts and inequalities, and where the reciprocal dynamics of disappointment prevail.

Winnicott (1965), theorising the phases of ordinary human psycho-social development, through which we all must transition, for better and for worse, suggests that this development involves a 'necessary disillusionment', which he links to our emerging from the *illusory* comfort of a more cossetted merger with primary care-givers into the un-comfortableness of having to think our own thoughts. Glover (2015) reminds us that the word 'illusion' itself derives from the Latin *ludere*, meaning to play, and that this 'necessary disillusionment', although painful, is potentially playful and creative. Moreover, it is psycho-socially connected to a capacity for *concern*, which might eventually enable us to take up our social roles and *appointments* in more or less respectful ways. Coleman (2014) suggests that to be disappointed in or by the other is central to the breakdown of many – if not most – intimate relationships. He further observes that not only is disappointment "an inevitable and necessary feature of the human condition", but in both its destructiveness and its potential creativity it is also "the glory and the tragedy of the human imagination" (Coleman, 2014, p. 24). Playing is a serious business.

The poet and social commentator David Whyte (2015) proposed that disappointment might also be thought of creatively as a "hidden, underground, engine" (Whyte, 2015, p. 49), and a potential source of trust and generosity that *may* provide an opportunity for transformation. However, to face the full depth of our (and others') disappointment requires what he describes as a "necessary and *merciful* heartbreak [our italics]" (ibid.). This confluence or intersection of disappointment and mercy calls to mind Portia's celebrated insight in the trial scene in *The Merchant of Venice*:

> The quality of mercy is not strained.
> It droppeth as the gentle rain from heaven
> Upon the place beneath. It is twice blest:
> It blesseth him that gives and him that takes.
> (*The Merchant of Venice*: Act 4, Scene 1
> (Shakespeare, 1600, p. 501))

This reflection on the 'twice-blessed' nature of mercy might help us to imagine disappointment as also 'twice-blessed' (or twice-cursed, depending on whether one experiences the proverbial cup as half-full or half-empty?) because there must also be a recognition of the impact upon both those who are disappointed *and* those who disappoint; and of the psycho-social crises at the intersection of experiences of 'disappointment', 'disrespect' and 'disillusionment'.

The disappointments and possibilities of dilemmatic spaces

Honig (1996) suggests that much (all?) 'psycho-social work' takes place in *dilemmatic spaces*, moments in time and space which open up when conversations about things that do not fit together, or which contain inherent antinomies and contradictions, *must* take place; and when actions are demanded that will inevitably disappoint someone or another. The implication is that within this reciprocally dilemmatic disappointment there will always be those who are disappointed and those who are disappointing – although, as we have already emphasised, in ways that are never equally distributed. The dilemma, then, is how to make best use of these psycho-social spaces to have the visions, to dream the dreams and then have the types of conversations that help us, painfully, to progress into something lighter rather than painfully to remain stuck or regress further into the darkness. By

166 Reclaiming the agora

Honig's reckoning, there can be no meaningful psycho-social change without conversations about experiences of disappointment.

Not only are we either disappointed or disappointing, but we must also face the more complex double-edged, twice-blessed (or cursed), inside-out or outside-in, both/and psycho-social moebius reality that we are all simultaneously both disappointed and disappointing. We are disappointed in others *because* we feel so disappointed and disappointed in ourselves *because* we are so disappointing, and so there is nowhere to run and nowhere to hide from the inherently painful nature of this *appointment*. The 'twice-blessed/cursed' nature of this (dis)appointment, then, could also be understood as an aspect of *ressentiment* or 'double-suffering' (Frost and Hoggett, 2008; Hoggett, Wilkinson and Beedell, 2013); or what we have termed reflexive violence (see Chapter 4). A double movement, involving a reciprocal and simultaneous attack on self-and-other, arises when a disappointing insult is added to a disappointed injury (and vice versa) in ways that eat away at our body and soul, and so interferes with our capacity to be concerned about or engaged with our own experiences of loss, the losses of our neighbours and, ultimately, in the loss of our shared home, the planet Earth. In these inhospitable or hostile systems, we lose touch with both our ideals and the wider reality of *our* very real existential crisis, and the need for change is avoided. We become displaced, redundant, rootless and disconnected from ourselves, each other and our environment – without even the relative comfort of a barrel to which we can retreat.

Too often in this ambivalent reciprocally painful psycho-social world of want and wanting, shame turns to contempt, and grief turns to grievance; the longing for connection that we believe is at the heart of our shared ordinary human vulnerability is denied or disavowed, and anger and *ressentiment* prevail in ways that are not only emotionally distressing but also corrosive of the structures and the cultures of the very social institutions that we have been traditionally invited to depend upon for our sense of social security. Mixed feelings run high but are difficult to *articulate*, links are not made, needful or imaginable compromises are not made, and the open public exchange of *psycho-social goods* is impossible.

Whilst some of us might be in agreement – at least on our better days – about the potentially transformative power of conversation, we might also notice the ways in which collectively we have spectacularly failed to maintain an effective conversational participation in the democratic process and how our personal, familial, social, communal and civic lives have become impoverished – and disappointing – as a result. Rather than co-exist in difference, we are sleep-walking into a deeply disappointing post-truth, dis-interested future. For some of us, the more privileged, these failures to engage involve different kinds of psycho-social retreats into our gated communities, private schools and private healthcare; as well as privatised psychotherapy conversations in which a false security is generated through a collusive turning away

Practices of disappointment 167

from the darkness without by offering imaginary psychological solutions for very real social problems (Scanlon, 2015).

Practising disappointment

> This dis-ease is beyond my practice.
> (*Macbeth*: Act 5, Scene 1 (Shakespeare, 1623, p. 1122 [our hyphen]))

In Chapters 2 and 3 we set out the frame of our 'Diogenes Paradigm' using numerous stories collected by various authorities about that dogged psycho-social practitioner/consultant. We kept one of them back in order to share it here, as we approach our conclusion. In this particular legend, Diogenes was found kneeling with his begging bowl (and his dog) at the feet of a statue. When asked the reason why he was engaged in this apparently futile pursuit – allotting himself this self-appointed impossible task (Roberts, 1994) – he replied that he did so in order to "get practice in being refused" (Diogenes Laertius, 3rd century BCE, 6.49; Navia, 2005, p. 215).

Here we find Diogenes engaged in one of his favoured *praxes* of parody. By publicly *practising disappointment* in this way, he invites his interlocutors to perceive, with him, that one might as well beg alms of a lump of stone as seek a more Cosmopolitan *accommodation* for him and his *praxes* by the Metropolitan in-group. He does not hesitate to lampoon those who accost him for the naïveté of *their* petitions. Yet his *praxis*, upon closer examination, is intricately multi-layered.

On one level, Diogenes' offering is simply a counsel of his prototypically Stoical wisdom of lived experience. He wants to suggest that getting oneself accustomed to having one's application for accommodation turned down may be a key life skill for any member of the incohesive out-group ambivalently in search of asylum or accommodation of their experience of being othered, of being located on the outside. There is also a counsel of humility – as who should say, "who am I to expect that these statues should provide me with soothing or sustenance?" On a further level, as we shall go on to explore, Diogenes is working to practise disappointment so as to get the better of it or, more subtly, to *get better at it* – so as not to be waylaid, disheartened or confounded by it. He wants to inhabit his disappointment in a particular way, so as to sharpen the edge of it, bring it into his life and make it work for him, rather than find himself tangled up in self-defeat; mired in that sense of shame and failure which the 'in-group' violently locates in him.

It will also be Alexander, in our paradigm, who must taste that fruit of disappointment; after all, Diogenes declines his offer of an appointment. However, it is the figure of Diogenes in this fraught and futile encounter who most likely will be blamed and disdained as feckless and indigent – 'attention-seeking' – for not doing it properly, for not being in his *proper place*; and (which is held to be much worse still) for doing it 'deliberately'. Diogenes knows to expect disappointment and so makes it part of his *praxis*. Alexander, who has never before been either refused or disappointed, is *caught out*. Alexander denies disappointment as a possibility; Diogenes practises it as an inevitability.

In effect, and notwithstanding what we have said thus far, it is not so much that Diogenes practises disappointment: it might be more accurate to say that he practises not identifying with the feeling of disappointment and the role of being 'dis-appointed', when he is invited to do so. Rather, he stands his ground and, like Rosa Parks, states that he *shall not be moved.* Diogenes, we might imagine, declines to identify as disappointed because he declines to recognise Alexander's authority to offer him appointments of any kind in the first place. Of Alexander himself, unlike his modern-day Metropolitan counterparts perhaps, we might imagine that this particular excursion, and the fruit of the disappointment he encountered in Diogenes' challenge, if not exactly sweet, was not so bitter, in that he stayed with Diogenes and continued talking with him. Perhaps it even made him think a little of both the reach and the limits of his (and Diogenes') power, privilege and positioning in their momentarily shared disappointment.

The question of how we engage with our own and with others' disappointment is important, because in 'late' capitalism we are invited and expected, as good consumers, to be locked into an eternal circle of disappointment – in the goods and the 'entertainment' services we procure and in the political classes and the media moguls who 'bestow' or provide them homogenously across the globe. This is why Berry (1993) writes of the importance of "sales resistance" (p. ix). As in the contemporary supermarket, so too in the 'globalisation-minus' hyper-mediated super-society, we are supposed to dissociate both from our desire and our disappointments as we consume, hypnotised by the lighting, the ambient sounds and smells, and the pseudo-science of product placement and shelf-dressing in the shopping outlets as we buy all the shiny new disappointments we didn't go hunting for in the first place.

This is also why Postman (1984) argues that the purpose of certain forms and modes of public entertainment is like the 'soma' in Aldous Huxley's *Brave New World* (1932), to put us to sleep: that we are in real danger of 'amusing ourselves to death'. He contrasts Huxley's vision with that of George Orwell, who suggested that the "ultimate subtlety" of this violently perverse modernity was "consciously to induce unconsciousness, and then, once again, to become unconscious of the act of hypnosis you had just performed" (Orwell, 1949, pp. 38–39). Sales resistance, on the internet as in the supermarket, in part then involves practices of resistance, such as consciously blinking, so as not to be lured from one's own avowed purpose of knowing one's own mind, thinking one's own thoughts and acting accordingly.

We are therefore invited to wake up from our sleepiness and to notice the acts of hypnosis that we have performed upon ourselves; to notice the dependency that keeps coming back for more of the same, and the pressure upon us, in our dissociation, to accept disappointment as the driving force propelling the not-to-be-questioned 'good' of economic growth, and the built-in obsolescence of the products it touts. As we saw in Chapter 7, the fantasy, the hypnotising invitation or lullaby, whispers that Gaia can always be framed as *in itself* disappointing – disappointingly finite, disappointingly, well, Earth-bound. Come on, people, runs this discourse: lighten up, think positively, there's always Mars …. To which assault upon our sense, the first line of resistance must be to *not* allow ourselves to *remain* disappointed in our planet, in the finite nature of its resources and delicate ecological balance of its operative systems. It behoves us instead to understand and respect the reality of disappointing exhaustibility – to acquiesce as little as possible to the invitation to be, and to remain, disappointed, to be in contact with the finite, limited and limiting nature of our individual and global existence – and to get out much, much more (though perhaps not using internal combustion engines).

Making new appointments: Resisting the widening of the gyre

> And in that Heaven of all their wish
> There shall be no more land, say fish.
> (Brooke, 1913, p. 36)

As we discussed in Chapter 8, numerous authorities, perhaps first and foremost Frantz Fanon, invite us to consider that protest – perhaps even violent upheaval and revolution – is the only way to overthrow the powers that be. We recognise the logic and moral force of these arguments. However, whether the conversations we have in mind take place before we take to the streets in protest and revolt, or after the Metropolitan structures that generated and perpetuate slavery and dehumanisation have been finally overthrown, it seems to us that we still need to find better ways to talk to each other. Zeldin (1998) argues that the right type of conversation, in the right place and at the right time, has the power not only to change minds but also to transform the social world: Margaret Mead suggested that "it is the only thing that ever has".[1]

Zeldin charts the changing nature of conversation, from the *agora* and the *fora* of ancient times, through to the *salons* and *cafés scientifiques* of French 'high society' as the nineteenth century drew to a close. He then explores the 'public conversations' that gave rise to social (r)evolutions, workers' rights, women's suffrage, and universal civil and human rights – and how the momentum generated by those conversations stalled or faltered. We hope that our own current concerns, to engage with conversations to explore our whiteness in the context of the #BlackLivesMatter movement (see Chapter 8) and our masculinity in the turbulent wake of the #Me Too movement, do not similarly result in impasse and further disappointment.

For Benjamin (2018), the aim of creating places for these conversations requires what she describes as a *moral* third space in which members-as-citizens can listen to each other's stories, see each other reflected in each others' pain and come to recognise all our own fragilities and interdependent vulnerabilities. This includes bearing witness to and affirming the reality of others' traumas and disappointments so that we might be better able, psychosocially, to *re-member* ourselves and each other.

On the wider socio-political stage in recent times, we have seen different kinds of 'reflective conversations' being deployed to bring peace to conflict zones, and would like to suggest that these might be usefully integrated to address both externally driven and internally generated disappointments. Restorative justice, conflict resolution and other (inter-)mediation methodologies have been brought to bear as a means of enabling the types of reflective conversations that allow different parties to share their profound sense of disappointment through truth telling, reconciliation, understanding and perhaps even forgiveness (Elworthy and Rifkind, 2006; Hoggett, 2009; Kleinot, 2012; Ofer, 2017; Weinstein, 2018; Drennan, 2018; Donoso, 2018).

These kinds of conversations have brought peace (or at least a cessation or reduction of organised violence) notably in South Africa and in (Northern) Ireland, and have allowed truths to be told about historical Church/State institutional abuse in Ireland and elsewhere. Such conversations have begun, in parts, to address the genocidal destruction of indigenous people by colonial powers and to acknowledge the inestimable human cost of the historical and contemporary trade, trafficking and enslavement of millions of people – whilst in other parts of the world, wars persist, conflict continues and truths about other types of institutionalised abuse, territorial occupation and the widespread exploitation of children and vulnerable adults are stories yet to be told.

Erlich, Erlich-Ginor and Beland (2013) deploy psychoanalytic, psychosocial and systems-psychodynamic approaches in their experiential working conferences exploring German–Jewish group relations in the aftermath of the Holocaust. They suggest a metaphorical development in such conversations from violence through sorrow to the finding of words. De Maré, Piper and Thompson (1991), discussing the 'median' group as a site for democratic deliberation and contestation, propose a movement "from hate, through dialogue to culture" that is necessary to allow neighbourhood and communities to grow and develop. They evoke the concept of *Koinonia*, meaning the gift of active participation that is linked to a desire to take up membership of the community group – to *belong*.

From a psycho-social point of view, a number of theorists, from different, overlapping traditions, have taken up the challenge of how we might better enable people to take up their membership of neighbourhoods and communities with reference to the notion of the 'Reflective Citizen' (Kraemer and Roberts, 1996; Gould, Lucey and Stapley, 2011; Mojović, 2019). Dubouloy (2011) suggests that to become a more reflective citizen requires that individuals, families and neighbourhoods, as sub-systems of wider communities, must ask the questions that will allow them to find their place, to take up their membership of that place, whilst allowing and enabling others to do the same. Krantz (2011) suggests that whilst it is *necessary* to be reflective, it is not in itself *sufficient* to bring about change, and so proposed a further movement from reflective citizen to 'deliberative citizen', within which we must first think and feel, after which we must find our voice(s) and then act accordingly. In this use of *deliberative*, Krantz is drawing attention to a double movement in the use of this word because it is *deliberate* in the sense of intentional and purposeful, but also because it involves *deliberation* in the sense of thoughtfulness in order to inform and enable this purposive action. Building on the work of our senior colleagues and friends, David Armstrong (2005) and Earl Hopper (2003), we then propose a move from 'Reflective Practice in the traumatised-organisation-in-the-mind' (see also Scanlon, 2012, 2017, 2019) towards what we are here imagining as 'deliberative action in the traumatised-community-in-the-mind'. This is then a move from hate and blood (somatic experience), by way of tears (emotional experience), to words and dialogue (relational and social experience).

What these and other related psycho-social methodologies[2] have in common is that they are *deliberative actions* that all aim to "rekindle democracy" Russell (2020) by inviting the "interested citizens" to re-occupy the agora Bauman, 2000; see Chapter 5). The key question here is how to enable us to come out from our psycho-social retreats to join with others to create new *appointments* for more ordinary conversations in the public sphere.

Gordon Lawrence (2000) explored the psycho-social attitude and relatedness necessary to enable the more effective development of such communities of practice. He contrasted the *politics of revelation* with the *politics of salvation* and suggested that one way of allowing something to be revealed is through 'social dreaming'. Social dreaming is a structured methodology, which rather than offering us 'salvation' from disappointment, and associated losses and hatreds, instead allows our interconnected disappointment to be *revealed* (Lawrence, 1998). The social and organisational power of the *politics of revelation*, and the impact of the shared dream in enabling a meaningful 'mission' and relevant 'social action' to emerge, was perhaps never more clearly illustrated than by Dr King Jnr, who famously dreamed a *social dream*:

> I dream ... that my four little children will one day live in a nation where they will not be judged by the color of their skin but by the content of their character ...
>
> (King, 1963)

Parsing the parcel

The penultimate word in this book belongs to the work of a tireless psycho-social commentator, the British writer, actor and director Alan Bennett, and

172 Reclaiming the agora

to his 2001 play, *The History Boys*. The General Studies teacher, Hector, discussing the inherent disappointments of living and learning, urges the 'boys' to take up their place in their own historical disappointing conversations:

> Pass the parcel. That's sometimes all you can do. Take it, feel it, and pass it on. Not for me, not for you, but for someone, somewhere, one day. Pass it on, boys. That's the game I want you to learn. Pass it on.
>
> (Bennett, 2001, p. 109)

At the heart of Hector's invitation is his evocation of the experience of the children who, when the music stops, excitedly tear open the newspaper wrapping in the hope of a reward – only to be faced with the disappointment of the empty wrapper, and the awful possibility that the prize will have been secured by another – before the parcel makes its way around the circle again. In late modernity, such is the fear of disappointment that the game has been re-invented so that there is a present *every* time that the music stops. We might also ask whose idea it was to create these children's games, in which children must learn unprocessed and public experiences of disappointment, in the first place, and what is thus revealed about power relations between adults and children?[3]

Hector invites us to relinquish all hopes of and desires for instant personal and psychological gratification. He instead demands of us that, through participating in the game and embracing the practice of disappointment, we might invest in and commit ourselves to a shared future in (creative) common. If we can somehow manage to pass it on, and hand it down, and not cling for dear life to its promise, that parcel may lead, if collectively unwrapped (and who knows whether gently or more violently?), to conversations that just might make a difference. The invitation offered by Eliot earlier could then be re-imagined in terms of how, as *psycho-socialists*, we might make links between the darknesses within 'the organisation-in-the-mind' (Armstrong, 2005), and the darkened-ness of the organisation-of-the-social without: between the 'good' society and the internal world (Rustin, 1991). We could then be better placed to respond to Eliot's invitation not to forget to be good. We might even leave the place in a better s(S)tate than we found it.

****

We want to conclude by noticing that, in the process of writing this book, we haven't each had exactly the same experiences in and of its composition – and by no means have we always been 'of one mind'. We have set ourselves to be of two minds and each of us has tended, annoyingly at times, to insist upon his having a separate identity, a different mind and an obstinate insistence on thinking his own thoughts. For each of us, in different ways, this book would have been very different if the other had not been there:

notwithstanding that we two have twenty years' experience of thinking and writing together and alongside each other.

We have certainly disappointed ourselves and each other on many occasions during those two decades. We have gone along with stuff – not woken up, when alarm bells were ringing – and not spoken out as often as we might have. We have stood in Alexander's shoes as we acted un-self-critically as agents of State, when resistance was ethically called for. We continued – and continue still – to take the shilling from various organisations who have not repudiated certain manifestly oppressive discourses. We wince now to contemplate just how much we left out of some of our earlier writings, on matters that now appear to us as central (such as race, and migration, and climate disaster).

We also can't help but worry that there is no escape from a shared, reciprocally disappointing destiny in which we-the-authors are going to disappoint you-the-reader, just as you-the-reader will also disappoint us-the-authors in the process. However, this is not a counsel of despair, at any level: it is merely an observation. We, none of us, can know if we are on the right track, and the best that can be hoped (and planned for) is that our disappointments can be put to work so that we might all be more strongly connected. If we can listen to the many layers of Diogenes' *praxis* and the performance of his critique, satire, parody, admonitions and public service announcements – all in the micro-moment of his kneeling before that statue, with his dogs by his side, his lamp at his feet, his stick in one hand and his begging bowl in the other – we may glimpse the possibility that Metropolitan power might yet be set aside; that the sun will continue to shine and to warm us all (within sustainable limits); and that the ground upon which we stand together will be neither morass nor maze nor quicksand.

Notes

1 Margaret Mead (1901–1978) was an anthropologist and social commentator who was 'in conversation' with some of the leading thinkers of her era. This quote is used here with the permission of the Institute of Intercultural Studies (https://www.interculturalstudies.org/Mead/biography.html).

2 Under this heading we would include group relations (Sher, 2018); large groups (Kreeger, 1975); median groups (De Maré, Piper and Thompson, 1991); social dreaming matrices (Lawrence, 1998, 2000); visual matrices (Manley, 2018; Mersky and Sievers, 2018); communities of practice (Wenger, 1998); listening posts (Khaleelee and Stapley, 2018); reflective citizens (Gould, Lucey and Stapley, 2011; Mojović, 2019); thinking spaces (Lowe, 2013); race conversations (Ellis, 2021); Tree of life (Ncube-Mlilo, 2021); death cafés (https://deathcafe.com/); climate cafés (https://climatecafes.org/); and other extra-mural programmes in the 'public sphere' (Maile and Griffiths, 2014; Diamond, 2014; Morgan, 2019).

3 We are grateful to David W. Jones for deepening our parsing of this particular parcel game.

References

Armstrong, D. (2005) *Organization in the mind: Psychoanalysis, group relations and organizational consultancy*. London: Karnac.

Bauman, Z. (2000) *Liquid modernity*. Cambridge: Polity Press.

Benjamin, J. (2018) *Beyond doer and done to: Recognition theory, intersubjectivity and the third*. London: Routledge.

Bennett, A. (2001) *The history boys*. London: Faber and Faber.

Berry, W. (1993) *Sex, economy, freedom & community: Eight essays*. Reprinted 2018. Berkeley, CA: Counterpoint.

Bion, W.R. (1961) *Experiences in groups*. London: Tavistock.

Blake, W. (1794) 'The human abstract', in Yeats, W.B. (ed.) (1905) *Collected poems*. Reprinted 2006. London: Routledge Classics, p. 77.

Brooke, R. (1913) 'Heaven', in Keynes, G. (ed.) (1946) *The poetical works of Rupert Brooke*. Reprinted 1981. London: Faber and Faber, p. 36.

Clancy, A., Vince, R., and Gabriel, Y. (2011) 'That unwanted feeling: A psychodynamic study of disappointment at work', *British Journal of Management*, 23, pp. 518–531.

Coleman, W. (2014) 'The intolerable other: The difficulty of becoming a couple', *Couples and Family Psychoanalysis*, 4 (1), pp. 22–41.

Craib, I. (1994) *The importance of disappointment*. London: Routledge.

De Maré, P., Piper, R., and Thompson, S. (1991) *Koinonia: From hate, through dialogue, to culture in the large group*. London: Karnac.

Diamond, M. (2014) 'Reflections on the meaning and experience of public space', in Boros, D. and Glass, J.M. (eds) *Re-imagining public space. The Frankfurt school in the 21st century*. New York: Palgrave, pp. 45–63.

Diogenes Laertius (3rd century BCE) *The Life of Diogenes of Sinope*. Translated by R. D. Hicks. Reprinted in Navia, L. (2005) *Diogenes the Cynic*. New York: Humanity Books, pp. 203–235.

Donoso, G. (2018) 'Psychosocial implications of political trauma and social recognition II: Experiences from the Truth Commission of Ecuador', in Adlam, J., Kluttig, T., and Lee, B.X. (eds) *Violent states and creative states: From the global to the individual. Volume 1: Structural violence and creative structures*. London: Jessica Kingsley Publishers, pp. 101–116.

Drennan, G. (2018) 'Restorative justice applications in mental health settings: pathways to recovery and restitution', in Adlam, J., Kluttig, T., and Lee, B.X. (eds) *Violent states and creative states: From the global to the individual. Volume 2: Human violence and creative humanity*. London: Jessica Kingsley Publishers, pp. 181–194.

Dubouloy, M. (2011) 'Is recognition a requisite for citizenship for managers?', in Gould, L., Lucey, A., and Stapley, L. (eds) *The reflective citizen: Organizational and social dynamics*. London: Karnac, pp. 131–149.

Eliot, T.S. (1934) 'Chorus VI', in *Collected poems* (1974). Reprinted 2002. London: Faber and Faber, pp. 151–174.

Ellis, E. (2021) *The race conversation: An essential guide to creating life-changing dialogue*. London: Confer Books.

Elworthy, S. and Rifkind, G. (2006) *Making terrorism history*. London: Rider Press.

Erlich, H.S., Erlich-Ginor, M., and Beland, H. (2013) *Fed with tears; Poisoned with milk: The Nazareth group relations conferences.* Geissen, Germany: Psychosozial-Verlag.

Fanon, F. (1952) *Black skins, white masks.* Translated by R. Philcox, 2008. New York, NY: Grove Press.

Fanon, F. (1961) *The wretched of the earth.* Translated by C. Farrington, 2001. London: Penguin Modern Classics.

Frost, L. and Hoggett, P. (2008) 'Human agency and social suffering', *Critical Social Policy*, 28 (5), pp. 438–460.

Gilligan, J. (1996) *Violence: Reflections on our deadliest epidemic.* Reprinted 2000. London: Jessica Kingsley Publishers.

Glover, N. (2015) 'Between comfort and disillusionment: Becoming a self at play', *Chiasma*, 2, pp. 81–95.

Gould, L., Lucey, A., and Stapley, L. (2011) *The reflective citizen: Organisational and social dynamics.* London: Karnac.

Habermas, J. (1962) *The structural transformation of the public sphere: An inquiry into a category of bourgeois society.* Translated by T. Burger with F. Lawrence, 1989. Cambridge: Polity Press.

Hoggett, P. (2009) *Politics, identity and emotion.* Bristol: Great Barrington Books.

Hoggett, P., Wilkinson, H., and Beedell, P. (2013) 'Fairness and the politics of resentment', *Journal of Social Policy*, 42 (3), pp. 567–585.

Honig, B. (1996) 'Difference, dilemmas, and the politics of home', in Benhabib, S. (ed.) *Democracy and difference: Contesting the boundaries of the political.* Princeton, NJ: Princeton University Press, pp. 257–277.

Hopper, E. (2003) *Traumatic experience in the unconscious life of groups: The fourth basic assumption: Incohesion: Aggregation/massification or (ba) I:A/M.* London: Jessica Kingsley Publishers.

Huxley, A. (1932) *Brave new world.* Reprinted 2007. London: Vintage.

Jones, D.W. (2018) 'Terror, violence and the public sphere', in Adlam, J., Kluttig, T., and Lee, B.X. (eds) *Violent states and creative states: From the global to the individual.* London: Jessica Kingsley Publishers, pp. 147–160.

Khaleelee, O. and Stapley, L. (2018) 'OPUS Listening Posts: Researching society', in Long, S. (ed.) *Socioanalytic methods: Discovering the hidden in organisations and social systems.* London: Routledge.

King James Bible (1611) *Standard Version.* Available at: https://www.kingjamesbibleonline.org/ (Accessed: 2 January 2021).

KingJr, M.L. (1963) 'I have a dream by Martin Luther King Jr; August 28, 1963'. The Avalon Project, Yale Law School. Available at: https://avalon.law.yale.edu/20th_century/mlk01.asp (Accessed: 30 April 2021).

Kleinot, P. (2012) 'The Bereaved Families Forum: Finding the Other within', in Adlam, J., Aiyegbusi, A., Kleinot, P., Motz, A., and Scanlon, C. (eds) *The Therapeutic milieu under fire: Security and insecurity in forensic mental health.* London: Jessica Kingsley Publishers, pp. 186–199.

Kraemer, S. and Roberts, J. (1996) (eds) *The politics of attachment: Towards a secure society.* London: Free Associations Books.

Krantz, J. (2011) 'Reflective citizenship: An organisational perspective', in Gould, L., Lucey, A., and Stapley, L. (eds) *The reflective citizen: Organizational and social dynamics.* London: Karnac, pp. 149–162.

Kreeger, L. (1975) *The large group: Dynamics and therapy.* London: Karnac.

Laughland, O. (2021) 'Claudette Colvin: The woman who refused to give up her bus seat – nine months before Rosa Parks'. Available at: https://www.theguardian.com/society/2021/feb/25/claudette-colvin-the-woman-who-refused-to-give-up-her-bus-seat-nine-months-before-rosa-parks (Accessed: 25 February 2021).

Lawrence, W.G. (1998) *Social dreaming at work*. London: Karnac.

Lawrence, W.G. (2000) *Tongued with fire: Groups in experience*. London: Karnac.

Lowe, F. (2013) *Thinking space: Promoting thinking about race, culture and diversity in psychotherapy and beyond*. London: Routledge.

Maile, S. and Griffiths, D. (eds) (2014) *Public engagement and social science*. Bristol: Policy Press.

Manley, J. (2018) *Social dreaming, associative thinking and intensities of affect*. London: Palgrave.

Mersky, R.R. and Seivers, B. (2018) 'Social photo matrix and social-dream drawing', in Hinshelwood, R.D. and Stamenova, K. (eds) *Methods for research into the unconscious: Applying psychoanalytic ideas in social science*. London: Karnac, pp. 145–169.

Mojović, M. (2019) 'Serbian reflective citizens and the art of psychosocial listening and dialogue at the caesura', *Journal of Psychosocial Studies*, 12 (1–2), pp. 81–95.

Morgan, D. (2019) *The unconscious in social and political life*. London: Phoenix.

Navia, L. (2005) *Diogenes the Cynic*. New York: Humanity Books.

Ncube- Mlilo, N. (2021) 'Tree of life'. Available at: https://phola.org/tree-of-life/ (Accessed: 30 April 2021).

Ofer, G. (ed.) (2017) *A bridge over troubled waters: Conflicts and reconciliations in groups and society*. London: Karnac.

Orwell, G. (1949) *1984*. Reprinted 2000. London: Penguin Classics.

Postman, N. (1984) *Amusing ourselves to death: Public discourse in the age of show business*. York: Methuen.

Roberts, V.Z. (1994) 'The self-appointed impossible task', in Roberts, V.Z. and Obholzer, A. (eds) *The unconscious at work: Individual and organizational stresses in the human services*. London: Routledge, pp. 110–121.

Russell, C. (2020) *Rekindling democracy: A professional's guide to working in citizen space*. Eugene, OR: Cascade Books.

Rustin, M. (1991) *The good society and the inner world: Psychoanalysis, politics and culture*. London: Verso.

Scanlon, C. (2012) 'The traumatised-organisation-in-the-mind: Opening up space for difficult conversations in difficult places', in Adlam, J., Aiyegbusi, A., Kleinot, P., Motz, A., and Scanlon, C. (eds) (2012) *The therapeutic milieu under fire: Security and insecurity in forensic mental health*. London: Jessica Kingsley Publishers, pp. 212–228.

Scanlon, C. (2015) 'On the perversity of *imagined* psychological solutions to very real social problems of unemployment (*work-lessness*) and social exclusion (*worth-lessness*): A group-analytic critique', *Group Analysis*, 48 (1), pp. 31–45.

Scanlon, C. (2017) 'Working with dilemmas and dis-appointment in difficult places: Towards a psycho-social model for team-focussed reflective practice', in Vaspe, A. (ed.) *Psychoanalysis, the NHS, and mental health work today*. London: Karnac, pp. 115–134.

Scanlon, C. (2019) '"Practising disappointment": From reflective-practice-in-the-organisation to deliberative-practice-in-the-community', in Thornton, C. (ed.) *The art and science of reflective practice in the organisation*. London: Routledge, pp. 76–84.

Shakespeare, W. (1600) *The comical history of the Merchant of Venice.* Reprinted 1986, in Wells, S., Taylor, G., Jowett, J., and Montgomery, W. (eds) *William Shakespeare: The complete works.* Oxford: Oxford University Press, pp. 479–508.

Shakespeare, W. (1623) *The tragedy of Macbeth.* Reprinted 1986, in Wells, S., Taylor, G., Jowett, J., and Montgomery, W. (eds) *William Shakespeare: The complete works.* Oxford: Oxford University Press, pp. 1099–1126.

Sher, M. (2018) *The dynamics of change: Tavistock approaches.* London: Routledge.

Stopford, A. (2020) *Trauma and repair: Confronting segregation and violence in America.* Lanham, MD: Lexington Books.

Weinstein, L. (2018) *7 principles of conflict resolution.* London: FT Publishing International.

Wenger, E. (1998) *Communities of practice: Learning, meaning, and identity.* Cambridge: Cambridge University Press.

Whyte, D. (2015) *The solace, nourishment and underlying meaning of everyday words.* Washington, DC: Many Rivers Press.

Winnicott D.W. (1965) *The maturational processes and the facilitating environment: Studies in the theory of emotional development.* London: The Hogarth Press and the Institute of Psycho-Analysis.

Zeldin, T. (1998) *On conversation: How talk can change your life.* London: Harvill Press.

Index

Adlam, J. 55, 81, 94
Afropessimism 63, 138
Afuape, T. 66
Agamben, G. 23, 24, 44
agora 74; agoraphilia and agoraphobia 75–6, 83; in ancient Athens 74–5; attacks on 82, 83–4; Diogenes in 28–9, 42; enclosure and expropriation 79–83; evacuation 76–9, 87n8; holographic 84–6; intermediate, as a therapeutic milieu 86
Agricultural Revolution 16, 79
Aiyegbusi, A. 94, 103
Alexander, C.F. 55
Alexander, the Great 173; and the *agora* 76, 77, 86; as an insulter 65; and disappointment 167–8; and disrespecting authority 96; fraught encounter with Diogenes 23, 32–5; and metropolitan citizenship 43–7, 49; and power differential 135–6; and reciprocal violence 56–7
Angelou, M.: on racial segregation and trauma 54–65, 141; on safety 5
Anthropocene 50, 51, 113, 116
Armstrong, D. 171
attachment 5; and blood ties 48
Augustine, Saint: *Confessions* 4; on Diogenes 30, 35

Baldwin, A. 50, 51, 121
Baldwin, J. xxii, 5; *Another Country* 12, 141, 144, 146
Bangladesh 118, 127n9
Banksy 85
Bartleby 66–7, 97, 149, 162; bartlebian politics, and passive resistance 67, 69, 150
Bate, J. 80

Bauman, Z. 49; on the 'agora' 50, 76–7, 78, 83, 85; and the post-Panoptical society 107–8n2
Beckett, S. 139
Beland, H. 170
Bendell, J.: on 'deep adaptation' 114
Benjamin, J. 169–70
Bennett, A.: *The History Boys* 171–2
Bentham, J.: and the Panopticon 99, 101–2
Berger, B. 6
Berger, P. 6
Berry, W. 80, 85, 115, 124, 148, 168
Bettini, G. 50, 51, 121
Bevington, D. et al.: on dis-integration 104
Bion, W.R.: and group membership 39, 42, 51n2, 57, 97, 163; and the mind as a house 4; on speaking lies 77
#BlackLivesMatter 137, 138, 144, 151, 169
Black Panther Party for Self-Defense: Ten-Point Platform and Program 133
Blake, W. 79, 80, 163
blame 16; and disappointment 163, 167; and dis-organisation 94, 105
Breivik, A. 82, 83
Brooke, R. 169
Brown, G.: *Psychoanalytic Thinking on the Unhoused Mind* 4
Buchwald, A. 106
Burke, E. 15, 17, 83
Bush, G. (former US President) 114
Butler, J. 139; on reflexivity and subjection 64; on social inclusion 136, 137, 139
Byron, Lord G. 80, 86n3

Cambridge Analytica 77–8
Cameron, D. (former UK PM): on immigration 19n9, 119; on prisoners' voting rights 82
Camus, A.: *La Peste (The Plague)* 100–1, 123–4
capitalism: British, and globalisation 50; and disappointment 168; pre-industrial, and social structure 15; and racialisation 142; *see also* carbon-fuelled capitalism
carbon-fuelled capitalism 50, 56, 58, 77; and climate change 50, 112–13; creation of hostile environments 116–17, 119
care system (health and social): and citizenship 46, 50; and disappointment 160–1, 164, 166; and group inclusion/exclusion 17, 42, 44, 46–7, 48; and the holographic agora 86; and homelessness 3, 7; and inequality 145, 153n5; and self-harming 59, 61; surveillance and shame 102–3; and traumatised dis-organisation 94–9, 104–7; understanding of trauma 13, 14
Carlen, P.: on homelessness 10
Carlyle, T. 18n5, 79
Carter, G.: on racial trauma 145
Carter, R.T.: on racism 140, 143, 146
Cesarani, D.: *Arthur Koestler: The Homeless Mind* 6
Chakrabarty, D.: on the climate change crisis 112, 115, 116, 117
Charlie Hebdo killings 82
citizenship: climate change and migration 50–1; and communalism 48; metropolitan *vs.* cosmopolitan 43–50; and racism 138; reflective, and disappointment 170–1
Clancy, A. 163
Clare, J. 79; 'The lament of Swordy Well' 80
climate change and disaster 50, 51, 111, 173; and carbon-fuelled capitalism 112–13; Climate March 83–4; Climate Strike 32, 46, 65; exhaustibility of resources and consumerism 114–17; as a *psycho-social* problem 112; taking positive action 124–5
climate migration 111, 114; identification of climate migrants 117–19; and

power relations 50–1; and racism 119–20, 121; reframing 120–2
clinic/clinical, and psycho-social approaches contrasted 5, 24, 33; beyond the clinic 145
Clinton, H. (former US Secretary of State): on migration 91
Coleman, W.: on disappointment 165
colonialism 17; and enclosure 81, 100; and migration 56; Orientalism, and othering 67–9; and othering 64, 141; and reciprocal violence 57
Conan Doyle, A.: on the Diogenes Club 25–6
Conrad, J. 119
consumerism: and climate disaster 115; and practices of disappointment 168
contagion: and dis-organisation 94; and the Panopticon 99–100; zoonotic, and pandemics 123–4
conversations: and absent members 39; disappointing 165–7, 172; in public sphere 75, 161, 169; about racism 144; reflective 170; in traumatised dis-organisations 99, 106
Cooper, A.J.: on equality 146
Cosmopolitan/Cosmopolitanism: in contrast to Metropolitan systems 43–50; philosophy 43–51; term coined by Diogenes 43; *see also* Metropolitan
COVID-19 51, 84, 123; and prisons 87n7; and racial trauma 145
Craib, I.: on disappointment 163–4
cross-cultural, theory 9
Crutzen, P.J. 113
Cynics: *askesis* 60; cynicism 36n1, 36n7; and disregard of authority 34; and globalisation 50; Greta Thunberg as 32; *kynikos* 28; Saint Augustine on 30; withholding of societal laws 31–2; workforce, and trauma 98; *see also* Diogenes, of Sinope

Dalby, S. 56
Dante Alighieri 18n
death: Diogenes' and Alexander's 35; self-denial and political commitment 61; and structural violence 10, 56, 123–4
Declaration of Independence (1776) 136, 149

180 Index

Declerck, P.: on homelessness as a structural necessity 9–10, 23–4
DeLapp, R.C.T.: on racial trauma 146
De Maré, P. 170
democratic/democracy 87n5; and the *agora* 78, 84; creating new appointments 171; Sinope as 27
Derrida, J.: and 'hostipitality' 86, 107
Dickens, C.: *David Copperfield* 8; *Dombey and Son* 36n2; racial prejudice 18n5
Dio Chrysostom 35
Diogenes, of Sinope (the Cynic) 23, 25; and the *agora* space 75–6; and citizenship 43–7, 49; and disappointment 167–8; fraught encounter with Alexander 32–5; life in a barrel, as a societal challenge 28–32, 35; reciprocal violence with Alexander 56–7; and reflexive violence 61–2; shame and displacement 27–8
Diogenes Club 25–6
Diogenes Laertius 26–30, 34, 35, 43, 167
Diogenes Paradigm xxii, xxiv; and the agora 76; Diogenes encounter with Alexander 33–5, 43, 45, 49, 96; and disappointment 167; and equality 150; and the master-slave relationship 63–5; and reciprocal violence 57–9; and reflexive violence 61; and the traumatised planetary system 111
'Diogenes Syndrome' 26
disappointment 160, 172–3; and deliberative citizenship 171; and dilemmatic spaces 165–7; disappointed-ness and disappointing-ness 160–1; and disillusion 164–5; and disrespect 164; embracing 171–2; and the holographic agora 84; and the politics of revelation 171; practice 167–8; recognition of our failures 163–4; and reflective citizenship 170–1; and reflective conversations 169–70; self-engagement in 162–3; 'twice-blessed/cursed' nature 165, 166
discourse xxiv; on housedness 16–17; of domination 44, 62, 67; in- and out-groups 24–25, 28; neoliberal 77, 82, 120
dis-organisation 93; aggregated states 97–8; and dysfunction 94; massified states 98–9; responses to, and

surveillance 99–103; social exclusion of the workforce 104–7
displacement 4, 5, 6, 9, 13, 81, 106, 166; blame for, as a lifestyle choice 16; Diogenes 27–31; and migration 50, 56, 58, 117, 118, 119, 120, 121; and racial trauma 65
Donne, J. xxii, 42
Dostoyevsky, F.: *The brothers Karamazov* 57–8
'doublethink' 115, 117
Douglass, F. 143
Du Bois, W.E.B 64, 112; on double consciousness 101; on racism 18n8, 135, 139, 141; on whiteness 142, 143
Dubouloy, M. 170
Dylan, B. (singer/songwriter) xxi, 34

ecology *see* climate change and disaster
Edgerton, D. 50
Eliot, T.S.: 'Choruses' 161, 172
Ellison, R.: *The Invisible Man* 3, 6, 14, 16, 63–4
enclosure: and expropriation of the commons 79–81; and fear of contagion 100–1
Engels, F. 15, 63
equality/inequality 136–7; and approximation 137–8; Diogenes claim 43, 45; empowerment and emancipation 146–8; impact of pandemics 123–4; racial, and common humanity 138–9; racial, and social exclusion 135–6; racial, and trauma 139, 144–6; radical, and anti-racism 149–52; and structural violence 11
Erlich, H.S. 170
Erlich-Ginor, M. 170
exclusion, out-groups 3, 17, 41; absent members 39–43; and the agora 76, 82–3, 85–6; and behavioural violence 11; and citizenship 48; Diogenes displacement 28–31; disregarding authority 34, 35; and fear of contagion 122–3; othering 63–7; and power differentials 23–5, 56; and racial inequality 135–7, 150; self-harming practices 59, 61; traumatised dis-organisations 94–6, 105–6; of the unhoused 15–16; *see also* inclusion, in-groups

Fanon, F. 64, 137, 148, 152, 169; on colonialism and reciprocal violence 57; on decolonisation 68, 150; on disappointment 162–3; on racism 144
Fielding, H. 23, 45
Floyd, George, murder of xvi, xx, 58, 84
'45' (Donald Trump) xx, 138
Foresight 122
fossil capitalism *see* carbon-fuelled capitalism
Foster, A. 4
Foucault, M. 24, 25, 45, 64, 80, 96, 122; on the Panopticon 100, 102; on *parrhesia* 34
Foulkes, S.H. 39, 57
France 9, 152; homeless policy 10
Francis, Pope 111, 117
fraught encounters: concept 23
Freire, P. 148
Freud, S. xi, 4, 12, 65; on agoraphobia 86n2; on the ego 61, 62
Frosh, S. 12

Gabriel, Y. 163
Gaia 50, 78; and citizenship 51; and disappointment 169; and fossil capitalism 113; self-regulation 117
Galtung, J.: on structural violence and social injustice 11
Ghosh, A. 118, 120
Gibbon, E.: *Decline and Fall of the Roman Empire* 41
Gilligan, J.: on disrespect 164; on male rape in US prison system 93; on Republican Party 125n1; on structural violence 11, 123
Global North/Global South xix, xxiii, xxv; and the Great Acceleration 87n10; securitisation of migrants 120, 122, 125; and structural violence 108n4
global warming *see* climate change and disaster
Glover, N. 164
Godwin, W. 101
Goffman, I.: on shaming rituals 93
The Great Acceleration 84, 112, 113, 116
Grenfell Tower 55–6, 70n5
Groucho Marx 49
Group Analysis xi–xiii
groupishness, disturbances of 57, 97

Habermas, J. 82
Haitian Revolution 87n5, 152
Hall, S.: on colonialism and displacement 4, 17n2; on 'othering' 64, 67, 68, 141
Hamilton, C. 112, 113–14
Healy, J.: *The Grass Arena* 7
Heaney, S.: *The Haw Lantern* 30
Hegel, G.W.F.: on the feudal slavery society 63, 64
Heidegger, M.: on homelessness 5
Henderson Hospital Democratic Therapeutic Community xi, xxviii
hermits 41–2
Hierocles: on attachment and dilution of blood ties 48; metaphor of the concentric circles 47, 48, 49
Holocene 51, 113, 116, 122
homelessness 3; French policy 10; modern philosophy on 4–5; and othering 8, 9–10; and societal violence 10–12; as a state of mind 4, 6; UK death rates 10
Honig, B. 165–6
Hopper, E. 171; on groupish disturbances 97
'hostipitality' 86, 107
housing, house, home: as a metaphor for mind 4; and safety 3–4; and un-housing 6; *see also* un-housed, un-housedness
Hughes, L.: 'Vagabonds' 1, 3
human mobility 111; reframing 120–2; *see also* climate migration
Hurricane Katrina: and climate migration 121; and structural violence 56
Huxley, A.: *Brave New World* 103, 168

inclusion, in-groups 24, 25, 41, 125, 144; and the agora 76, 82, 85–6; and citizenship 43–6, 48, 50, 52n7; and disappointment 162, 167; and equality/inequality 12, 136, 137, 148, 150, 152; and fear of contagion 122; and housing/unhousing 6, 16, 17; and practices of violence 56, 5759, 61, 62, 67; refusal of 28, 31, 34, 39–42; responses to otherness 106–7; *see also* exclusion, out-groups
India xix, xx, 52n8

Index

industrialisation 79–80; Industrial
  Revolution 16, 81, 126n5
injury 94; moral, and traumatised
  dis-organisations 94; to the political
  body 59; self- 59–60; and societal
  violence 58
injustice: and inequality 124; and
  structural violence 10–12; and
  trauma 58
Institute for Economics and Peace 117
insult 18n6, 57, 59, 107, 146; and
  othering 67; and reflexive violence 62,
  65, 166
International Organization for Migration
  (IOM) 118, 120–1
Intersectionality/intersectional theory:
  othering 8; disappointment, disrespect
  and disillusion 164–5; free trade and
  slavery 154n11; globalisation and
  climate disaster 120; pandemics
  and structural inequalities123;
  self-harming practices 60

Jacotot, J. (1770–1840) 146–8, 150
James, C.L.R. 87n5, 115, 152
Johnson, B. (UK PM): and COVID-19
  policy xx; populist leadership style xx, 78
Jones, D.W. 82
Jones, J. 140
Joyce, J. xxi, 144, 151
Jung, C.G. 4
Juvenal 93, 102

Kellner, H. 6
King James Bible: John 14:2 4; Leviticus
  25:23 1; Matthew 22:21 46; Psalms
  146:3 160
KingJr, M.L. 143; on social dreaming
  171; on societal violence 10, 11–12
Kinouani, G.: on whiteness 142–3
Klein, N. 9, 44, 67, 121
Klepp, S. 50; on human mobility 121
Krantz, J.: on deliberative citizenship 171

Lamming, G. 148
Lancet: on climate migration 118
Latour, B. 50, 51, 123, 125; on the
  coronavirus 50, 51, 123, 125
Lawrence, G.: on practices of
  disappointment 171
Lear, J. 124; on unjust societies 58
Lebron, C.J. 143, 151

Lee, B.X. 11
Lee, G. 11
Lenkiewicz, R. 26
Levi, P. 55
Levi-Strauss, C. 106
Levy, A.: *Small Island* 143
Lewis, J., Freedom Rider 133
Lincoln, A.: on equality 136–7
Linebaugh, P. 80–1; on enclosure 80–1
Lorde, A. 140, 151; on intersectional
  identity 139; on oppression 135

MacIntyre, A. 138
MacKenzie, Edward 'Diogenes' 26, 29
Main, T. (Cassel Hospital) 24
Malcolm X 149, 152
Mann, T. 125
Marley, B. and the Wailers: 'War' 151
Martin, W. 47
Marx, K. xi, 5, 15, 63
Masters, A.: *Stuart: A Life Backwards* 7–8
May, T. (former UK PM): on
  citizenship 48
McQueen, S.: *Red, White and Blue* 152
Melville, H.: *Bartleby the Scrivener* 66–7;
  Moby Dick 51n3
Metropolitan/Metropolitanism 63,
  70n2, 173; citizenship, and inclusion
  43–6, 49, 52n7; and practices of
  disappointment 167, 168; response to
  Gaia problems 50–1; securitisation of
  migrants 56; systems of care 46; and
  traumatised dis-organisations 98; *see
  also* Cosmopolitan
migration: and colonialism 56; and
  politics 50–1, 91; and racism 68;
  securitised 56, 120, 121, 123, 125; *see
  also* climate migration/human mobility
mind: fear of contagion 100; as a
  metaphor for home 4, 6
Mitchell, J. (singer) 83
Mitchell, T.: *Carbon Democracy* 84–5
Monbiot, G. 82
Morant Bay Rebellion 18n5
Morlock, F. 147
Morris, W. 76
Morrison, T. 151
Motz, A. 59

Neo-liberalism 16, 44, 143; neo-liberal
  turn 111; and racism 120–1, 125n1;
  and the retreat from the agora 77

Nietzsche, F. xxiv, 5, 17
9/11 attacks *see* World Trade Centre attacks

Obama, B. (former US president) 137–8
Occupy movement 82
Olusoga, D.: on the slave trade 142
Orientalism 67–9
Orwell, G. 9, 168; on 'doublethink' 126n4
othering: and colonialism 64, 67–9; and political/psychological superiority 17; and racism 68, 141; as a social structural violence 9–10, 17; as a toxic phenomenon 8

pandemics: and citizenship 51; and connection to other issues 124–5; and fear of contagion 122–3; and structural inequalities 123–4; *see also* contagion; COVID-19
Panopticon 99–101; 107n2; perverse 101–3
Parenti, C. 122
Parks, R. 152, 168; engaging in disappointment 162; practice of radical equality 149–50
parrhesia 34, 42, 50, 57, 76
Patterson, O.: on 'natal alienation' 63, 64
Peace of Westphalia 52n5
Pelletier, C. 45, 51n1, 136
Pericles 27, 28
Pickett, K.E. 12
Piper, R. 170
Plato 45, 74; on Diogenes 30; *Republic* 4
Plutarch 33, 44; on citizenship 47
Poor Laws 15
Pope, A.: *Epistle IV* 46, 48
Postman, N. 168
power, power relations 135–6; colonisation, and 'othering' 67–8, 69; and disappointment 162, 171–2; and dis-organisation 106; in- and out-groups 24, 57; master-slave dynamics 63; Metropolitan 44–7, 49–51, 56, 173; in the Panoptical society 100, 102; and racism 140, 141, 143, 151–2; speaking truth to 34, 35, 45–6, 77, 78, 162; unequal, and structural violence 11, 56
Printz, D.M.B. 146
prison, prisoners: denial of rights 82; PIPE practices 107n1; and racism 144–5; shaming and violence 11, 93

protest politics: and the 'agora' 82, 83, 84–5; against the enclosure 79–80; and self-denial 61
psycho-social, psycho-social trauma 18n6; climate disaster 112; disorganised 94, 95–9; homelessness, unhousedness 4, 6, 7, 9, 12–15, 31; practices of disappointment 161, 162, 163–6; psycho-social studies, field of xi, xxv; psycho-social ailments, responses 17, 24, 57, 61; and racism 143, 146; and reciprocal violence 57–8; resistance 45, 66–7; and self-harming 59–60, 61; spaces 74, 75, 76, 83, 86n1; and structural violence 11–12, 14, 16; and survivor movements 65

quarantine: and exclusion of out-groups 11, 64, 104; and fear of contagion 100, 122, 127n13

Rabelais, F. 70n2; *Pantagruel* 36n6
racism 18n2; anti-, and radical equality 149–52; colonialism, and reciprocal violence 57; ideology 139–41; inequality, and social exclusion 135–8; invisibility, and reciprocal violence 63–4; and migration 68, 119–20, 121; racial trauma 105, 144–6, 148; segregation, and structural violence 56; and whiteness 141–4
Rancière, J. 25, 114, 147; on border control 122; on equality 148–9, 150; on protest politics 85
reciprocal violence *see* violence, reciprocal
reflexive violence *see* violence, reflexive
Republican Party xv, 114, 125n1
Rilke, R.M. 5, 16; on the 'disinherited' 5, 16
Roberts, V.Z. 4
Rousseau, J.J.: *The social contract* 91
Russell, C. 171

sacrificial zones xix, 44, 115–16
safety and security: and agoraphobia 75; and attachment 5; and 'globalisation' 9; and housing 3–4, 51; identity adaptation, and trauma 64
Said, E. 121; on Orientalism 67–9
Sartre, J.-P. 137
Scanlon, C. 108n5, 161, 167, 171
Scheuermann, T.D. 140, 143

184 Index

Scranton, R.: on protest politics 84–5
Selassie, H.: on racial equality 151
self-harming 57–8, 59; culturally accepted 60; objectification and othering 67; politically motivated 61; and re-traumatisation 60; revealed as a body text 62; and self-denial 60; and self-neglect 60
sexual abuse 7; anxiety, and dis-organisation 102; trauma, and the survivor movement 65
Shakespeare, W.: *Macbeth* 167; *The Merchant of Venice* 165; *Othello* 17n1; *The Tragedy of King Lear* 32; *As you Like it* 3
shame and shaming: Diogenes 27–31, 167; and disappointment 163, 164, 167; in prisons 11, 93; and surveillance 100–3; and traumatised dis-organisation 95, 97, 106; and whiteness 143–4
Shelley, P.B. 79, 80
Simeon Stylites, the Elder, St. 41–2, 51n3, 60, 62, 69–70n1
slavery, slave trade 18n5, 43, 51n4, 58, 142; master-slave dialectic 63–6; race issues 136, 142–4
Smith, B. 12, 16
Sophocles: *Antigone* 61
Star Trek 52n6
Steiner, G. 15
Stoics, Stoicism: and Cosmopolitanism 47–8; and disappointment 167
Stopford, A. 96, 145; on racial trauma 161
superiority: and dis-organisation 98; political leading to psychological 17; race 140, 146, 151; and violent exclusion 24
surveillance, and shaming 100–3
'syllogomania' *see* 'Diogenes Syndrome'

Tennyson, A. 39
Thatcher, M. (former UK PM) 125n1; on immigration 119–20
Thelwall, J. 80
Thompson, E.P. 79, 81
Thompson, S. 170
Thucydides 28, 29
Thunberg, G. 65; and Cynical praxis 31–2; school strike, as a rediscovery of public spaces 83

trauma, re-traumatisation 11, 18n6, 56, 66, 111, 164, 170, 171; Diogenes 27–31, 45; and dis-organisation 94–9, 104–7; and 'othering' 64; psycho-social understanding 12–15; racial 141, 143, 144–6, 148, 154n13, 161; and reciprocal violence 57, 58; and self-harming 60, 61; and social injustice 58; survivor movements 65
Trump, D. see '45'

UK Commission on Race and Ethnic Disparities 152n1
un-housed, un-housedness: blame, as a lifestyle choice 16; definition 5–6; *vs.* homelessness 6; hostility towards 8, 9–10, 15–16, 17; as a psycho-social experience 6–7; rejection of the societal system 28–32, 35; speaking for 25; and trauma 12–15
United Kingdom: care system, and globalisation 50; enclosure of the commons 79–82; homeless death rates 10; hostility towards migrants 119–20; housing policies 17; racial inequality and trauma 105, 145
United Nations 16, 117, 118, 151
United States 86n2, 125n2; anti-racism 137–8, 149–50; climate disasters 56, 118, 121; prisons, shaming and violence 11; racial trauma 141, 144–5, 161

vagabondage 1, 3; hostility towards 3, 15
Vince, R. 163
violence, reciprocal 15, 55, 58, 117, 136; and colonialism 57; and disappointment 160, 166; and exclusion 25; and 'groupish' disturbance 57, 97; racism, and invisibility 63–4; in traumatised dis-organisations 94, 95; *see also* self-harming
violence, reflexive 61–2, 64, 106, 166; as deliberate 62; and disappointment 166; and insult 62, 65; and othering 67
violence, structural: and biosphere destruction 55–6; and dis-organisation 94, 105, 107, 108n4; and the enclosure of the commons 79–81; and inequality 123–4, 138; and injustice 10–12; in the master-slave relationship 63–4; and

othering 8–10, 17; and racism 56, 120, 139–42, 144–6

WASP democracies 78
wa Thiong'o, N.: *Petals of blood* 115, 117, 142
Weil, S. 58, 67; self-denial 61
Whyte, D. 165
Wilderson III, F.B.: Afropessimism 70n3, 138
Wilkinson, R.G. 12
Williams, M.T. 146

Williams, R. 69, 80
Windrush scandal 120
Winnicott, D.W. 4, 164
World Trade Centre attacks 56

Yeats, W.B. 95, 98
Young, J. 11

Zeldin, T. 169
Zeno, of Citium 47, 49
Žižek, S. 11, 13, 66; on ecology and global capitalism 116

Taylor & Francis eBooks

www.taylorfrancis.com

A single destination for eBooks from Taylor & Francis with increased functionality and an improved user experience to meet the needs of our customers.

90,000+ eBooks of award-winning academic content in Humanities, Social Science, Science, Technology, Engineering, and Medical written by a global network of editors and authors.

TAYLOR & FRANCIS EBOOKS OFFERS:

A streamlined experience for our library customers

A single point of discovery for all of our eBook content

Improved search and discovery of content at both book and chapter level

REQUEST A FREE TRIAL
support@taylorfrancis.com

Printed in the United States
by Baker & Taylor Publisher Services